DISPOSING DICTATORS, DEMYSTIFYING VOTING PARADOXES

We decide by elections, but do we elect who the voters really want? The answer, as we have learned over the past two centuries, is "not necessarily." That is a negative, frightening assertion about a principal tool of democracy! This negativism has been supported by two hundred years of published results showing how bad the situation can be. This expository, largely nontechnical book is the first to find positive results showing that the situation is not nearly as dire and negative as we have been led to believe. Instead there are surprisingly simple explanations for the negative assertions, and positive conclusions can be obtained.

Donald G. Saari is Distinguished Professor of Mathematics and Economics and Honorary Professor of Logic and Philosophy of Science at the University of California at Irvine, where he is Director of the Institute for Mathematical Behavioral Sciences. He previously served on the faculty of Northwestern University from 1968 to 2000, where he held the Pancoe Professorship of Mathematics. A member of the U.S. National Academy of Sciences, Fellow of the American Academy of Arts and Sciences, and Fellow of the American Association for the Advancement of Science, Professor Saari is the former Chief Editor of the *Bulletin of the American Mathematical Society*. The author of more than 170 published papers, he has also written numerous books, including *Basic Geometry of Voting* (1995), *Decisions and Elections: Explaining the Unexpected* (Cambridge University Press, 2001), *Chaotic Election! A Mathematician Looks at Voting* (2001), *The Way It Was: Mathematics from the Early Years of the Bulleting* (2003), and *Collisions, Rings, and Other Newtonian N-Body Problems* (2005).

Disposing Dictators, Demystifying Voting Paradoxes

Social Choice Analysis

DONALD G. SAARI

University of California, Irvine

CAMBRIDGE UNIVERSITY PRESS
Cambridge, New York, Melbourne, Madrid, Cape Town, Singapore, São Paulo, Delhi

Cambridge University Press
32 Avenue of the Americas, New York, NY 10013-2473, USA

www.cambridge.org
Information on this title: www.cambridge.org/9780521731607

First published 2008

Printed in the United States of America

A catalog record for this publication is available from the British Library.

Library of Congress Cataloging in Publication data

Saari, D. (Donald)
Disposing dictators, demystifying voting paradoxes : social choice analysis /
Donald G. Saari.
p.   cm.
Includes bibliographical references and index.
ISBN 978-0-521-51605-1 – ISBN 978-0-521-73160-7
1. Social choice.   2. Voting.   3. Elections.   I. Title.
HB846.8.S26   2008
324.6–dc22   2008029663

ISBN   978-0-521-51605-1 hardback
ISBN   978-0-521-73160-7 paperback

For my sister
Katri Saari,
*a creative artist and dedicated educator who has influenced many.
Among our many shared memories, several are associated with
growing up in the forested, northernmost reaches of the United States.*

Contents

Preface

In part, this book reflects my Condorcet Lectures delivered at the Centre de Recherche en Économie et Management, Université de Caen, Caen, France. Perhaps anticipating paradoxical election behavior of the kind exhibited by the "Nader effect" in the 2000 election, which would have added spice to the already lively discussions, these lectures were purposely scheduled for the week after the November 2004 U.S. presidential elections.

The Condorcet Lectures are named after the prominent eighteenth-century French scholar and politician Marie-Jean-Antoine-Nicolas de Condorcet. As one must expect, a lecture series named after the Marquis de Condorcet must emphasize contributions made to social choice and voting theory. Appropriately, the inaugural Condorcet Lectures were delivered by Kenneth Arrow in September 2002. My lectures were the second in this series, and the third were given in June 2005 by Amartya Sen. What a delight to be sandwiched, perhaps serving as a comma, between these two great thinkers, who have influenced the field of social choice in so many ways. Indeed, certain of their seminal results play key roles in Chapter 2 of this book.

My hosts, Vincent Merlin and Maurice Salles, also organized a small conference centered around the general topic of my lectures – "The Subtle Mathematical Structure of Social Choice." In order of presentation, the speakers, all eminent contributors to this area, were

- Luc Lauwers (Catholic University of Leuven), who spoke on the topological approach to the aggregation of preferences

- Bernard Monjardet (Université de Paris 1), who described discrete mathematics in social choice
- Nicholas Baigent (University of Graz), who provided a general perspective on social choice in generalized metric spaces
- Christian List (London School of Economics), who directed his emphasis toward strategic-proof judgment aggregation

In this book, I describe some of List's work; Baigent and Lauwers have made contributions about topological social choice other than that discussed in Chapter 2; and Monjardet has played a major role in extending notions from social choice to areas such as consensus.

Sponsoring groups include the Université de Caen, CNRS, and the Centre de Recherche en Économie et Management (CREM). CREM, created years ago by Maurice Salles, is currently being jointly run by Salles and Vincent Merlin. Salles was the originator and organizer for the Condorcet Lectures, and both Salles and Merlin did an excellent job with everything associated with my lectures, the conference, and the accompanying social aspects.

Adding to my delight was the fact that these lectures were presented in Caen. Caen is special for me because several of my choice theory ideas were honed and advanced by visits to this delightful region of France. Inspiration and insights were gained from discussions with Professors Salles and Merlin, faculty, students, and the many visitors who regularly pass through CREM. As such, my thanks to Professors Merlin and Salles go beyond the invitation to deliver the Condorcet Lectures to include the several other visits from which I have greatly benefited over many years!

You know the problem – good intentions going astray. Rather than quickly writing up the lecture notes, which were projected to be the length of an average journal article, the manuscript started to grow, and grow, and grow. Then there was the temptation, which I can never resist, of adding new results plus developing appropriate structures (Section 4.5) to encourage others to join us in this fascinating search for new conclusions.

An expanding manuscript translates into delays, which meant that other invited lectures came about. So this book is primarily based on my

Condorcet Lectures at the Université de Caen, but significant portions also reflect comments from my July 2006 Condorcet Lecture at the Society for Social Choice and Welfare meeting in Istanbul, Turkey, and my April 2006 plenary talk at the European Public Choice Society meeting in Turku, Finland. My thanks to the respective hosts Remzi Sanver and Hannu Nurmi. Sanver – a young, energetic, clever researcher – is a future leader in this area; Nurmi is an influential leader of public choice in the Nordic countries.

Professor Nurmi influenced my decision to make choice theory one of my areas of research. The story starts about twenty years ago when, although I had written papers in this area, choice theory was an avocation; my research life was consumed with issues from celestial mechanics (mathematics of astronomy) such as the evolution of the universe. I am notoriously horrible about keeping abreast of any literature, but my interest in voting theory sufficed to keep me reasonably current with the latest research. I found, however, that most articles were written in an overly technical language that obscured for an outsider the main themes of this area.

Then I stumbled on Nurmi's book [43]. I was unaware of the main players in this field, so I read it primarily because as a Finnish-American I was curious about this book written by a Finn. In it I found a clear, well-written, selective overview of the difficulties of the area. As Nurmi's books prove, clear exposition with insightful results are influential. His writings helped me develop a personal sense about what topics are crucial and should be pursued. Quickly thereafter, choice theory became a major research focus.

For me, the central issues at that time included:

1. The so-called axiomatic approach of characterizing procedures with axioms so that "we know what we are getting"
2. The search for new voting paradoxes
3. Arrow's and Sen's seminal but negative theorems that imposed significant barriers for progress by suggesting that whatever you do is flawed because "all methods are unfair"
4. Strategic behavior

In what follows, I address three of these issues in an expository manner. For instance:

1. The axiomatic approach clearly has not lived up to its promises as measured by the lack of consensus about "what we are getting." As described in Chapter 3, the unexpected explanation is that, often, this approach is used incorrectly in the social sciences.

2. Finding voting paradoxes may seem to be more of a game of creating amusing oddities than contributing anything of value. This is not the case. After describing the crucial rule played by paradoxes (Chapter 3), I characterize all positional voting paradoxes that can be associated with fixed profiles. Then, in Chapter 4, with a slightly different perspective offered in Chapter 5, I explain why all of these voting paradoxes, which add mystery and content to this field, occur. This analysis does explain what we are getting from voting rules.

3. Arrow's and Sen's theorems erect huge barriers for this area: They suggest that much of what we want to do is impossible. But, as shown in Chapter 2, by understanding *why* these results occur, both assertions admit benign interpretations that remove those previously perceived obstacles to progress.

4. I do not explain "how to be manipulative if you must" only because I already published a fairly nontechnical description about how to identify and characterize all strategic possibilities in my paper [78] and in a chapter in my book [74].

Any writing project involves help and assistance from others. I am delighted to thank Vincent Merlin (a frequent coauthor) and Maurice Salles for helping in so many ways (e.g., Maurice made several useful suggestions about an earlier draft of this book). My thanks to Katri Sieberg (another coauthor) for her helpful suggestions about an earlier version of the manuscript that she used in her 2006 minicourse in Turku, Finland. Thanks to Jack Stackpole for finding some subtle errors. My thanks to the reviewers; I was impressed by their exceptionally useful comments. Thanks to my friend Dao Vuong, a computer whiz who keeps me current and operating. The always important financial support for this research came from the National Science Foundation; the more recent being grants NSF DMI-0640817, where the project of developing ideas from choice theory to address issues of multiscale design in engineering has sharpened my insights into aggregation processes, and NSF DMS-0631362, which supports my development of a mathematical approach for voting theory. My thanks for the privileges offered by the library at Michigan Technological University, which is near where I do most of my writing. Also, I appreciate the help from Cambridge University Press and Mary Paden and her staff in preparing the book for publication!

As always, my deepest thanks go to my wife and best friend, Lillian Saari, for her patience, which remains surprisingly intact even when I develop a glassy look during a conversation because my mind suddenly made an unexpected left turn to become hopelessly snarled with some aspect of my research, and, in particular, for her insights, constructive criticisms, and comments during our many discussions on these topics and my other research endeavors. She is a delight and is a true partner!

Let me conclude by warmly inviting students and researchers to join this area. (Exercises available at http://www.math.uci.edu/~dsaari will permit using this book in the classroom.) After all, beyond the intriguing academic mysteries, this is a research area in which results can be of value far beyond the walls of academia! This is a rare discipline in which research conclusions can, should, and must have an impact on the future directions of society.

Donald G. Saari
Irvine, California

ONE

Subtle Complexity of Social Choice

1.1 Does *Everything* Go Wrong?

Remember your last important election? Maybe it was to select the chair of a department, business unit, or social group. Maybe it was to determine who to hire, what alternative to select, which material to use in a construction project, or where to locate a new plant. Maybe it was in a presidential primary. Were you happy? It is not uncommon to be disappointed with the outcome and complain that the wrong choice won. A natural response is to dismiss such complaints as sour grapes: "Get over it already! You lost!" But surprisingly often the "wrong person" did win. The mathematical study of whether decision and election rules elect "whom the voters really want" is called *social choice*.

For an outsider, the area of social choice can leave the impression of a mysterious subject discouragingly consumed with disturbing voting paradoxes. These examples of voting inconsistencies, which permeate the literature, produce realistic worries about whether we might elect someone whom the voters really do not want. It is worth worrying about this fear because, in fact, surprisingly often that is precisely what happens.

Even more bothersome is the fact that this disease where societal outcomes can flaunt voters' wishes appears to have reached the epidemic level by afflicting *all* conceivable voting rules. Worse news comes from the seminal Arrow's and Sen's theorems, which are introduced in Chapter 2. These theorems state that it is impossible to do what seems to be quite natural to do. There is also a severe language barrier where many of these published articles, which seemingly promise darker and deeper levels

1

of dismal assertions and conclusions, are described in dense technical terms that even a mathematician can find difficult to parse. I know; I am a mathematician.

But the news isn't all bad. In recent years, positive conclusions have been discovered, while negative assertions have been put to rest or placed in perspective. In this book, I will put a cheerier tone on central issues in the field by replacing gloom with some "good news."

I do so by providing new perspectives for essential difficulties in this area. This includes addressing those troubling dictators and ubiquitous voting paradoxes by explaining what causes them. The explanations range from identifying the source of Arrow's discouraging result about a dictator and the cause of Sen's result, which asserts that there can be a fundamental conflict between societal needs and individual liberties, to all of those voting paradoxes that professionals in this field have learned to love. We should love them; they keep us employed.

What "Subtlety?"

There does not seem to be anything subtle or complex about election rules. For some methods, such as the standard plurality vote where each person votes for a favorite candidate, simple counting is about the heaviest mathematics required to tally ballots. Even children in a kindergarden class can handle a "show-of-hands" – nothing complex about this.

As we have learned over the past two centuries, voting rules, including the plurality vote (also called "vote-for-one" or, in Europe, "first past the post"), are far from being simple or transparent. Instead, as frustrated voters in many countries may wonder in the aftermath of almost any election season, and as experts in this academic field have known since the work of Jean-Charles de Borda during the pre-revolutionary days of eighteenth-century France, so many things can go wrong with elections that we must worry whether election results accurately reflect the voters' beliefs. The complexity of voting rules, then, does not derive from the definitions or implementation of the rules but from their subtle discomforting consequences.

Mind you, I am not talking about those widely discussed problems caused by malfeasance of election officials – actions explicitly directed toward "stealing" the election. Instead, I am referring to unexpected consequences caused by hidden properties of our standard and widely used election rules. Bluntly stated, even with the idealistic assumption that all procedural aspects of an election are honest and carefully followed, the choice of an election rule can seriously distort the outcome away from what arguably is the "true choice of the voters." To illustrate with widely discussed contemporary examples, did George W. Bush's victory over Albert Gore in the 2000 U.S. presidential election accurately reflect what the American, or even Floridian, voters wanted? I do not think so. Did the French electorate truly respect Jean-Marie Le Pen enough to justify advancing him to the runoffs in the 2002 French elections? I doubt it. These worrisome kinds of problems are discussed here.

1.2 And the Proud Father Is...

The field has a delightfully interesting history spiced with conflict thrown into the mix. Even though concerns about the choice of an appropriate voting rule can be traced back to the earliest of times, the academic pursuit started when Jean-Charles de Borda [6] worried in his June 1770 presentation whether the "wrong people" were being elected to the Paris Académie des Sciences.[1] With an insightful, explicit example, Borda proved that the academy's election method allowed them to elect individuals who, in fact, the voters collectively viewed as being *inferior.* What a serious indictment!

What was this problematic election rule that allowed inferior conclusions? The culprit was the *plurality vote,* which is widely used across the world; it is the rule responsible for the questionable outcomes in the earlier mentioned American and French elections. Borda then introduced a voting rule (assign 2, 1, 0 points, respectively, to candidates who are positioned first, second, and third on a ballot) to resolve the difficulty. His "Borda Count" rule *does* solve the problem; at least, it works for examples of the type that he described.

By planting seeds of doubt about standard voting rules and by calling academic attention to this issue, Borda rightfully is the *Father of Social*

---

[1] The academy was abolished in 1793 during the Reign of Terror and later reestablished in the Institut de France.

Choice; without question, his insights and presentation initiated this academic field. With that said, however, I am left with the feeling that when he delivered his 1770 address, Borda viewed voting theory as a side fling where his objective was not to start a new academic area, which he did, but to correct a troubling peculiarity afflicting the quality of newly chosen academy members. Perhaps recently elected classes of academy members failed to match expected standards, and this slip in quality provoked Borda into searching for the cause and a cure.

To place his contribution in a proper perspective, all of us, at one time or another, have worried about flaws within organizations in which we are members. To redress the problem, we explain to our colleagues what is wrong while suggesting ways to correct the deficiency. It might involve, for instance, inefficiencies in assigning students to classes or evaluating graduate students for advancement to Ph.D. candidacy. We point out the problem, argue for change, and then move on to what we view as our real work.

At least initially, this probably was the level of intensity that Borda assigned to the voting question.[2] He identified a serious defect in the academy's election rule, made his insightful change now called the Borda Count, explained why it was an improvement, and then moved on to his academic pursuits. After all, Borda, a mathematician and one of France's most notable experimental physicists, was more interested in the mathematics of astronomy and fluid dynamics and in his central role in creating

---

[2] Borda returned to this topic after issues and challenges were raised by Condorcet. But Borda's efforts were directed toward hydrodynamics, mathematical physics (the Borda harp remains of interest within partial differential equations), and the mathematics of astronomy (e.g., the research that resulted in his election to the French Académie des Sciences in 1753 at the age of 23 involved the behavior of projectiles). With his use of calculus and experimental methods, he helped to unify areas of mathematical physics. His "repeating circle" device, which had profound nautical applications because of its significant accuracy, was used to define the length of a meter! This distinguished man also played a central role in the establishment of the famous Bureau des Longitudes in Paris serving as its first president. As a side-note indicating the historical importance of this bureau, today the Prime Meridian passes through the original site of the Royal Observatory in Greenwich England. Before 1884, however, navigation was complicated by several choices – the French one was defined by a line embedded in the second floor of the Bureau des Longitudes and passing through the center of the clock on the wall of the Palais du Luxembourg that overlooks the outdoor pool.

Author pointing to the French "Prime Meridian" in the astronomy institute founded by Borda.

the metric system: Some research issues he raised then are still studied today.

My interpretation is consistent with that of Duncan Black, who writes in his classic book [7] *The Theory of Committees and Elections*:

The initial step [to develop a theory for voting] was taken by Borda, who ... [had] achieved distinction as a mathematician and had for the centre of his life the Academy of Sciences. It was no doubt elections to the Academy, membership of which was for him the most valuable of all privileges, and not the wider problems of politics that first directed his mind to the theory. In it he showed the same eye for the significant fact and for the simplifying assumption as in his other researches, and he broached the subject in a new way. His work has the robust good sense of the practical man.

Although Borda's contributions to voting remain central to this field, a rough measure of the relative insignificance that Borda might have placed on them compared to his many other mathematical and scientific contributions is that in Marcart's [31] 636-page biography of Borda,

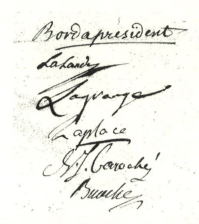

The signatures of Borda, as president, and other notable mathematicians and astronomers on a document establishing the Bureau des Longitudes in Paris.

only 7 pages are devoted to Borda's interest in and contributions to voting theory.

Borda was a surprisingly well-rounded, productive researcher who was active in several scientific pursuits as well as a recognized naval officer. In recognition of his leadership of a fleet of six ships involved in the American Revolutionary War and winning notable victories, Borda was made a member of the American "Order of Cincinnatus." Borda's contributions include being a recognized military figure and a renowned experimental physicist, establishing the definition of the meter, creating the Bureau des Longitudes in Paris, discovering several mathematical results in hydrodynamics, initiating the study of voting rules, and on and on. His accomplishments were certainly a nice start for a curriculum vitae!

For voting theory, it was the Marquis de Condorcet [12] who nurtured and raised the child sired by Borda. Condorcet moved beyond addressing the voting problems facing the academy to initiate a general theory for voting rules. His masterful work is, and deserves to be, studied today. Without Condorcet, the development of a theory for voting most surely would have been delayed for at least another century. Combining Borda's fleeting affair with social choice – a fling with unexpected and lasting consequences – with Condorcet's more fatherly devotion, it is

Two streets in Paris; a concrete recognition of the founders of social choice.

appropriate to designate both gentlemen as the founding fathers of this area.

1.3 Enemies?

Condorcet was a major figure in French history whose many contributions were honored in 1989 when his remains[3] were moved into the Panthéon in Paris. His academic accomplishments, intellectual friendship with Thomas Jefferson, leadership role in the French Revolution, service to the French Academy, and deep contributions to social choice made him a major figure.

Let me offer a short, incomplete list of these contributions: Four score years before the American Civil War, Condorcet wrote persuasively against slavery and the slave trade. He took strong stands on issues being contested today, such as his opposition to the death penalty and his support for the equality of rights for women and the Jewish. During those days it was necessary to fight to protect Protestants, and he did so. As if this were not enough, he was the founder of the Condorcet jury theorem, a version of the central limit result, and the founder of a more general investigation of "social mathematics." A particularly insightful message of his is that selecting the appropriate voting rule is just one step:

---

[3] As Maurice Salles reminded me, his "remains" were symbolically moved to the Panthéon; it is unknown where his actual remains are located or if they even exist.

The rule is a tool that can be useless if not accompanied by a civilized and informed discourse. He was an incredible, courageous, perceptive man!

Perhaps of interest only for those in the area of social choice are the persistent assertions that Condorcet viewed Borda as an enemy. An enemy? Left unexplained, these comments resemble a meal without wine: Something of significance is missing. We want to know why, so it is worth exploring this issue.

From what I learned, this "enemy" notion was merely an irrelevant passing stage reflecting Condorcet's insecurity and immaturity at a younger age exacerbated by political battles and a resource allocation problem – affairs that rarely bring out the best of anyone. Problems seemed to dissipate after Condorcet gained confidence in his leadership roles.[4]

As I write this, I have an amusing thought. Condorcet was elected to the Paris Académie des Sciences in 1769; in June of the next year, 1770, Borda explained to the academy how their voting rule could elect inferior choices. This timing forces one to wonder whether Borda was referring to the "inferiority" of Condorcet's class of academy members. Did Condorcet wonder whether Borda was pointing to him? If so, this would explain Condorcet's rumored enmity toward Borda. We may never know, but I wonder.

Let me start my commentary with an exemplar of mathematicians' self-deprecating sense of humor – a joke widely circulated within our profession:

How can you tell which mathematician is an extrovert?

The answer:

The one who looks at *your* shoes when talking to you.

Converting this joke into a measure of social behavior, it appears that during his younger years and the early part of his career (when the "enemy" comments occurred) Condorcet was a world-class introvert striving to overcome a warped upbringing. To learn more about this, I highly

---

[4] Keith M. Baker, the author of *Condorcet* [5], suggested in an email exchange that this statement is consistent with his understanding of the situation.

recommend Baker's fascinating book *Condorcet* [5], which is a principal reference for this man of great importance to French history. In Baker's book we learn (p. 3) how Condorcet's twice-widowed mother "sought to preserve herself from further loss by smothering the child in a mantle of piety. Dedicated for his protection to the virgin (so the tradition goes), he was kept in white dresses until the age of eight."

White Dresses and Other Humiliations

White dresses until the age of 8! This humiliation brings to mind the Shel Silverstein song, recorded in 1969 by Johnny Cash, entitled "A Boy Named Sue." As the daddy who left home explains years later, right after the son finally finds him and they have a knockdown physical brawl to exact revenge over his given name of Sue, the father knew he would not be around,

> So I give ya that name and I said goodbye
> I knew you'd have to get tough or die
> And it's the name that helped to make you strong

It is easy to appreciate the consequences of Condorcet's white dress experience. Perhaps out of necessity, like the boy named Sue, he would develop street-brawling skills. In the physical sense of good ole fisticuffs, this did not occur, but in the sense of verbally and intellectually taking on opponents, this bare-knuckled trait served the feisty politician Condorcet quite well during the French revolutionary years. Even earlier, Mme Suard remarked (Baker [5], p. 5) that

Between the malice of his mind and the goodness of his heart, there was a contrast that I always found singularly striking. . . . His intolerance in matters of political opinion was incredible.

One must wonder whether Condorcet, who was carrying all of this emotional baggage, strived to dismiss lessons carefully learned at his mother's knee.

It got worse: Condorcet's Jesuit education did not reward him with happy years. Read Baker's description ([5], p. 3) of Condorcet's thoughts:

Among the Caribs [according to Condorcet], it was the customary practice to render newborn children completely stupid by flattening their heads between two boards. The mongols relieved themselves of the fear that a prince of the blood might foment trouble by the application of a narcotic potion producing imbecility by degrees. . . . Of all the known methods for reducing man to the intellectual level of the beast, however, Condorcet regarded as the surest that . . . [used by the monks]. A moral education fit to make debauched and hypocritical atheists or fanatically bigoted imbeciles; a philosophical education comprised of scholastic jargon and theological dreams; a closed educational environment calculated to foster and perpetuate the adolescent tendency to homosexuality; these were the principal aspects of his education at the hands of the Jesuits that Condorcet remembered at the age of thirty.

Wow! This description trumps all complaints I have ever heard about bad educational and scar-producing childhood experiences. It is easy to appreciate why Condorcet's later mentors strived to make him socially more acceptable. The year he was elected to the Paris Académie des Sciences (1769), Mlle de Lespinasse still labored

to repair the defects of Jesuit education by schooling [Condorcet] in the social graces. . . . Condorcet was admonished to leave off biting his nails and gnawing his lips in company; to refrain from folding himself in two while talking, . . . , to keep his ears free of chalk and his hair cut less close to his head; to leaven the madness of his long days of study with some cultivation of the science of love. ([5], p. 23)

Presumably Condorcet was also carefully coached to look at the other person's shoes during conversations.

Enemies and Money

Take a talented, brilliant, quick-tempered young man with limited social graces, no history of tolerance, and a "malice of mind," mix in a fight over scarce resources, and what would you expect? It occurred, and it might explain Condorcet's "enemy" attitude toward Borda. Again, I encourage you to read Baker's book ([5], pp. 35–47). For a brief synopsis, the strategic machinations of d'Alembert and Condorcet with the goal of making Condorcet the academy leader required a significant pot of money. They discovered one – 12,000 livres designated to support experimental research. Could they divert this cache of cash for their purposes? Coconspirator Turgot used the power of his office of controller-general to redirect almost half of this money, 5,000 livres, to Condorcet.

Imagine the reaction when money dedicated for academic research projects suddenly is diverted to an administrator's pay. It happened;

the experimentalist complained, and Turgot changed course. One must believe that Borda was effective in this fight because it was in Condorcet's counterresponse, to justify taking this cash, where Condorcet makes his widely quoted condemnation of Borda as abandoning mathematics for "petty applied science."

Condorcet's silly comment, which Peyton Young [121] rejects as exhibiting "a certain amount of personal venom," can be dismissed as "so-is-your-father" name-calling, merely reflecting the heat of battle. After all, Borda already was a recognized mathematician – where Borda's seminal contribution defining the meter in our metric system was a direct consequence of his "petty applied science" and some of his research remains relevant within mathematics today. In contrast, none of Condorcet's work in mathematics – distinct from social mathematics – has survived.[5]

Adopting an equal-opportunity approach, Condorcet attacked *everyone* doing empirical research. Fortunately, his myopic views were not taken seriously, even by a later version of himself. Imagine the ill effects this would have had where several rewards of contemporary science and society are based on empirical insights. I prefer to dismiss Condorcet's comments as a young man's natural elbow-swinging reaction in the midst of an appropriation squabble; far worse commentary comes from contemporary politicians. Condorcet should be, and is, judged by his many positive accomplishments including his efforts to advance science – even the empirical sciences.

Now toss in political disagreements. Prior to the money appropriation incident, academy members were upset because, rather than following tradition where *they* would select who would occupy the powerful position of secretary, the academy members were forced to ratify the choice of Condorcet. This choice-of-one, which was determined with the approval of a minister with the authority of the king, was part of the political plotting of Condorcet's supporters. I cannot discover whether Borda was for

---

[5] Early in his career, Condorcet was called one of the top ten mathematicians of his time. I can find no mathematician who knows anything about him other than through social choice and French history, so what is the source of this comment? The best I can determine is that Condorcet used series to compute certain integral calculus problems, now standard but then relatively new. His research on social mathematics, of course, remains important both historically and in substance.

or against this foisting of Condorcet on the academy, but because Borda took the academy very seriously, one must suspect that his voice was well heard. If so, this action would have contributed to Condorcet's negative attitude. Borda did fight against the academy leadership's censorship of publications – actions that would affect and limit Condorcet.

What strikes me is that everything I can find about Condorcet's negative attitude toward Borda occurred during the hot and heavy events associated with Condorcet striving to secure his position of secretary. Remember, this happened when Condorcet was in his thirties – when his supporters and managers were laboring to have him socialized.

Blocking Borda's Publication

A serious, persistent charge is that Condorcet blocked the publication of Borda's seminal paper – the written version of his 1770 presentation. That may be true, but the history is more complicated. Remember, when Borda gave his presentation, Condorcet was 27 years old, a recently elected member with no authority over academy publications. Moreover, the early 1770s saw an increase in the number of scientific papers to be handled by the then ailing secretary Fouchy. The obvious occurred; during this time *all* publications suffered lengthy delays where "much scientific material was lost for years... in 'the bottomless pit of the secretariat'" ([5], p. 35). Condorcet is blameless for these delays; the fault lay with Fouchy's negligence, which was exacerbated by an increased workload and limited help.

After Condorcet assumed power, that backlog had to be handled. Then, as anyone who has served as an editor must wonder, a legitimate mistake might have been made. Rather than suppressing Borda's contribution, it may have taken time for Condorcet to recognize the importance of Borda's paper, albeit through his own new research interests and with characteristic bumbling to cover his delay. After all, only with hindsight was the seminal value of Borda's paper applauded. In fact, it is reasonable to question whether even Borda appreciated the significance of what he did in 1770; as speculated previously, he probably viewed this work as a valued *internal* contribution to the functioning of the academy. Personally, I prefer to give Condorcet the strong benefit of the doubt.

The two of them most surely exchanged harsh words in the 1780s with their arguments over voting rules. This is nothing new; this happens whenever strong-willed individuals differ over something they view as being important. However, extrapolating from contemporary debates in this area, which can be strongly contested on a professional basis but seldom extend to a personal level, why should we equate professional disagreements with bitter personal relationships? Condorcet definitely had difficulties with personal interactions early on, but by the mid-1780s he appeared to have mellowed.

My favorable views are further shaped by the reality that Borda and Condorcet worked together, seemingly well, on committees. In 1790, for instance, Borda chaired a committee to develop the metric system, and Condorcet served along with mathematicians such as Laplace and Lagrange. Did they have disputes? Probably. Were they enemies? After Condorcet matured and became confident with his academy leadership role, I doubt it. After reviewing the issue, my sense is that these often expressed "enemy" comments have been overblown: I believe they are irrelevant and should be ignored.

I've said enough on this topic; as my main interest involves the theory of social choice, I now concentrate on the important and pragmatic issue of addressing, and trying to resolve, the difficulties that continually afflict this field: Here the seminal ideas of Borda and Condorcet continue to dominate. Thus, expect their ideas to play an important role in what follows.

1.4 Curse of Dimensionality

From the start – with Borda's original article and with Condorcet's subsequent analysis – mathematics has played a central role in the theory of social choice. There is an excellent reason: The problems in this area can be so difficult that, typically, they require the muscle power of mathematics to sort out what happens and to analyze the situation.

An often unrecognized source of this complexity is the *curse of dimensionality*. This curse is the primary cause for all voting paradoxes as well as the controversy about which voting rule is "optimal"; it is responsible for our inability to comprehend what can occur in voting theory and social choice. The effects of this curse are illustrated throughout this book.

To explain, by using modern computer graphing methods, say with a Maple program, we can develop intuition even about a particularly complex function $y = f(x)$. Just have the computer draw a graph on the two-dimensional space – the horizontal axis is the one-dimensional domain while the vertical axis is the one-dimensional range. The resulting picture displays behaviors and properties. Similarly, we can even appreciate the subtleties of problems where the domain – the space of inputs – is two- or three-dimensional. But the excessively high dimensionality of voting prevents us from using standard, illustrative graphs for even a three-candidate election.

To identify the villain, notice that even after excluding ties, there are $3! = 6$ transitive ways to rank three candidates; for example, if the candidates are A, B, C, then a voter might prefer $A \succ B \succ C$ (i.e., A is preferred to B and C, and B is preferred to C), or $B \succ C \succ A$, or .... Just listing how many voters have each of six possible preferences defines a vector in a six-dimensional space. The space of outputs – where each candidate's tally is specified – is in a three-dimensional space. Thus, a standard "graph" requires a nine-dimensional space. There are ways (Saari [64]) to reduce the three-candidate election problem to a five-dimensional domain with a two-dimensional space of outputs, or a seven-dimensional setting. *Seven* dimensions is unfathomable! I have trouble visualizing geometric settings beyond our comfortable three dimensions, so forget a graph in a seven-dimensional space.

It gets worse; six candidates require a 719-dimensional domain where the range, the space of outputs, is a 129-dimensional space![6] A standard $y = f(x)$ graph would require an 848-dimensional space! Ouch! The impossibility of comprehending such a representation reflects the curse of dimensionality – a curse that plays a major role in muddling up the theory of voting.

---

[6] To explain these numbers, the domain involves the $6! = 720$ ways to rank six candidates. As for the range, the six-candidate rankings are in a six-dimensional space, the six five-candidate rankings consume another $6 \times 5 = 30$ dimensions, and so forth. With some tricks, the sum of numbers for the range dimension reduces to 129.

Mathematics is the only discipline currently available where we can transcend our experiences, and it plays a valued role in handling this dimensionality problem, which complicates social choice. For instance, nobody I know has experienced life beyond our three-dimensional world, yet even a college undergraduate armed with a first course in linear algebra can handle aspects of the geometry associated with a six-, or ten-, or twenty-dimensional setting. Topological, combinatoric, algebraic, and other mathematical techniques lead to a better understanding of this field: Mathematics is a required tool. Indeed, the muscle power of mathematics has uncovered results that might never have been discovered otherwise. A prime example is when Kenneth Arrow [2] skillfully used combinatoric methods from mathematics to prove his stunning, seminal result about voting theory (see Chapter 2). Arrow showed that the only decision rule satisfying certain desirable and seemingly innocuous conditions is a dictatorship! Without question, the enormous life injected into the theory of voting by this counterintuitive result ushered in the true Golden Age of voting and social choice. Many other results, discovered through mathematical reasoning, quickly followed.

As a mathematician who loves his discipline, I am expected to promote the virtues of mathematical approaches. I do, but with words of caution. For mathematicians, mathematics is a way of thinking; for non-mathematicians it usually is a tool – that can be misused. Mathematics has significantly advanced social choice, but at times (see Chapter 3) its misuse has lead the field in directions that I find to be futile because they mask the real issues. An appropriate use of the tools of mathematics requires finding the "correct" mathematical framework for understanding social choice. The necessary, subtle mathematical frameworks needed to advance the area of social choice must be developed.

1.5 Outline

Finding an appropriate mathematical framework to analyze social choice, to conquer that dimensionality curse, has been my objective since I stumbled on this fascinating academic area. This book will describe only a portion of my findings, so let me state what is not covered.

First, even though my research has been associated with developing the *geometry of voting* and even though this approach has provided several new insights, this topic will not be covered here. Indeed, an exposition is in my article [73]. Also, I emphasize concepts rather than mathematical details: Supporting details are in the original referenced papers and in a planned, more technical book.

1.5.1 Dethroning Dictators, and Then Paradoxes

Chapter 2 addresses the frustration caused by all of those impossibility results, such as Arrow's theorem. The jist of these well-known results is that we cannot do what we may want to do when designing voting rules. Is this true? The conclusions stated by these eminent authors are, of course, correct. But, as I will explain, their *interpretations* can be misleading. The central difficulty is that explicitly stated information that we believe is being used is not. Once we understand why these conclusions arise, it is easy to find benign interpretations for many of them and, of great importance, to discover positive conclusions.

A second theme, in Chapters 3–5, is to discover "What causes all of those voting and social choice paradoxes?" The intent of these chapters, which provides a convenient framework to analyze voting rules, is to go beyond the negative results in the field to find appropriate mathematical structures to systemetically discover positive conclusions. It is reasonable to think of this work as exploring how to tame the dimensionality curse.

What connects these two themes is the mathematical perspective that provides a way to analyze voting and decision rules. The idea is captured in Figure 1, which is just a standard representation of a mapping from its domain to the range. In voting, the domain is the space of profiles – a list of possible voter preferences – while the range is the space of election or decision outcomes and the mapping F is the decision rule.

As described in Chapter 2, after specifying the domain and range, Arrow's approach emphasizes the structure and properties of the decision rule. He proves that for a decision rule, or mapping, to satisfy certain desirable conditions, the outcome strictly depends on the preferences of

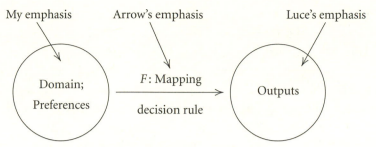

Figure 1. Schematic for choice analysis.

one particular voter – a dictator. In mathematical terms, F is equivalent to a function of a single variable.

Stimulated by his result, an extensive literature developed showing how to restrict the domain, or extend the allowable kinds of election outcomes, with the goal of trying to relax Arrow's negative conclusion. In other words, after specifying the properties of a decision rule, the only variables left to explore are the structures of the domain – usually in terms of profile restrictions – and range – moving from complete, transitive societal rankings to quasi-transitive, or acyclic, or other kinds of societal rankings. Arrow's powerful influence on this field is reflected by how his emphasis on the properties of decision and election rules continues to dominate the field.

A second approach was developed in the 1950s. While the initial intent was to analyze individual decisions, it is easy to translate these results into a discussion of voting methods. R. Duncan Luce [29] pioneered this conceptually different methodology where he stressed the structure of the admissible societal outcomes, rather than the properties of a decision rule. More precisely, Luce admitted only election outcomes with certain desirable properties that are stronger than Arrow's central requirements. Luce's conditions admit a nice interpretation whereby each alternative can be viewed as having an intrinsic level of strength, or support, that is preserved over all possible subsets of alternatives.

By specifying the allowable outcomes, the variables left to attain Luce's desired conclusions are the choice of the decision rule and profile restrictions. That is, the actual decision rule with its corresponding profile restrictions is determined in terms of Luce's choice axiom. By mandating that only desirable election outcomes can occur, positive conclusions do emerge. The cost, which involves restrictions on the admissible preferences, is not overly high. For instance, Luce's approach yields stronger properties than usually allowed with restrictions such as Black's single-peaked condition [7]. Yet, in a real manner, Luce's restricted preferences are more relaxed than Black's single-peaked condition (Saari [81]). (A purpose of [81] was to use advances from social choice theory to extend Luce's approach; much more can be done in this direction.) It is worth noting that an important consequence of Luce's axiom is the now familiar Logit model from statistics.

1.5.2 The "Will of the Voters": What Is It?

My approach reflects my belief that the major intricacies of social choice are due to the curse of dimensionality. To understand the nature of the culprit causing the excessive dimensionality, which is the domain, my emphasis is to identify natural structures for the space of preferences.

Of course, in order to capture the "will of the voters," we must determine what the voters want. Be assured; I am not advocating surveys. Instead, mathematical structures are used to identify data structures, or configurations of preferences, with which it is arguable that the resulting societal outcome should be of a certain kind. It is easy, for instance, to construct configurations of preferences where the election outcome should be a tie. So if an election rule fails to provide a tie with this configuration, we have added information about the inner workings of the rule. A related, but slightly different approach is described in Section 4.4.

In particular, these data structures serve as a filter. If a voting rule has an expected outcome for a profile configuration, it "passes." If the rule does not have an anticipated outcome, then we can better understand why the rule can admit unexpected outcomes. Stated in more mathematical terms, these configurations of profiles, which correspond to level sets of different rules, define a coordinate system for profile space where one class of rules may have ties in one direction of profile space, but other rules do not.

As this approach creates a coordinate system, it is agnostic: You decide, not I, whether you want certain data structures to define certain election outcomes. After you decide, your choice identifies the permitted election rules. This approach of emphasizing the structure of preferences – the level sets of the decision rules – continues through much of what follows; it is the basis for Chapter 4. Indeed, this coordinate system significantly tames the dimensionality curse while providing a much quicker way to analyze election systems.

TWO

Dethroning Dictators

Rarely does a proposal enjoy a complete consensus; however, the proposition that the field of social choice owes an enormous debt to Kenneth Arrow would pass unanimously. Even though we can debate who should receive credit for siring this academic discipline – Borda, Condorcet, or both – Arrow's insights clearly inspired the modern rebirth of the field. The startling, counterintuitive conclusions of his Ph.D. thesis [2] served as a powerful magnet to attract talented researchers to this area.

Arrow's profound result is negative; it states that it is impossible to do what seems to be obviously possible to do. The astounding nature of his assertion unleashed an avalanche of negative conclusions that seemed to bury us with exasperation: "Is everything that we want to do impossible to do?" The persistence of this theme created a frustrated sense that positive conclusions in this area probably do not exist. This was the prevailing attitude when I moved into this field: The researchers, resembling a gaggle of partying morticians, cheerfully greeted me with this pessimistic commentary. In this chapter, I will provide some hope by showing how and why the situation is nowhere near as dire as these results suggest.

I found it surprising that many of the major negative conclusions have amazingly similar explanations. The value of knowing *why* these negative results occur is that, often, this information can be used to replace the frustrating negativity with positive assertions.

2.1 Major Negative Conclusions

Before explaining why so many things can go so wrong, it is worth reviewing these negative conclusions that have so strongly influenced our thinking. The granddaddy, of course, is Arrow's result. After introducing Sen's influential conclusion, I describe an interesting but negative topological result discovered by Chichilnisky. This is followed by several voting examples that have raised questions beyond voting theory to include concerns within the legal world and even philosophy.

After reviewing what can go wrong, the next step is to identify what causes these negative assertions. As a preview, they occur because *information we believe is being used by the decision rule is not being considered at all.* To discover the nature of this ignored information, which by not being used makes these negative conclusions obvious rather than surprising, I will examine the domain – the space of individual preferences.

2.1.1 Arrow's Theorem

A convenient way to view Arrow's theorem is to specify the domain and range and then the specific properties that are imposed on decision rules.

1. *Domain:* The space of "inputs" consists of all possible individual preferences in Arrow's setting; it is where each voter has a complete, transitive ranking of all alternatives. That is, if a voter prefers Anni to Bobbie and Bobbie to Connie, then the voter prefers Anni to Connie. No restrictions are imposed on which transitive ranking a voter chooses. The domain, then, consists of all possible arrangements of how the voters rank the candidates.
2. *Range:* The requirement on the range, or space of election outcomes, is that the candidates are ranked in a transitive manner. This makes sense. Otherwise, if the voters prefer Anni to Barb, Barb to Connie, and Connie to Anni, who do they prefer? To avoid such cyclic conclusions, Arrow insisted on transitivity.[1]

---

[1] In a personal conversation (January 2006), Arrow told me that when he developed his theorem, he did not know about "acyclicity" where, weaker than a transitive

It remains to select properties for the decision rule. A natural condition specifies the societal outcome when all voters agree on the relative ranking of a pair of alternatives.

3. *Pareto:* For any pair of candidates, if all voters rank the pair in the same way, the common ranking is the pair's societal ranking.

Beyond unanimity, shouldn't the societal ranking of a pair be based strictly on what the voters think of this pair? After all, it is reasonable to expect that a group's ranking of a CD featuring Mozart with a CD featuring Sibelius is independent of their thoughts about a CD featuring Beethoven. If, for instance, some voters gain an appreciation for Beethoven, why should this affect the Mozart–Sibelius ranking?

4. *Binary Independence, or IIA (Independence of Irrelevant Alternatives):* The ranking of a pair of alternatives depends only on how the voters rank this particular pair; information about other alternatives is irrelevant. More specifically, if $\mathbf{p}_1$ and $\mathbf{p}_2$ are any two profiles for which each voter has the same relative ranking of some specified pair, then the societal ranking for this pair is the same for both profiles.

These innocuous appearing conditions seem to be standard: The surprise – and it is a stunning surprise – is that they are incompatible.

Theorem 2.1 (Arrow [2]): With three or more alternatives, the only decision rule that satisfies the preceding four conditions is a dictatorship. Namely, there is a specified voter so that the societal outcome always agrees with that voter's preference.

---

outcome, the rankings cannot be cyclic. A nice feature of his theorem is how it excludes nontransitive acyclic settings. As an example, pairwise voting over three candidates where a winner needs more than a two-thirds vote satisfies Pareto, independence of irrelevant alternatives (IIA), and it *never* admits cycles. Yet this rule is subsumed by Arrow's theorem because it allows nontransitive outcomes such as where $A \sim B$, $B \sim C$ (in each pair, neither candidate received more than two-thirds of the vote), but $A > C$. A ten-voter illustrating profile is where three each prefer $A > C > B$, $C > B > A$, and $B > A > C$, and one prefers $A > B > C$.

A dictator! Viewed in terms of power, the situation is worrisome because Arrow's dictator is absolute rather than benevolent. The societal outcome depends strictly on the dictator's preferences, while everyone else's wishes are totally ignored.

The voting rules we normally use are not equivalent to an absolute dictator, so this theorem ensures that settings exist whereby our rule violates at least one of Arrow's conditions. An obvious example is the 2000 presidential vote in Florida. Even though Bush beat Gore, the polls indicated that, with a smaller Nader support, Gore would have beaten Bush (i.e., the plurality vote violates binary independence). The point is that for *all* nondictatorial election rules, settings exist where Arrow's conditions fail to be satisfied. This leads to the traditional interpretation of Arrow's theorem that there does not, and cannot, exist a "fair" election method. Is this interpretation correct? After raising doubts, I will show why it is not.

To indicate where my argument is going, notice how easy it is to identify the binary independence (IIA) condition as the culprit causing this difficulty. The goal is to move beyond suspecting *that* IIA creates this dictatorial problem and to understand *why*. Moreover, because IIA is the primary reason for Arrow's conclusion, it is useful to discuss the reasonableness, or lack of reasonableness, of this condition.

2.1.2 Sen's Seminal Result

When I ask men in my audience "What a nice shirt you have on. Who said you could wear it?" a frequent answer is "My wife."

Choosing a shirt to wear is a personal decision, which is the intended point of my question. Certain aspects of personal life are one's own, so the decisions should remain private rather than be submitted to a community discussion. As a corollary, these kinds of personal decisions and choices should remain strictly within the domain of a particular individual. With the man in the audience, the decisive person is his wife.

Sen's theorem addresses this interaction between societal and individual concerns, but leads to another troubling, negative conclusion. As with Arrow's theorem, I introduce Sen's insightful result by first specifying the domain and range, and then the conditions that are imposed on the decision rule.

1. *Domain:* The domain, or space of individual preferences, is where each voter has a complete, transitive ranking of all alternatives. No restrictions are imposed on the ranking a voter chooses.

Sen's choice for the range is more flexible than that in Arrow's setting. Instead of insisting upon transitive rankings, Sen merely requires the election outcomes to avoid cyclic rankings.

2. *Range:* The range, or space of potential outcomes, consists of all rankings of the candidates that have no cycles.

Two conditions are imposed on the decision rule. The first is the obvious Pareto condition.

3. *Pareto:* For any pair of candidates, if all voters rank the pair in the same way, then that common ranking is the societal ranking for the pair.

The next condition ensures that some individuals can make a choice over specified pairs of alternatives. To illustrate with the earlier shirt example, the man's wife had the option of choosing between two different shirts that he could wear: She, and only she, could make the selection.

4. *Minimal Liberalism (ML):* At least two individuals are each assigned at least one pair of alternatives. For each of these *decisive agents*, their ranking of the pairs of alternatives assigned to them is the societal ranking of the pair.

These conditions appear to be innocuous and quite natural; nevertheless, they are incompatible.

Theorem 2.2 (Sen [102]): With three or more alternatives, no decision rule satisfies these four conditions.

To indicate the ubiquity of Sen's conclusion while illustrating his result, consider the following example, which, essentially, is from my paper with my graduate student Lingfang (Ivy) Li [27]. The example involves a search committee, consisting of Adrian and Erik, charged with selecting one of the candidates Anni, Brigid, or Claudia for a tenured position in an economics department. Information about the candidates follows:

Name	Micro Papers	Macro Papers	Hair Color
Anni	40	16	Blond
Brigid	21	19	Brown
Claudia	10	17	Black

(2.1)

The decision rule satisfies Sen's theorem: Erik is an expert in microeconomics, so he determines the committee ranking of Anni and Brigid because both claim expertise in this area. Similarly, as an expert in macroeconomics, Adrian determines the committee's ranking of Anni and Claudia because both applied for a position in this area. Of course, should Adrian and Erik agree about how to rank a pair, that is the committee ranking.

According to the data in Equation 2.1, Erik's ranking is Anni $\succ$ Brigid $\succ$ Claudia, while Adrian's ranking is Brigid $\succ$ Claudia $\succ$ Anni. The committee's outcome, which illustrates Sen's conclusion, is as follows:

- Erik imposes the "Anni $\succ$ Brigid" committee ranking.
- By unanimity, the committee ranks "Brigid $\succ$ Claudia."
- Adrian imposes the "Claudia $\succ$ Anni" committee ranking.

This leads to indecision caused by a cycle! ("Hair color" is used in Section 2.3.2.)

Sen's conclusion commonly is described as pinpointing a serious conflict arising between individual rights, as captured by minimal liberalism, and community concerns, as reflected by the unanimity of the Pareto condition. After all, because these are the only two substantive conditions imposed on the rule, where else could discord arise? I will again raise serious doubts about this traditional interpretation. In particular, after describing a radically different explanation for the conflict captured by Sen's result, we will discover that while Sen's theorem raises issues about individual rights and community concerns, new concerns arise that can differ significantly from traditional interpretations. For instance, rather than infringing on individual rights, in some settings Sen's cycles more accurately capture the frustrations of a dysfunctional society – or search committee.

2.1.3 Topological Dictators

"What a beautiful day!" It is too nice to stay in the office, so some of us, who happen to live on a circular island, are planning a party at the beach. Where? Well, the beach resembles a circle, designated by S^1, so we'll adopt an appropriate decision rule for circles to select the party site. Although it is not clear what rule to use, desired properties of the decision method follow:

1. *Domain:* Each person can select any point on S^1 – the beach. There are no restrictions.
2. *Range:* The outcome can be any point on S^1 – the beach.

Now that the domain and range have been specified, it remains to designate the properties of the decision rule. The first is the ever-present condition of unanimity.

3. *Unanimity:* If everyone agrees on the location for the party, then that is where it will be. In more formal terms, if $\theta_j \in S^1$ is the position preferred by the jth person, and if the n voters agree as $\theta_1 = \theta_2 = \cdots = \theta_n = \theta \in S^1$, then

$$F(\theta_1, \theta_2, \ldots, \theta_n) = \theta$$

The next two technical conditions are crucial. Continuity is needed because without it an infinitesimal change in even one person's choice could cause an undesired change or jump in the outcome. Without continuity, for instance, should a person's opinion change even by the half-width of a grain of beach sand, the outcome could jump.

The second condition avoids obviously unacceptable outcomes. For example, if only two people are planning to party and one wants to be on the east part of the beach while the other prefers moving slightly to the south to enjoy more sun, they would both be upset with a decision rule that selects a location directly to the west.

4. *Continuity:* The decision rule, $F : S^1 \times \cdots \times S^1 \to S^1$, is continuous.
5. *Pareto:* With $n = 2$, if there is a unique shortest distance between the two voter choices, the outcome is on that arc.

For the motivating beach example, the Pareto condition requires the outcome to be essentially in an eastern direction, somewhere between the two preferred choices. Notice how the Pareto condition includes "unanimity" as a special case. As it turns out (see [24]), the Pareto and unanimity conditions can be significantly relaxed. After stating the result, the sole remaining technical term of *homotopy* will be defined.

Theorem 2.3 (Chichilnisky [11]): Any continuous mapping

$$F(\theta_1, \theta_2) : S^1 \times S^1 \to S^1$$

that satisfies unanimity and the Pareto condition is homotopic to a dictator.

Chichilnisky's beautiful results are more general; they admit any number of voters where F represents a mapping that allows each person to select a point in the k-dimensional sphere, denoted by S^k, with the outcome also in S^k. (Also, see the nice work of Baigent [3].)

A graduate student of mine, Jason Kronewetter, and I [24] generalized this theorem in different directions. We sought conclusions that would address more general economic and choice settings. A typical example is to position an industrial plant on a rectangular piece of land that is full of holes. One hole might be created, for instance, by a lake or a mountain, while other holes might identify where the plant cannot be built because the sites are already occupied, maybe by schools or personal property.

Another example involves positioning a satellite somewhere over the Earth; the problem is to select a point on a two-dimensional sphere S^2. If, in addition, the satellite's orientation must also be determined, which may be true for communication or weather satellites, then the domain is $S^2 \times S^2$. I could go on and on, but the main point is that whenever regions have "holes," expect the selection mapping to be "homotopic to a dictator."

To understand the term *homotopic*, recall that topology is the study of mathematical properties that remain constant even after an object is twisted, shrunk, deformed, and/or stretched. This leads to the joke that a topologist cannot distinguish between a donut and a coffee cup: Each object has one hole so if either one consists of a pliable material, it could be stretched, twisted, pushed, and pulled into the other. With this background, the topological dictator conclusion sounds horrible: It projects the image of a twisted, wrinkled, shrunk despot! What is it in reality?

Think of a decision rule $F(\theta_1, \theta_2)$ as being homotopic to a dictator if it is possible to continuously diminish, or "shrink," an agent's influence from what it actually is to where the agent now has absolutely no impact. When the agent no longer can influence the outcome, the other agent is free to make the decision; he has become a dictator. For example, consider the beach party where the first agent selects the location for the picnic, while the second one makes modifications, perhaps to move out of the sun. By continuously reducing the influence of the second person to nothing, we end up where what the first person wants is what we get; he is a dictator! It is important to note that the original rule is *not a dictatorship*. Only when the rule can be continuously transformed or collapsed into a dictatorship is it homotopic to a dictator.

The actual description provides a calmer image than that twisted despot, but what Kronewetter and I established still sounds horrible; it asserts that whenever there are holes in a domain, then some variable or agent dominates! As I also will show, there are many natural ways to avoid these negative conclusions.

2.1.4 "Paradox of Voting" and Condorcet's Triplets

One of the oldest mysteries in social choice is the *paradox of voting*.[2] The issue is to understand why the three-voter profile with transitive preferences

$$A \succ B \succ C, \quad B \succ C \succ A, \quad C \succ A \succ B \qquad (2.2)$$

defines a majority vote cycle. The vote tally leading to this cycle is illustrated in the following table where each ranking is divided into its binary

---

[2] For a comprehensive description of the Condorcet paradox, see William Gehrlein's book *Condorcet's Paradox* [20]. Gehrlein, a professor in the business school at the University of Delaware, has made important contributions to social choice, particularly with his pioneering insights about the likelihood of various behaviors. For an interesting description of the role of this paradox in law, see Cheryl Block's article [8].

parts. In each column, one candidate beats the opponent by a 2 : 1 vote; the cyclic outcome is listed in the bottom row.

Ranking	$\{A, B\}$	$\{B, C\}$	$\{A, C\}$
$A \succ B \succ C$	$A \succ B$	$B \succ C$	$A \succ C$
$B \succ C \succ A$	$B \succ A$	$B \succ C$	$C \succ A$
$C \succ A \succ B$	$A \succ B$	$C \succ B$	$C \succ A$
Outcome	$A \succ B$	$B \succ C$	$C \succ A$

(2.3)

The significance of this example starts with Condorcet's belief that the best societal decision is for a group to use majority voting over pairs. In honor of his pioneering efforts, a candidate who beats all others in pairwise majority votes is called the *Condorcet winner*, while the candidate who loses to all others is the *Condorcet loser*.

What I like about the example in Equation 2.3 is that when something is proposed, both its advantages *and* known flaws should be reported. Condorcet, who is credited with the example in Equation 2.3, proves there are settings where his approach fails because neither a Condorcet winner nor a Condorcet loser is defined.

The troubling example in Equation 2.3 cannot be dismissed; it is central for much of what is discussed throughout this book. A version of this triplet, for instance, forms the core of my example in footnote 1 in this chapter. I highly recommend that you try to explain why these three transitive preferences in Equation 2.3 cause a cyclic conclusion and what it means. (See the explanation in Section 2.2.2 and the more complete discussion in Chapter 4.)

2.1.5 List's Lists

Christian List,[3] an active participant in the Caen conference that accompanied my Condorcet Lecture, and his coauthors have explored several troubling philosophical and legal issues. (See, for example, [28].) Rather than exploring one of his discursive paradox examples, let me introduce

---

[3] Christian List, who is on the faculty of the Department of Government of the London School of Economics, is interested in a variety of topics ranging from philosophy to social choice.

one that connects the flavor of these arguments with the common experiences of many readers.

Suppose a three-member faculty committee must determine whether or not a student should be advanced to Ph.D. candidacy (or whether an assistant professor should receive tenure or ...). A majority vote is required to advance. Each faculty member's decision is based on the student's performance on both a written and an oral exam. If a faculty member feels that the student failed one or both of these exams, she is instructed to fail the student. The results follow where a "yes" or "no" indicates the judge's opinion on an exam and whether to advance.

Judge	Written	Oral	Decision
1	Yes	Yes	Yes
2	No	Yes	No
3	Yes	No	No
Outcome	Yes	Yes	No

(2.4)

The student is denied advancement (the last column) because two of the three judges found him deficient in at least one category. On the other hand, a majority of the judges found that the student passed the written exam (the second column), and a majority found that he passed the oral exam (the third column). Had the committee used a decision rule that first assesses the student's performance over each criterion and then makes the final decision based on these outcomes, he would have passed! The career of a student and the integrity of a program are on the line, so which approach is appropriate? Should the student be judged on each criterion, or on the whole? How do you explain this conflict?

2.1.6 Anscombe

I discovered the Anscombe paradox [1] by reading one of Hannu Nurmi's[4] delightful books [44]. The worrisome phenomenon occurs when

a majority of the voters can be on the losing side on a majority of the issues.

---

[4] Hannu Nurmi is an Academy Professor at the Academy of Finland and a Professor of Political Science in the University of Turku, Turku, Finland. He is a leader of public and social choice activities in the Nordic countries.

A quick way to introduce this paradox is with an example where voters 1, 2, and 3 constitute the suffering majority, and voters 4 and 5 form the minority that always prevails. Suppose there are three issues where a "yes" or "no" vote indicates a voter's support or disapproval.

Voter	Issue 1	Issue 2	Issue 3
1	Yes	Yes	No
2	No	Yes	Yes
3	Yes	No	Yes
4	No	No	No
5	No	No	No
Outcome	No	No	No

$$(2.5)$$

Voters 1, 2, and 3, a majority of the voters, are on the losing side two out of three times; voters 4 and 5, however, always are on the winning side.

Alternatively, when viewed in terms of a political party, even though the majority coalition of voters 1, 2, and 3 approves of all three concerns, they lose in a majority vote on all three issues each with a $3:2$ vote. Beyond providing a paradox, this example illustrates a reason behind the political reality where political parties enforce "party discipline."

2.1.7 A Standard Requirement

An interesting commonality among Arrow's theorem, Sen's theorem, the voting paradox, List's lists, and Anscombe's paradox is that they all require three or more alternatives or two or more pairs. This is not an accident, as will be explained in the next section. The curse of dimensionality is involved.

2.2 Commonality

I could provide many other examples not found in the literature.[5] But to avoid bombarding you with a barrage of negative results, particularly

---

[5] See my book [75] for examples that have related explanations that involve apportionment problems (e.g., the apportionment of congressional seats in the United States); economic supply and demand; interpersonal interactions in psychology, finance, and gambling; and even basic questions from probability and statistics.

after promising to eventually offer some cheer, let me move to the next stage by showing what is common among the last three results. After that, I will explain why they all occur.

My explanation emphasizes the structure of the space of individual preferences because this is the domicile of the dimensionality curse. By describing this structure, you will discover how to create all sorts of new examples illustrating troubling conclusions for a wide selection of other themes. The analysis starts with the Condorcet triplet.

2.2.1 Condorcet's Ideas Dominate

Even though the Anscombe paradox, List's lists, and the Condorcet cycle appear to identify distinctly different phenomena, they do not; *each is a special case of the same behavior*. In fact, it takes just a "name change" to convert each example into one of the others. For example, by changing the Condorcet triplet (Equation 2.3) names into "Yes" and "No" labels, we discover that all of these troubling behaviors become special versions of Condorcet's example.

From Condorcet to List and Anscombe

To create the example in Equation 2.4, which illustrates one of List's lists, simply replace $A \succ B$ in the Condorcet table with "Yes" (so $B \succ A$ is replaced with "No"); $B \succ C$, with "Yes"; and $A \succ C$, with "Yes". Equation 2.4 immediately emerges. This tight connection suggests that, while novel philosophical concerns may be attached to the tables, all of List's three-judge examples are, in fact, rewordings of the Condorcet triplet. As shown in the next section, this always is the case.

The same argument holds for Anscombe's paradox. Here the assignment of "Yes" or "No" differs only in the "Issue 3" column. In this column identify $A \succ C$ with a "No" vote. The first three voters in the majority coalition turn out to be nothing more than the Condorcet triplet where "Yes" will win in a 2 : 1 vote over each issue. To create the Anscombe paradox, just introduce two more voters – constituting the minority party – who are negative over each issue. Again, the key component for all examples illustrating Anscombe's paradox is essentially a rewording of the Condorcet triplet.

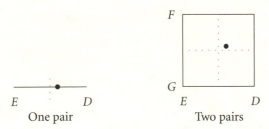

Figure 2. Pairwise voting.

They Always Are Related

A one-to-one "name change" identification between any mysterious majority vote phenomena and the Condorcet triplet argument holds for all three alternative settings. The following geometric argument establishing this fact comes from a paper [89] I wrote with Katri Sieberg.[6]

To review our argument, start with a pair of alternatives, say $\{D, E\}$, maybe "David" and "Elaine." The $\{D, E\}$ majority vote outcome can be represented with a point on a straight line with endpoints labeled D and E. If, for instance, D beats E by receiving 60 percent of the vote, then, as indicated with the point ($\bullet$) on the line in Figure 2, place the point 60 percent of the way from E to D. For one pair, this point represents both the election outcome and the profile: D received 60 percent of the vote and 60 percent of the voters prefer $D \succ E$.

Now add a second pair $\{F, G\}$; suppose the same voters give 55 percent support to F over G. By placing the D–E and F–G axes, respectively, in the horizontal and vertical directions to create a square, the joint outcome is represented by the point $(0.6, 0.55)$ in the Figure 2 square.

Adding a second pair unleashes the "curse of dimensionality." In particular, even though the point in the square accurately specifies both election outcomes, it *no longer identifies the profile*. For instance, using

[6] Katri Sieberg, a frequent coauthor of mine who studies a wide variety of topics from power indices to game theory to conflict to crime (e.g., see her book *Criminal Dilemmas* [109]), is a political scientist at the State University of New York, Binghamton. She currently holds the Erkko chaired professorship at Tampere University, Tampere, Finland.

an example Sieberg developed for our paper, is there significant support for the joint outcome because

55 percent of the voters prefer the actual $D \succ E$, $F \succ G$ outcome, while 45 percent disagree as 5 percent prefer $D \succ E$, $G \succ F$ and the remaining 40 percent prefer the opposite $E \succ D$, $G \succ F$,

or is the support for the joint outcome questionable because

only 15 percent prefer the actual $D \succ E$, $F \succ G$ outcome, while a huge 85 percent of the voters express discontent by disagreeing with at least one outcome? The 85 percent of the voters splits where 45 percent of all voters prefer $D \succ E$ but disagree with the outcome by preferring $G \succ F$ and 40 percent prefer $F \succ G$ but disagree by preferring $E \succ D$.

To describe this example as Sieberg does, consider the common situation where local school teachers are underpaid and have poor health benefits. To correct the problem, suppose two proposals are put forth for a vote: One is to increase wages, and the other is to improve benefits. Each axis in Figure 2 is a "yes"–"no" vote on one issue; let D be a vote *against* a salary increase and F a vote *against* improved benefits.

A rewording of Sieberg's first example is that

the community is so unsympathetic with the teachers that 55 percent of the voters voted against both proposals. Only 40 percent of all voters voted for both proposals, and 5 percent of the voters voted to increase benefits but not wages.

In contrast, the community might be highly sympathetic to the plight of their teachers. In keeping with the second scenario,

a full 85 percent of the voters want to help the teachers! Budgetary concerns, however, make it impossible to approve both salary advances and benefit changes so a choice must be made. In doing so, 45 percent of all voters, worried about health costs, support improved benefits but not a salary increase. On the other hand, 40 percent of all voters support a salary increase over improved benefits. Only 15 percent of the voters are against both propositions.

Both scenarios have identical election outcomes: A salary increase loses with the 60 percent vote against it, and a change in benefits loses with the 55 percent negative vote. In the first scenario, this outcome accurately reflects the voters' views. In the second, however, the election outcomes grossly violate the majority's (85 percent) intent to help the teachers. This is Sieberg's point: It is possible for a significant number of the voters to strongly disagree with the election outcomes. This kind of structure, involving lost information, allows us to create those election paradoxes that all theoreticians have learned to love. As shown next, these inconsistencies are caused by a dimension curse, which is a theme of this book. See Section 2.2.2 for a more general explanation, which identifies a disturbing feature of majority votes.

Adding this second pair unleashes the dimensionality curse: The domain for the two-pair problem jumps from a one-dimensional line to a *four*-dimensional space. Each direction represents a voter type: The types are the number of voters preferring (E, G) or (E, F) or (D, G) or (D, F). (Sieberg and I [89] show how to represent all possible profiles – including all paradoxical settings – that support any specified election outcome over pairs. As a corollary, our representation permits us to compute the likelihoods of different outcomes.)

To understand what is happening, recall from high school algebra that when solving a problem with more unknowns than equations, the solution can be a line or even a higher dimensional space. Similarly and in general, each joint outcome for the two pairs is supported not by a unique point but by a *two-dimensional* space of profiles.[7] As a result of this dimensional jump, which introduces enormous flexibility in selecting voters' preferences, finding profiles that appear to conflict with the election outcome is easy. The situation resembles a trip to a flea market: Who knows what can be found!

Three or More Pairs

If significant ambiguity between the outcome and a profile emerges just by introducing a second pair, imagine what happens with three or more pairs! To provide a measure of the increased complexity, Sieberg and I [89] proved for two pairs of alternatives that all supporting profiles must include *some* voters whose preferences agree with the actual outcome. But we also proved that this no longer is the case with three or more pairs. Instead, it could be that *nobody* likes the complete conclusion!

The "curse of dimensionality" emerges because, with three pairs, profile space now is *eight-dimensional*. In general, as we know from that

---

[7] Each outcome is given by an equation in the four variables. With two equations and four variables, a solution is supported by a $4 - 2 = 2$ dimensional space of profiles.

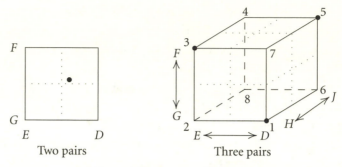

Figure 3. From two to three pairs.

high school algebra course, each joint outcome is supported by a *five-dimensional subspace of profiles. Five* dimensions are difficult to imagine! Our familiar physical world has only three dimensions, so three pairs create an even more complex setting with two extra directions in which trouble-making examples can reside! Of course, for many profiles in this five-dimensional space, the common outcome is reasonable. What creates interest are the many outliers lurking in the dark corners of this five-dimensional space for which the outcome appears to be incompatible and strange. In other words, the curse generated by these added dimensions is to encourage electoral mischief – including the existence of profiles where *everyone* disagrees with the outcome!

Fortunately, this eight-dimensional space of profiles can be visualized by using a simple cube. Much of what follows uses the familiar structure of a common box with its eight corners, or vertices, so it is worth pulling out a box – even a discarded cereal carton will do – label the corners as described, and trace out the arguments. To minimize abstract comments, assign names to the letters.

The phenomenon where nobody likes the outcome can be illustrated with the cube in Figure 3. To reduce the ever-present problem of notation contamination, the cube's vertices are labeled with numbers from the translation key.

Vertex	Ranking	Vertex	Ranking
1	$D \succ E, G \succ F, H \succ J$	2	$E \succ D, G \succ F, H \succ J$
3	$E \succ D, F \succ G, H \succ J$	4	$E \succ D, F \succ G, J \succ H$
5	$D \succ E, F \succ G, J \succ H$	6	$D \succ E, G \succ F, J \succ H$
7	$D \succ E, F \succ G, H \succ J$	8	$E \succ D, G \succ F, J \succ H$

To create a joint majority vote outcome over the three pairs where no voter totally agrees with the conclusion, notice that if the three voters have preferences given by vertices 1, 3, and 5, the outcome is closest to vertex 7; thus, this $D \succ E$, $F \succ G$, $H \succ J$ set of rankings is the outcome. So, this example is constructed by selecting a vertex for the outcome and then selecting each of the three neighboring vertices to define the three-voter profile.

To verify this assertion, check your cereal box, compute the majority vote tallies, or connect the three vertices to create an equilateral triangle. Using the geometry of the triangle, the election outcome, with the $D \succ E$, $F \succ G$, and $H \succ J$ joint outcome (where each wins with a $2:1$ vote), is located at the triangle's center. As promised, this example has an election outcome where each voter disagrees with at least one ranking for the outcome.

Five different profiles support this $D \succ G$, $F \succ G$, $H \succ J$ conclusion. Because they play central roles in what follows, each profile deserves a name. The unimaginative choices, listed next, merely use the vertex labels from the cube:

Profile Name	Voter 1's Type	Voter 2's Type	Voter 3's Type
$\mathbf{p}_1$	8	7	7
$\mathbf{p}_2$	1	4	7
$\mathbf{p}_3$	2	5	7
$\mathbf{p}_4$	3	6	7
$\mathbf{p}_5$	1	3	5

$$(2.6)$$

For the first four profiles, the first two voters completely disagree. For example, for the $\mathbf{p}_1$ example, the type 8 voter prefers $D \succ E$, and the type 7 voter prefers the opposite $E \succ D$; this contrariness holds for all pairs. By having diametrically opposite preferences on the cube, or opposite vertices on your cereal box, the two voters' opposite beliefs create a tie, which is broken by the third voter. For these four profiles, then, the joint outcome of a vertex 7 ranking is easily justified.

There remains an outlier. The only profile for which it may be difficult to justify its outcome is profile $\mathbf{p}_5$ where *nobody* fully agrees with the full outcome; on the cereal box, this profile consists of the three vertices surrounding vertex 7. This outlier, of course, directly manifests the curse of dimensionality; increasing the dimension of the space of profiles permits more outlier profiles that appear to be in conflict with the outcome. Sieberg and I [89] made this notion precise by proving that

majority vote pairwise outcomes always reflect the *average of all possible supporting profiles, but not necessarily a specific profile.*

This assertion resembles lessons from elementary statistics; a particular point need not resemble the "average." Similarly in voting, an outlier profile could be associated with a seemingly inconsistent outcome.

The Role of Outliers

Wait a minute. If an outlier p_5 is not representative of the outcome or of any other supporting profile, why is it of any interest? Can't we just dismiss it? Actually, we can't; this outlier profile plays a central role in choice theory. By using name changes, this outlier can be identified with the Condorcet profile, List's examples, and the soul of the Anscombe paradox.

To connect the Condorcet profile with the outlier profile, use the name changes

$$H = A \succ B, \; D = B \succ C, \quad \text{and} \quad F = C \succ A \, (\text{so } J = B \succ A, \text{etc.})$$

By carrying out the name change details, and it is worth doing so on your cereal box, it follows that Condorcet's transitive rankings become the outlier p_5 profile. This name change also shows that each of the four profiles where the outcome is compatible, profiles p_1 to p_4, *involve cyclic preferences.* For instance, the outlier p_5 is identified with the Condorcet triplet

$$A \succ B \succ C, \quad B \succ C \succ A, \quad C \succ A \succ B$$

where all three voters have transitive preferences, and p_1 is translated into

$$[A \succ B, \, B \succ C, \, C \succ A], \quad [A \succ B, \, B \succ C, \, C \succ A],$$
$$[B \succ A, \, C \succ B, \, A \succ C]$$

where *all voters are cyclic*. The cyclic outcome generated by Condorcet's profile fails to reflect the actual outlier profile with its transitive preferences because the rule must capture the "average of *all possible* supporting profiles," even though most of them are explicitly forbidden.

In more bothersome terms, this argument proves that the Condorcet triplet causes cyclic rankings because *the pairwise vote cannot distinguish whether or not the profile is transitive*. The actual profile is transitive because transitivity is explicitly required. However, the majority vote possesses no features to permit it to detect what is intended.

Compare the behavior of the majority vote with that of a pet dog being trained to roll over. We know what our command means; does the dog? Similarly, as far as the majority vote is concerned, we know that only transitive profiles are allowed, but does the rule understand this? If not, just like the dog who looks at the trainer in a confused manner while wagging his tail, the majority vote can ignore *our* intent. This statement becomes particularly significant with outlier profiles where, as shown previously, our intended meaning for the profile should be, and is, ignored. The rule reflects the average of all supporting profiles rather than the specified outlier.

Restating these comments, the cyclic outcome occurs because the pairwise vote is incapable of recognizing the explicit assumption that voters have transitive preferences. The cyclic outcome reflects the average over all supporting profiles – even over cyclic profiles that are explicitly forbidden!

To generalize this discussion, notice from the geometry of the cube that for a majority vote outcome to differ from all of the voters' preferences, at least three voter preferences must be at vertices that surround a fourth vertex – as is true with the previous description. This fact holds for any majority vote setting, including any three-alternative example of the kind List explores. Indeed, with the name change that identifies D, G, and H with "Yes," the Equation 2.4 example jumps out. The same kind of analysis holds for the Anscombe paradox, or for *any* majority vote example where nobody agrees with the joint outcome. Thus, the Condorcet triplet, the List types of examples, and the Anscombe paradox are particular manifestations of what can occur with majority voting.

If so much confusion is created with only three alternatives and their associated three pairs, imagine the perverse delight emanating from the difficulties that arise with four alternatives and the associated six pairs! Could anything be more frustrating than five alternatives with their ten pairs or six alternatives with fifteen pairs? This curse of dimensionality, which assumes an even more mischievous nature, is nirvana for theoreticians seeking new, more frustrating negative examples.

Before introducing a different explanation for this behavior, notice how this discussion requires "three or more pairs." This requirement should ring a loud bell because Arrow's theorem and Sen's result both require three or more alternatives, which generate three or more pairs. You might wonder whether the cube diagram explains these results. It does, as described later in this chapter. (Also see Saari [64, 75] and a paper that I wrote with my graduate student Ivy Li [27].)

2.2.2 Can We Trust the Majority Voting over Pairs?

All too often, faculty receive still another ballot to elect colleagues to this or that university panel. To ensure an appropriate balance across disciplines, we may be asked to vote for one candidate from each department, or from each school.

To illustrate what we all have encountered, consider a hypothetical setting where each of three schools puts forth two candidates: One of these two will be elected. To simplify the tallying of ballots, suppose the election voters are the three deans where each dean votes for one candidate from each of the three lists: The majority winner from each school is selected.

Suppose the candidates are

Engineering	Social Sciences	Sciences	
David	Harry	Fred	(2.7)
Elaine	Joyce	Gloria	

If David, Harry, and Fred were each elected by a $2:1$ vote, does this outcome reflect what these three deans – the three voters – wanted?

Without knowing how each dean voted, about the only way to address this question is to list all possible supporting profiles. This is easy: Each majority vote has a 2 : 1 tally, all possible profiles are listed in Equation 2.6 where, to simplify the identification, the first letter of each name corresponds to a letter on the cube (i.e., identify H with *Harry*). In this manner, $\mathbf{p}_2$ represents where one dean voted for David, Harry, and Gloria, and another voted for Elaine, Joyce, and Fred to create a tie in each school. The third dean's vote of David, Harry, and Fred breaks the tie.

If the actual profile is the same as one of the first four ($\mathbf{p}_1$ through $\mathbf{p}_4$), then, as noted, it is arguable that the election outcome accurately reflects the aggregate views of the voters. Moreover, in each of these settings, at least one voter's preferences completely agree with the election outcome. The following translates these four profiles into the dean election setting where the first two deans completely differ and the third breaks the tie:

	Dean One	Dean Two	Tie Breaker
$\mathbf{p}_1$	David, Harry, Fred	Elaine, Joyce, Gloria	David, Harry, Fred
$\mathbf{p}_2$	David, Harry, Gloria	Elaine, Joyce, Fred	David, Harry, Fred
$\mathbf{p}_3$	David, Joyce, Fred	Elaine, Harry, Gloria	David, Harry, Fred
$\mathbf{p}_4$	Elaine, Harry, Fred	David, Joyce, Gloria	David, Harry, Fred

Suppose that the actual profile is $\mathbf{p}_5$. Other than asserting that each candidate won by 2 : 1, it is not clear whether the voters would, or would not, be happy with the outcome. For this outlier profile,

- One dean votes for Elaine, Harry, Fred.
- A second one votes for David, Joyce, Fred.
- And the third votes for David, Harry, Gloria.

Suppose each dean wanted to have a man and a woman on the committee: This assumption is consistent with their votes. If so, each dean would be dissatisfied with the all male joint election outcome. An obvious objection is that this mixed gender pairing is expecting far too much! After all, how can the election rule suddenly incorporate new "connection information" where each voter wants a mixed gender outcome. There is no reason to expect that an election outcome can satisfy some implicit constraint or desire of the voters unless the constraint is explicitly built into the voting rule.

This inability of the majority vote to reflect an "extra" condition is my main point. After all, with the name changes

$$\text{David} \to A \succ B \quad \text{Elaine} \to B \succ A$$
$$\text{Harry} \to B \succ C \quad \text{Joyce} \to C \succ B$$
$$\text{Fred} \to C \succ A \quad \text{Gloria} \to A \succ C$$

the "all candidates of the same gender" become "cyclic rankings," and *any mixed gender vote is identified with a transitive ranking.* The importance of this name change comes from the demonstrated fact that the majority vote is incapable of handling, or even recognizing, side constraints such as the mixed gender condition. The name change proves that this inability is equivalent to the assertion that the *majority vote is incapable of handling, or even recognizing, transitivity.* This makes sense: Think of the majority vote as a rule forced to wear blinders in that the decision rule must concentrate strictly on what happens with a particular pair – any connections this pair has with other pairs, such as transitivity, is irrelevant and ignored.

Incidentally, a version of this mixed gender election example actually occurred at Wheaton College. A nice description, along with a solution, is described in Ratliff [48].[8]

2.2.3 A Common Explanation

The same explanation holds for the Anscombe and List problems. These examples are troubling because we expect connections across pairs, as identified with voter preferences, to survive the decision process. Instead, the majority vote completely severs all connections. In Anscombe's paradox, for instance, the majority group is well defined; each of the first three voters supports two of the three party positions. The point, however, is that *the pairwise vote cannot recognize, hence it cannot respect, the connection of belonging to the majority party.* Consequently, the outcomes

---

[8] Tommy Ratliff is the chair of the Math Department at Wheaton College and the chair of the Northeastern section of the Math Association of America. Trained as an algebraic topologist at Northwestern University, he proved several highly counterintuitive, important results about Dodgson's voting rule after he turned to voting theory [49–51].

are connected to the majority or minority party strictly by coincidence; the majority vote has stripped away all membership connections. The impact of Anscombe's paradox remains, but these comments remove the mystery.

As described in my paper with Sieberg [89], the same argument explains Sieberg's example (Section 2.2.1). In her second scenario, 85 percent of the voters relate the two choices; they wish to help the teachers, but they differ in how this should be done. The pairwise vote, however, severs this intention and creates frustrated voters, which is Sieberg's point.

A similar explanation holds for the examples created by List and his colleagues. In my example of evaluating a student, each faculty member's views on the oral and written exams determines his or her final recommendation. Even though the intended relationship is to determine each evaluator's belief based on information from two sources – the written and the oral exam – the majority vote completely severs this crucial connection when the views of voters over each exam are determined separately.

Stated simply, the majority vote ignores all possible and intended relations among pairs. If relationships over parts are of value, stay away from the majority vote, or any rule such as Kemeny's rule that is based on pairwise voting. Using such a rule violates your objectives because the rule must, and will, ignore intended relationships such as transitivity of preferences.

2.3 Why Do These Negative Results Occur?

To show why the same argument explains Arrow's and Sen's theorems, I first convert their statements into "of course, that's obvious" versions. With Arrow's theorem, for instance, by ignoring the requirement that voter's must have transitive preferences, the new version loses all interest; the conclusion that a rule could have nontransitive outcomes becomes obvious.

After all, without Arrow's condition of transitivity, we can admit profiles where all voters have the cyclic preferences

$$A \succ B, \quad B \succ C, \quad C \succ A$$

Should this be the case, then Arrow's Pareto condition immediately ensures a cyclic societal outcome. This assertion is not surprising; if voters don't have transitive preferences, and/or if the rule cannot use information about transitive preferences, then why should we anticipate transitive outcomes? As we will see, this is the total explanation of Arrow's result.

2.3.1 Arrow's Theorem

Before describing why Arrow's theorem occurs, recall my example used to motivate Arrow's binary independence condition. This is the story about ranking three CDs, which feature Beethoven, Mozart, and Sibelius. Let me state that, perhaps reflecting my Finnish-American heritage, I *much* prefer Sibelius to Beethoven. Are my preferences transitive?

There is not enough information to answer this question. Transitivity is a condition that relates the rankings of all pairs. Consequently, to determine whether my preferences are, or are not, transitive, you need to know my {Sibelius, Mozart} and my {Mozart, Beethoven} rankings.

Now consider the problem of finding a societal ranking of the three CDs. Binary independence, or IIA, requires that when determining the {Sibelius, Beethoven} societal ranking, the decision rule *cannot* use any information about how the voters rank other pairs: As such, this requirement means that *the rule cannot use any information about whether the voters have, or do not have, transitive preferences*; it dismisses the intended transitivity condition. Being slightly more technical, it is easy to show that if the decision rule F, which finds the societal ranking, satisfies IIA, then it can be written as

$$F = (F_{\text{Sibelius, Beethoven}}, F_{\text{Sibelius, Mozart}}, F_{\text{Mozart, Beethoven}}) \quad (2.8)$$

where the outcome of each F component is determined strictly by information about how the voters rank the two identified composers.

The expression in Equation 2.8 is identical to the one used when discussing pairwise voting; a difference is that the different F components, each of which determines the societal outcome for a specified pair, need not use the majority vote. Nevertheless, binary independence renders inoperative the crucial, explicit assumption of transitivity. As such, binary independence converts Arrow's theorem into a setting that removes the assumption of the transitivity of individual preferences. If the rule cannot use the transitivity assumption, however, Arrow's conclusion no longer is of any surprise.

Just as with the majority vote in the three dean example, binary independence effectively vitiates the assumption that voters have transitive preferences. Arrow's result requires three or more alternatives, which have three or more pairs. The reason is that, as described earlier using the argument I developed with Sieberg, three pairs is the first setting in which an outlier profile occurs where nobody agrees with the outcome. Indeed, a proof of Arrow's result in the appendix of my book [75], which uses the Figure 3 cube, shows that Arrow's theorem can be explained in essentially the same way as the paradox of voting; the decision rule must select from among four possible supporting profiles, where three of them involve cyclic preferences. Because the rule must ignore the transitivity assumption, it delivers the "average" of the four supporting profiles. Again, the curse of dimensionality introduces outlier profiles; they, with the accompanying loss of the transitivity assumption, cause Arrow's result.

My Granddaughter and Arrow's Dictator

As a slight digression, let me tell you about my granddaughter Tatjana; as is true of all of my grandchildren, she is very bright. Even at a tender age when she was just mastering how to crawl, Tatjana could navigate across a living room floor, cluttered with alphabet blocks. What was amazing is how she would pass the blocks in the correct alphabetic sequence! Without hesitation she would crawl by the "A" block first, the "B" block second, the "C" block third, and so forth. She was absolutely amazing!

A slight confession is in order. Before Tatjana would start her journey, I would carefully arrange the blocks in the appropriate order along the only path that she could take. All right, rather than my granddaughter's native abilities, her crawling precision more accurately captures the careful arrangement of the data.

The Tatjana effect

This "Tatjana effect" can be extended to standard approaches of "profile restrictions." We know how to create profile restrictions, such as Black's [7] single-peakedness condition, where even the pairwise vote delivers transitive outcomes. But, as was true with my granddaughter's crawling trajectory, the orderly transitivity of the societal rankings has little to do with the rule. Instead, any orderliness in the outcome reflects and mimics the carefully imposed orderliness of the data.

The same commentary applies to the various profile restrictions that circumvent Arrow's conditions. Just as IIA requires a rule to ignore the transitivity of individual preferences, we must expect (and it can be shown to be true) that whenever transitive outcomes occur, they more accurately reflect the orderly structure of the data rather than the merits or properties of the decision rule. Numerous articles describe profile restrictions that permit nondictatorial Arrovian rules to have transitive outcomes, where the weakest condition requires just one voter to leave out just one preference ranking (Saari [75]). But seldom does the associated rule assume a form whereby anyone could recommend it for actual use. These rules have a stilted structure for an obvious reason: The awkward structures reflect the reality that, with IIA, the rules cannot use the crucial individual rationality assumption.

An extreme profile restriction is to totally ignore everyone's preferences – except for those of one specified voter. The Pareto condition requires the associated rule to repeat the specified voter's preferences as the societal ranking. So, whenever this voter has transitive preferences, the outcome will be transitive. This profile restriction is, of course, Arrow's dictator. Namely, rather than a decision rule, we arrive at the radically different interpretation that *Arrow's dictator should be treated as an extreme profile restriction.*

2.3.2 Sen's Result

The same observation, about how certain assumptions imposed on decision rules dismiss the individual rationality assumption, completely explains Sen's result. To describe why, first notice that without requiring all voters to have transitive preferences, Sen's result becomes trivially obvious and of zero interest. If everyone had, for instance, the same $A \succ B$, $B \succ C$, $C \succ A$ cyclic preferences, then Sen's Pareto condition forces a cyclic outcome.

A way to illustrate my point about the effective loss of this assumption of individual rationality is with an example. Suppose that voter 1, with preferences $D \succ A \succ B \succ C$, is decisive over the pair $\{A, B\}$, and that voter 2, with preferences $B \succ C \succ D \succ A$, is decisive over $\{C, D\}$. All information a Sen decision rule needs is listed in the table in Equation 2.9 where a dash indicates a ranking that is irrelevant for the decision rule because another agent is decisive over that pair.

Voter	Preferences	$\{A, B\}$	$\{B, C\}$	$\{C, D\}$	$\{A, D\}$
1	$D \succ A \succ B \succ C$	$A \succ B$	$B \succ C$	—	$D \succ A$
2	$B \succ C \succ D \succ A$	—	$B \succ C$	$C \succ D$	$D \succ A$
	Outcome	$A \succ B$	$B \succ C$	$C \succ D$	$D \succ A$

$$(2.9)$$

To compute this cyclic outcome, the results for the first and third columns are determined by the particular decisive agent, and the outcomes for the second and fourth columns are determined by the Pareto condition.

This example proves that a cyclic outcome can occur; the next step is to understand why it can arise. To explain, notice that a voter's ranking over a pair is immaterial when that portion of the table has a dash. For voter 2, for instance, it is immaterial whether the voter's $\{A, B\}$ preference is $A \succ B$ or $B \succ A$. The first choice makes the preferences cyclic, whereas the second makes them transitive – a huge difference! Voter 1 and $\{C, D\}$ produce similar results: A $C \succ D$ choice makes the preferences cyclic, and $D \succ C$ makes them transitive. In other words, *minimal liberalism forces an associated rule to ignore the assumption of individual rationality!*

To underscore the importance of this statement, notice how one column in the table in Equation 2.1 lists the hair color of the applicants. Because this information is not used, it can be dismissed as being irrelevant. Similarly, once we firmly understand why the assumption of transitivity plays no more of a role than the hair color information, it too can be dismissed as being irrelevant, which reduces Sen's statement to an obvious one.

Creating All Possible Examples

To demonstrate this argument about the de facto loss of the crucial individual rationality assumption, let me show how easy it now is to construct any number of amazing examples to illustrate Sen's theorem; these examples can be as wild and convoluted as you desire. (See Saari [75].) With six alternatives, for instance, I will construct an example with interconnecting $A \succ B$, $B \succ C$, $C \succ D$, $D \succ A$ and $B \succ C$, $C \succ E$, $E \succ A$, $A \succ B$ cycles – a decade ago this might have qualified as a nice paper.

Start by assigning everyone these cyclic preferences. As shown in the following table, each societal outcome is determined by the Pareto condition.

Voter	$\{A, B\}$	$\{B, C\}$	$\{C, D\}$	$\{A, D\}$	$\{C, E\}$	$\{A, E\}$
Ann	$A \succ B$	$B \succ C$	$C \succ D$	$D \succ A$	$C \succ E$	$E \succ A$
Ivy	$A \succ B$	$B \succ C$	$C \succ D$	$D \succ A$	$C \succ E$	$E \succ A$
Katri	$A \succ B$	$B \succ C$	$C \succ D$	$D \succ A$	$C \succ E$	$E \succ A$
Outcome	$A \succ B$	$B \succ C$	$C \succ D$	$D \succ A$	$C \succ E$	$E \succ A$

$$(2.10)$$

Next, for each cycle and each agent, let someone else be decisive over at least one pair. If we start with Ann, this means that either Ivy or Katri must be decisive over a pair from each of the two cycles. For example, $B \succ C$ is in both cycles, so an easy way to satisfy this condition is to let, say, Katri be decisive over $\{B, C\}$. This choice satisfies the condition for both cycles for Ann and Ivy.

An easy choice to satisfy this condition for Katri is to let Ivy be decisive over $\{A, B\}$ because this pair is in both cycles. To involve all women and to illustrate the flexibility of the approach, let Ann be decisive over, say, $\{A, D\}$ in the first cycle, and Ivy decisive over $\{A, E\}$ in the second cycle. The only difference in the resulting information table is that the societal outcome now is determined by the decisive voter rather than the Pareto condition in the three columns with a decisive agent.

Voter	$\{A, B\}$	$\{B, C\}$	$\{C, D\}$	$\{A, D\}$	$\{C, E\}$	$\{A, E\}$
Ann	$A \succ B$	—	$C \succ D$	$D \succ A$	$C \succ E$	—
Ivy	$A \succ B$	—	$C \succ D$	—	$C \succ E$	$E \succ A$
Katri	$A \succ B$	$B \succ C$	$C \succ D$	—	$C \succ E$	—
Outcome	$A \succ B$	$B \succ C$	$C \succ D$	$D \succ A$	$C \succ E$	$E \succ A$

$$(2.11)$$

It remains to find transitive preferences for each voter. This is easy! In general, for each pair where a dash appears in the information table, just reverse the original binary ranking. In this manner, the original cyclic preference is converted into a transitive one. For instance, transitive preference rankings for the three women that are consistent with the table in Equation 2.11 are

Name	Ranking
Ann	$C \succ D \succ A \succ B \succ E$
Ivy	$C \succ E \succ A \succ B \succ D$
Katri	$A \succ B \succ C \succ D \succ E$

$$(2.12)$$

All Possible Illustrating Examples

Any example constructed in this manner reflects the inability of a rule satisfying Sen's conditions to distinguish between transitive and cyclic voters. By starting with cyclic preferences, the unanimity condition (from Pareto) determines the outcomes. Even after introducing decisive voters, the societal outcome must remain the same; the only difference is that the decisive voter, rather than the Pareto condition, determines the conclusion. The importance in the manner in which decisive agents are introduced is that in each cycle it is immaterial how each voter ranks at least one pair. By reversing the ranking of one pair from each cycle, the cyclic preference is transformed into a transitive ranking!

The important point, as proved in Saari [75] and again in Saari and Petron[9] [88], is that *all possible examples illustrating Sen's theorem can be constructed in this manner.* Consequently, all possible examples illustrating Sen's result indicate that the minimal liberalism condition requires the decision rule to ignore the assumption of individual rationality. Incidentally, in my paper coauthored with my graduate student Ivy Li [27], we provide the first direct proof of Sen's theorem[10]: Our proof shows how the cyclic outcomes in Sen's theorem arise because the rule "averages" over all supporting profiles, even over profiles with cyclic preferences that are explicitly forbidden. Our explanation is based on the one I developed for Arrow's conclusion by using the previously discussed cube construction. Our geometric approach captures all of the Sen conflicts, emphasizes the curse of dimensionality, and indicates all ways to escape Sen's consequences.

So, in direct contrast to what the literature asserts and emphasizes, Sen's result is *not* a conflict between individual rights and social welfare. Instead, Sen's result means that minimal liberalism prohibits the rule from using the crucial "individual rationality" information; consequently, the rule uses unintended cyclic information. Indeed, minimal liberalism and Pareto can be replaced with many other pairwise decision rules leading to the same conflict. For instance, if we replace Pareto with the pairwise vote and minimal liberalism with committee choices, the same conflict again arises because information about transitive preferences is ignored. I will explore other unexpected and surprising interpretations of Sen's cycles later in this chapter.

---

[9] Anne Petron is on the faculty of the Economics Department at the Université de Caen: She actively participated in the conference associated with my *Condorcet Lectures*. It was during one of her lectures at Caen, in her early stages of graduate school, that I started my approach toward understanding Sen's theorem. Later, the two of us examined other consequences.

[10] All "proofs" we have seen are based on creating examples. Strictly speaking, an example proves the result only in the specified setting, our proof handles all possibilities. Thus, this paper offers the first general proof of Sen's result.

2.3.3 Topological Dictators and Beach Parties

By now, I hope that you are conditioned into examining these negative results with the goal of determining what specified kind of information is not being used by a decision rule. Indeed, this loss of specified information does explain the beach party example; can you figure out what it is?

Before identifying what information is ignored, let me describe an unexpected conclusion, which seems to have been missed in this literature for the past quarter century – namely, asserting that an agent is a topological dictator need not mean very much. (This theme is examined more closely in my paper [24] with Kronewetter.) It is reasonable to expect that a topological dictator always has significant power; this is not true.

An Upset Child

To illustrate why a topological dictator need not mean what is often described, consider the upset child example that Kronewetter and I [24] created. (Also see my paper [67] and the appendix of this book.) In this example, a mother and her young son plan to picnic on the beach of a circular island. The decision rule is that, with minor exceptions, the mother decides that where she wants to picnic is where they will picnic. The exception occurs when the child is upset because his wishes are nearly directly opposite to those of his mother's. To handle this rare situation in a continuous manner that satisfies the Pareto condition, change the picnic site until it coincides with the child's choice whenever the child's and his mother's views are directly opposite one another.

To illustrate with Figure 4a, if the mother's and child's preferences are given, respectively, by θ_M and θ_C where angle θ determines a point on a circle, then the outcome (depicted by the arrow) is θ_M whenever the child's choice of θ_C is within 179° of the mother's, that is, whenever the child's choice is outside the two vertical lines at the bottom of each circle. Only for a small 2° arc on the circle, depicted in an exaggerated manner by the two vertical lines, does the child have a say. To determine this outcome, as indicated in Figure 4b where the child's choice now is in the bottom region, continuously change the outcome, while staying in the

Arrows point to the outcomes

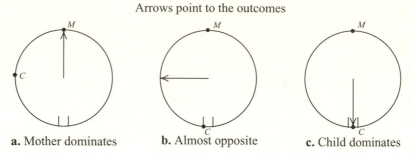

a. Mother dominates   **b.** Almost opposite   **c.** Child dominates

Figure 4. An upset child at the beach.

Pareto set, from the mother's choice to an outcome that is precisely the child's as the child's choice varies from being 179° (Figure 4b) to the 180° (Figure 4c) position directly opposite of his mother's wishes. To satisfy Pareto, as indicated in Figure 4b, the outcomes move on the side of the circle defined by the child's choice.

The mother clearly dominates; she is significantly more influential in making the decision. The topological dictator, however, is the *child!* To see this counterintuitive assertion, continuously reduce the region of dominance of the mother from 179° to 0°; the end result is where the child completely dominates. One might wonder whether it is possible to similarly decrease the child's region of influence, but this turns out to be impossible. A way to prove this fact and see that this example is about as extreme as possible is to describe the structure of the domain by using a "level set argument" as developed in our paper [24] and the appendix of this book. Because the structure of the domain and the curse of dimensionality are main themes of this book, these arguments are outlined in the appendix.

Is a Topological Dictator Misleading?
As this upset child example dramatically demonstrates, asserting that someone is a topological dictator can be highly deceptive. Even more, the concept of a topological dictator can be completely misleading. To explain, suppose a group wants to party somewhere along a straight beach. The decision is easy; take the average of the choices. This averaging rule satisfies the Theorem 2.3 conditions of continuity, unanimity, and

Pareto. Surely this rule that gives everyone an equal role in the decision is not homotopic to a dictator. Or is it?

It is. To demonstrate, let

$$F_{AV}(\mathbf{x}_1, \ldots, \mathbf{x}_n) = \frac{1}{n} \sum_{j=1}^{n} \mathbf{x}_j$$

be the averaging function, and let $F_{Dic}(\mathbf{x}_1, \ldots, \mathbf{x}_n) = \mathbf{x}_1$ be the rule where the first person is the dictator. To transform one rule into the other, use

$$F^*(\mathbf{x}_1, \ldots, \mathbf{x}_n, t) = \frac{\mathbf{x}_1 + t(\mathbf{x}_2 + \cdots + \mathbf{x}_n)}{1 + t(n-1)}, \qquad 0 \le t \le 1$$

Notice that $F^*(\mathbf{x}_1, \ldots, \mathbf{x}_n, 1) = F_{AV}$ and $F^*(\mathbf{x}_1, \ldots, \mathbf{x}_n, 0) = F_{Dic}$, which means that on a straight beach the averaging function is homotopic to the topological dictator. This homotopy, which continuously diminishes with the value of t the influence of $(n-1)$ of the voters to zero, is a huge, distorting change; it resembles the story about converting a donut into a coffee cup, and it reflects the flexibility of topology. Even though this flexibility provides a powerful mathematical tool, it can also spawn seriously misleading interpretations – such as the traditional description of a topological dictator.

Even more, it is easy to show that one dictator can be homotopic to another dictator. To do so, use

$$F^*(\mathbf{x}_1, \ldots, \mathbf{x}_n, t) = \frac{\mathbf{x}_1 + 2t(\mathbf{x}_2 + \cdots + \mathbf{x}_n)}{1 + 2t(n-1)}, \qquad 0 \le t \le \frac{1}{2}$$

and

$$\frac{\mathbf{x}_2 + (2 - 2t)(\mathbf{x}_1 + \mathbf{x}_3 + \cdots + \mathbf{x}_n)}{1 + (2 - 2t)(n-1)}, \qquad \frac{1}{2} \le t \le 1$$

When $t = 0$, the first voter is a dictator; when $t = \frac{1}{2}$, the averaging rule is recovered; and when $t = 1$, the rule crowns the second voter as dictator. To describe in words what is happening, start from average rule of $t = \frac{1}{2}$. Moving from $t = \frac{1}{2}$ to $t = 0$ diminishes the influence of voters 2 to n, but moving from $t = \frac{1}{2}$ to $t = 1$ shrinks to nothing the role of voters 1, 3,.... If one dictator can be homotopic to another, and both to the average rule, what does this concept mean? Seemingly, it means very little.

As an example on the circle, consider $F(\theta_1, \theta_2) = 10\theta_1 - 9\theta_2$, where θ_j is the angle determining the jth person's choice of location to picnic. This rule satisfies continuity and unanimity but not Pareto. (To see this, with $\theta_1 = \frac{\pi}{10}, \theta_2 = 0$, the two people want to picnic somewhere in an eastern position. The outcome, however, is $10(\frac{\pi}{10}) - 9(0) = \pi$, or directly to the west.) The homotopy $F^*(\theta_1, \theta_2, t) = \theta_1 + 9t(\theta_1 - \theta_2)$ has the property that $F^*(\theta_1, \theta_2, 1) = F(\theta_1, \theta_2)$; $F^*(\theta_1, \theta_2, 0) = \theta_1$, or a dictatorship. Again, this homotopy continuously diminishes one voter's influence to zero. In fact, it is difficult to conceive of any decision rule that is not homotopic to a dictator if the role of some voters is diminished. We are forced to ask, of what value is this concept?

Effectiveness

The preceding discussion forces us to question whether these earlier conclusions, such as Theorem 2.3, have any substantive meaning. They do, but only after replacing the topological dictator with a more relevant notion that captures what probably was intended. To do so, replace the topological dictator with an "I can do something that you can't do" asymmetry concept.

Start with an "I can do anything you can do" setting. Namely, for any choice I make, say $x_1 = a$, suppose you can select a $x_2 = b$ to force some societal outcome of d. If so, then I can do the same when the situation is reversed, that is, when you select $x_2 = a$, then I always can find some $x_1 = c$ so that the outcome is the same d. (Note that it may be that $c \neq b$.) However, I am *more effective* than you are if the situation is not reversed; this means I can attain certain outcomes that you cannot.

With the upset child example, the mother clearly is more *influential* than the child, but the child is more *effective*, that is, the child can force more outcomes than the mother. To see this, let the child select a position $\theta_C = a$, say, the northern part of the island, and the mother select a position $\theta_M = b$, say, the western part to force the outcome d, which would be the western part. When the situation is reversed and the mother selects $\theta_M = a$, the northern part, the child always has a θ_C choice to force the same d outcome, the western part. This assertion follows from Figure 4 because once the child's choice is nearly opposite his mother's, the societal outcome ranges through all values on the circle including this western point.

To see that the child can accomplish more than the mother, start with what the child can achieve. Let the mother select $\theta_M = a$, say, the northern part; then, let the child select the Figure 4c diametrically opposite point $\theta_C = b$, the southern part. According to the decision rule, the societal outcome is the child's choice of b, the southern part, because it is diametrically opposite the mother's. Now, if the child starts with $\theta_C = a$, the northern part, it is impossible for the mother to force the outcome that is diametrically opposite the child's. After all, what the mother wants, the mother gets – but only until her choice is nearly opposite of what the child wants. Here, the outcome rapidly reverts to the child's choice.

By using these new terms, we can replace Theorem 2.3 with a result that captures the sense that there is some one voter with more impact and effectiveness than another. This theorem has been extended to any number of voters and with much more complex settings.

Theorem 2.4 (Kronewetter and Saari [24]): Any continuous mapping

$$F(\theta_1, \theta_2) : S^1 \times S^1 \to S^1$$

that satisfies unanimity and the Pareto condition must be such that one voter is more effective than the other.

Our theorem, as stated in [24], is wider reaching. Beyond circles, for instance, it includes objects such as a region with a finite number of disconnected holes, which are of the type that might arise in a location problem.

A proof is in our paper [24], but let me offer some slightly technical insight as to why these results and many extensions hold. First, let $\mathcal{V}$ be a domain with holes – it may be a sphere, or a torus (the surface of a donut), or several spheres connected in a chain, or any number of geometric constructions. With $n \geq 2$ agents, the decision rule is

$$F : \mathcal{V} \times \cdots \times \mathcal{V} \to \mathcal{V} \tag{2.13}$$

The assumptions that this mapping is continuous and satisfies the una-nimity condition is not sufficiently restrictive for our purposes. As the $F(\theta_1, \theta_2) = 10\theta_1 - 9\theta_2$ mapping from circles to a circle illustrates, many functions can satisfy these two conditions. Check what this F allows: Holding one of the variables fixed, say $\theta_2 = 0$, the image of $F(\theta_1, 0)$ wraps around the circle *ten times* while θ_1 makes only one cycle. Clearly, several of the outcomes are diametrically opposite the input! Thus to have realistic "decision analysis outcomes," we must impose added conditions, such as Pareto, on the decision rule.

The mathematical effect of doing so is to fix the *index* of the mapping. To avoid getting too technical, think of these extra conditions as allowing the image of the mapping F, when one of the variables changes, to wrap around the image space $\mathcal{V}$ at most once. With the upset child, by holding the mother's choice fixed and varying the child's choice, the outcome covers the circle. The reverse effect does not occur. Holding the child's choice fixed and varying the mother's choice fails to cover the circle; there is a gap. If there had not been a gap for all but one of the agents, it would be possible to show that the rule allows pathological outcomes.

In other words, whatever form the various conditions assume, they have the mathematical effect of requiring one of the variables to be *more effective* than the other: The complete wrapping is caused by one variable (the boy in the upset child example), while the others create limited "folds" that can be unraveled. Consequently, expect conditions of the indicated type to lead to a conclusion that one agent is more effective than the others.

Missing Information?

The common thread that relates and connects all of the major negative results in this chapter is that certain specified conditions force the asso-ciated decision rules to ignore explicitly stated and crucial information about preferences. As such, we must wonder what information is miss-ing in Theorems 2.3 and 2.4. As a clue, the missing information in all earlier explanations involved a part–whole conflict whereby the whole – the transitivity of individual preferences – is vital to achieve the desired kind of outcome. Yet in Arrow's and Sen's theorems, an assumed condi-tion forced any associated rule to concentrate solely on the parts – binary rankings – and ignore the individual rationality condition specifying how the parts connect to construct the whole. If such an explanation holds for Theorems 2.3 and 2.4, then what causes the part–whole conflict where some variable, or some agent, is "more effective" than others?

The surprising culprit is *continuity*. Continuity is a local concept defined in terms of limits; if $x_n \to x_0$ as $n \to \infty$, then $f(x_n) \to f(x_0)$. This condition, then, requires that, for points x_n close to x_0, the images $f(x_n)$ be close to $f(x_0)$. Stated in words, after imposing any degree of accuracy, once points are so close to x_0 that they cannot be distinguished from x_0, we cannot distinguish their consequences, the points $f(x_n)$, from $f(x_0)$.[11] Notice how this emphasis on local behavior ignores the explicit global constructions.

A more complete description of why continuity contributes to this problem is in [24]. (See the appendix of this book.) It is easy to understand why emphasizing the local structure forces us to misinterpret – actually, ignore – the global structure of preferences. As described earlier, this feature of ignoring the global structure is the same local versus global problem that arises with Arrow's IIA and Sen's minimal liberalism. To see the idea, recall that when even bright people of ancient times emphasized the local and immediate structure of our planet, they had little reason to believe that the Earth was anything other than flat. Similarly, if we lived on a huge circle and used only local information, we would view the circle as being, essentially, a straight line. It is not a line; it is a circle.

Consequently, we treat the continuity condition of these theorems – when not supplemented with information about the global structure – as forcing rules to become mathematical versions of "flat Earth" proponents. By extracting and using only local information about the structure of the domain, there is nothing to prevent the rules satisfying Theorems 2.3 and 2.4 from treating the domain as a line, rather than a circle. This lack of information about the actual geometry makes a big difference: If the domain were a line, there would be no problems. The difficulties arise when the domain connects into the circular structure, and nothing is provided to permit the rule to bend around this crucial information.

---

[11] More precisely, with any specified degree of accuracy, the points $f(x_n)$ cannot be distinguished from $f(x_0)$ once another determined level of accuracy requires that all but a finite number of the x_n cannot be distinguished from x_0.

2.4 Positive Replacements

Now that we know *why* the various negative conclusions hold, we need to use this and related information to explain *how* to change the conditions to allow positive assertions. The approach is obvious; the negative results occur because the rules are forced to ignore valuable specified information. So, we must modify the conditions in a manner to permit the rules to use the vital information. I show how to do so for the three main negative conclusions.

2.4.1 Arrow's Result

If binary independence, or IIA, forces the associated rule to ignore the transitivity of individual preferences, then the obvious remedy is to modify the IIA condition so that an associated rule can use at least some of this individual rationality information. There are many ways to do this; the following suggestion is just one possibility.

Finding a Positive Result
Rather than using the full transitive ranking to determine the societal outcome, we need to find a way to preserve the intent of Arrow's IIA condition for each pair while leaving out information about the identities of the other candidates. The following approach, which captures a sense that the voters have transitive preferences, uses a minimal way to distinguish a binary ranking within a transitive ranking from a simple binary ranking.

A difference between binary rankings (e.g., $A \succ B$, $A \succ C$ and the same binary pairs within the transitive ranking $A \succ B \succ C$) is that *the connectivity of pairs in a transitive ranking allows them to be distinguished by the number of alternatives that separate them.* For instance, within $A \succ B \succ C \succ D$, zero alternatives separate the $A \succ B$ ranking: Represent this situation as $[A \succ B, 0]$. In the $A \succ C$ ranking, A and C are separated by one alternative, so this setting is represented by $[A \succ C, 1]$.

Definition 2.1: For a transitive ranking, the "intensity" of the ordinal ranking is the number of candidates that separate the two. If α alternatives separate the two specified alternatives in a ranking, say $A \succ B$, then represent this by $[A \succ B, \alpha]$. The intensity form of independence of irrelevant alternatives, or IIIA, is where the societal ranking of a pair is based strictly on how the voters rank the pair and the level of intensity.

To demonstrate how Arrow's IIA differs from IIIA, notice with the ranking $A \succ B \succ C \succ D$ that the IIIA information for the $\{A, D\}$ pair is $[A \succ D, 2]$ and that IIA uses only the $A \succ D$ information when determining the $\{A, D\}$ societal ranking. By replacing IIA with IIIA, both the $A \succ D$ ranking and the separating integer of 2 can be used.

Theorem 2.5 (Saari [64, 75]): By replacing the IIA, or binary independence, condition of Arrow's theorem with IIIA, the admissible rules include the Borda Count. This is where an n-candidate ballot is tallied by assigning $n - j$ points for the jth-ranked candidate. The candidates are ranked according to the number of points assigned to them. The Borda Count is the only positional method[12] that satisfies these conditions.

When finding the societal ranking for a specified pair, say $\{A, B\}$, tally the ballots by giving the higher ranked candidate one point more than the α value; this turns out to be equivalent to the Borda Count. For instance, suppose the intensity rankings for four voters over $\{A, B\}$ are

$$[A \succ B, 0], [A \succ B, 3], \quad [B \succ A, 1], [B \succ A, 1]$$

then A receives $1 + 4 = 5$ points, and B receives $2 + 2 = 4$ points leading to the societal ranking of $A \succ B$. Without using the intensity information, we have a $A \sim B$ tie.

Is IIA a Reasonable Condition?
Is the binary independence, or IIA, condition reasonable? Surprisingly, some still think so. Some have even argued that without this condition, nothing prevents a group from adding George Washington, Abraham Lincoln, and other irrelevant alternatives to an election list to complicate

---

[12] A positional method (Chapter 3) is where ballots are tallied by assigning a specified number of points to each candidate based on how they are positioned on the ballot.

the decision process. Others, including Iain McLean [37],[13] argue that "IIA is in there for a good reason, as Satterthewaite indirectly shows. Take out IIA and you have gross manipulability."

McLean's statement, which sounds nice and has been voiced by others, suggests that IIA prevents strategic behavior. It does not,[14] and we know this from many examples. To explain what is going on, recall that IIA severs all relationships among pairs of alternatives including the transitivity of individual preferences. Thus, IIA reduces the *rule* to either–or decisions for each pair: By rendering the outcome independent of what happens with other pairs, comparisons are not permitted. This comment is essential. Clearly, a setting is strategy-proof if, when determining a pair's outcome, it is forbidden to consider consequences associated with the outcomes of other pairs. However, although IIA severs comparison connections for the *rule*, *voters* still retain these relationships. Thus, voters can (and do) compare the personal implications of different outcomes over the pairs. It is *our* ability to compare, to be able to use the relationships severed by IIA, that reintroduces the if–then setting of strategic voting.

---

[13] Iain McLean, at Oxford University, has made valued contributions to the field of social choice by translating and making available many of the historical documents of this field. In particular, let me highly recommend his book with Urken [38].

[14] This refers to Mark Satterthwaite's beautiful result that a nonmanipulable system satisfies IIA. The converse, however, need not hold; satisfying IIA need not insulate a system from manipulation. Even though Satterthwaite used Arrow's result to prove his seminal statement about manipulability, it is convenient (and accurate) to view this connection as a number-counting conclusion to nicely identify when this particular curse of dimensionality can kick in (i.e., if there are enough alternatives for an Arrow-type result, there are enough for strategic settings). To see the dimensionality connection with Figure 2, on the line a new voter's vote moves the bullet toward one candidate and away from the other – this either–or vote is either sincere or counterproductive, but it is never strategic. With the square, his participation again moves the bullet toward the vertex representing his vote, but with *four* vertices, beyond the "either sincere or counterproductive (voting opposite of a sincere vote)," there are two others. Depending on how voters rank the alternatives, these other choices can be strategic. (See [74, 78].) A way to avoid strategic actions is to reduce the dimensions available to an agent. With several agents, such settings often have the flavor where an agent's action determines his or her *status*, but what the agent *obtains* is based on the actions of others. An example is the Vickery auction where the highest bidder gets the good at the cost of the second highest bid. As it is easy to compute, the optimal strategy is to bid sincerely. The originator of this scheme, William Vickery, received the 1996 Nobel Prize in Economics.

We know this; pairwise voting satisfies IIA, yet when interpreted with agendas, our ability to make comparisons unleashes well-known strategic voting opportunities. For another example, majority voting cycles must be interpreted when they occur in an election. They could represent selecting everyone, no one, a stalemate, or a specified alternative such as the status quo; maybe a tie-breaking rule is used. Whatever the choice, cycles introduce options that some voters may prefer to the sincere choice.

To illustrate with the stalemate option, suppose my preferences are $A \succ C \succ B$, a cycle defines a stalemate, and the sincere outcome of the pairs defines the transitive ranking $C \succ A \succ B$ where the $C \succ B$ pairwise tally is very close. Because I cannot elect my top-ranked A, it may be in my best interest to strategically vote for B over C to create a stalemate with a $C \succ A$, $A \succ B$, $B \succ C$ cycle. This is not a hypothetical comment; it commonly occurs in politics where, to avoid selecting what a politician does not want, the politician might do whatever is necessary to create a stalemate. The fact is that majority voting over three pairs *is susceptible to strategic action*. The same assertion holds for several other rules that satisfy IIA.

Even though the implication of this comment by McLean and others is false, it is worth staying with it to explore other consequences. To do so, remember from Arrow's theorem that accepting IIA along with Arrow's other conditions carries the cost of accepting a dictator. It seems to me that when faced with a choice between where someone might vote strategically or the certainty of having decisions determined by an absolute dictator, most of us would warmly embrace the possibility of strategic action as being, by far, the lesser evil. (In fact, we already made this choice because our election rules do not satisfy IIA.) After all, even with extreme strategic behavior, we have some voice in the outcome; with a dictator, we have none.

To motivate another issue, we all know people who can argue either for or against any specified condition. If challenged, some could even promote the virtues of smoking: Not that long ago arguments were made describing how smoking relaxes us, helps to maintain our weight, makes us look sophisticated, and so forth. A pragmatic evaluation, however, requires examining consequences. With smoking, the pragmatics include the increased likelihood of illness and death. For more and more people, this pragmatic baggage strongly outweighs other considerations. More generally, evaluations must include consequences.

What about a pragmatic evaluation of IIA? I doubt whether anyone really worries about a current ballot featuring George Washington. Yes, some ballots do include irrelevant alternatives, but history has proved that when voters are serious about voting, they tend to ignore the irrelevant choices. This was firmly illustrated with the 2002 California gubernatorial election involving more than 130 candidates. Some irreverent voters did support the professional stripper or the porn king, but the vast majority of the voters concentrated on the serious candidates. The principal role played by the irrelevant alternatives in this election was to provide amusing fodder for news articles. Of course, if voters are not serious about voting, expect bad things to happen with, or without, irrelevant alternatives. Recall from Section 1.3 that Condorcet cautioned about society's need for informed voters.

The pragmatic tradeoff in accepting IIA is that it drops the assumption that people have transitive preferences. A more accurate question about IIA, then, involves a cost–benefit exchange: We can have either IIA or the transitivity of voter preferences, but not both. The cost of this swap is clear and dear: Without requiring the voters to have some level of individual rationality, anything is possible. As such, it is doubtful whether many theorists would be willing to accept this IIA consequence.[15]

If one does accept IIA over the transitivity of individual preferences, then, for accuracy of presentation, the individual rationality assumption

---

[15] In a recent book [32], Anthony McGann describes natural settings, such as sport competitions, where transitivity is questionable. If team A can beat B, and B can beat C, why should A beat C? Because transitivity is doubtful, does IIA play a role? To examine this issue, notice how the need to rank teams creates a need for transitive outcomes. A standard approach, Copeland's rule, counts each team's victories. By summing pairwise victories, the approach cancels cyclic, nontransitive data; it becomes a special case of the Borda Count. (See, for instance, the discussions preceding Equations 3.6 and 3.10.) That this rule *fails to* satisfy IIA is reinforced each season when team C's fans cheer for team A over B because A's victory will advance C over B in the rankings. Anthony McGann is an Associate Professor in the Political Science Department of the University of California at Irvine and an active member of the Institute for Mathematical Behavioral Sciences.

should be dropped. After all, once IIA is assumed, further assuming that voters have transitive preferences is about as relevant for the conclusion as assuming that the preferences come from voters in Nordic countries. Both conditions are essentially ignored, so both can be safely dropped.

IIA Is Everywhere!

The discussion of whether to accept and include IIA as part of a decision rule is a theoretical concern. In reality, the original version of Arrow's result continues to speak very loudly about much of what we observe in society, economics, and decision making. Decisions are being made with rules depending on versions of IIA. Consequently, Arrow's theorem describes ever-present and continuing difficulties faced by society.

The foregoing analysis explains why these problems occur: Crucial information that is intended to be used to determine societal outcomes is not being used at all. Indeed, this tendency for voting and decision rules to ignore available and specified information plays a key role in the next chapters when I outline how to explain all voting paradoxes.

A way to indicate the ubiquity of Arrow's conclusions is to note that anywhere pairwise comparisons are being used – in surveys, in statistics, or in textbook selection – IIA and its attendant difficulties arise. Illustrations of these problems in engineering are described in a different paper that I wrote with Katri Sieberg [91]. Our basic idea reflects the reality that an engineer faces problems of costs and complexities when determining rankings of alternatives. As such, it is not unusual for engineering decisions to be based on pairwise, or partwise, comparisons. For instance, is this metal stronger than that one? How does a third choice compare with the better one?

Moreover, decisions about, say, the choice of the material and certain designs tend to be made separately. The engineers with whom we have worked are bright; they understand surprisingly subtle relationships that they want satisfied. But, as previously described, the pairwise vote, or even partwise decisions, must ignore these intended and necessary relationships. This reality, in turn, promotes inefficiencies. As we show in our paper, this is precisely what happens. Currently, I am analyzing multiscale engineering design where a generalized form of Arrow's theorem is central to the analysis. In other words, the message from Arrow's theorem, although now modified, remains central to concerns of contemporary society.

2.4.2 Sen's Result

How to evade Sen's result is not completely resolved, but I will give references and a brief commentary about how this can be done. First, I want to illustrate how the results described here lead to a radically different interpretation of Sen's conclusion.

New Interpretations

To explore new interpretations of Sen's result, we need the following definition that, in fact, is a mild extension of my earlier "intensity of ordinal rankings" in Definition 2.1.

Definition 2.2: If in Sen's theorem a decisive agent selects a ranking for a pair, and if a second agent has the opposite ranking with a positive intensity level, then the decisive agent has imposed a *strong negative externality* on the second agent.

This definition hints about what will happen. To be specific, in direct contrast to the traditional interpretation that Sen's result indicates a conflict between society and individuals exercising normal private rights, we must wonder whether situations exist where the actions of the decisive agent impose on others not just negative externalities, but *strong negative externalities.* If so, then rather than questioning the rights of individuals to make personal decisions as in Sen's theorem, we reach a radically different interpretation: Do individuals have the right to impose hardships on others? Not only can this happen, but these hardships are suffered by everyone!

Theorem 2.6 (Saari and Petron [88], Saari [75]): For any decision rule that satisfies Sen's condition, in each cycle, each and every agent suffers a strong negative externality that is caused by the choices made by some decisive agent.

It is easy to construct examples similar to the earlier example about hiring a new faculty member, where the strong negative externality reflects a standard, strong disagreement in views. Nevertheless, the image one carries away from Theorem 2.6 is of a dysfunctional society where everyone is seriously bothered by someone else. Even though not all settings are dysfunctional, this theorem identifies new, very rich avenues of exploration for Sen's results.

Natural illustrations of what I mean arise during states of social transition. An example that Petron and I use is the transition from that time when smoking in restaurants was permitted to the current smoke-free setting. Many years ago, no actions could be taken to prevent smoke from drifting over your dinner plate to mar your evening. Because only nonsmokers suffered strong negative externalities, the setting for Sen's theorem does not apply because the smokers could enjoy the evening. But once nonsmokers gained power, they could, and did, take action. During this period of transition, the actions taken by each group imposed a strong negative externality on the other.

So, Sen's cycles must always be associated with strong differences of opinion and the possibility of conflict. Instead of the traditional assertion about individual and societal rights, we made a broader interpretation that extends interest in Sen's theorem to a large class of other societal issues.

Resolutions?

It remains to find ways to circumvent Sen's negative conclusions. The technical approach is clear: Sen's cycles are caused because his requirements force a decision rule to ignore the individual rationality assumption. Consequently, all ways to evade the negative aspects of Sen's conclusion require changing his conditions so that the decision rules can resurrect and use this crucial information. Approaches exploring how to do so are described in my papers with Petron [88] and Li [27].

For instance, a difference between binary rankings and transitive binary rankings is that a "strong negative externality" cannot be defined with the former. Beyond capturing a sense of intensity, the intent of this externality concept is to include information about voters' transitive preferences. This suggests allowing an agent to be decisive only if his actions do not impose a strong negative externality on someone else. Unfortunately, this condition limits attention to a single pair without examining what happens with other pairs, so it returns to the concerns raised throughout this chapter. As described in my paper with Li [27], changes must be coordinated. Moreover, as social scientists, we want to go beyond technical descriptions to identify remedies that are natural and effective.

What is remarkable about Sen's assumptions is how they capture the spirit of what has happened in society for millennia. People do make decisions on their own, yet, in some manner, the decisions tend to be reasonably in accord with societal concerns. Some dysfunctional aspects of society are described in the press, but we also witness considerable accord. Thus, it is reasonable to explore why we don't always see cycles or dysfunctional societies as suggested by Theorem 2.6. Maybe lessons about how to sidestep the negatives associated with Sen's formulation can be found by examining how society has evolved to handle these situations.

Here is a situation (from [75]) we all have experienced – overly loud music played late at night when we are trying to sleep, or in public settings disrupting our intended activities. That can be a strong negative externality! Yet, in contrast to the message of Theorem 2.6, without power to respond we suffer; the boors do not.

It is clear what happens; eventually people will do something about this nuisance. We witness this banding with laws about smoking in public places and, in tune with our current example, noise abatement laws. With such laws and during a transition stage, we *do experience* the strong negative externalities promised by Theorem 2.6. If you play loud music that only slightly bothers someone else, they may do nothing. But if the noise seriously bothers them, creating a strong negative externality, they will call the police, which will impose a strong negative externality on you.[16]

To model this, let Boor's preferences be "Play loud music" $\succ$ "Play music softly" $\succ$ "Interact with the police." Suffering Citizen's preferences are "Play music softly" $\succ$ "Interact with the police" $\succ$ "Play loud music."

[16] Using an economist's measure of whether the externality is strong, calling the police incurs a personal cost, so the precipitating action must be stronger than just displeasure.

The information table, which displays the cycle and the strong negative externalities, becomes

	{**Loud, Soft**}	{**Soft, Police**}	{**Loud, Police**}
Boor	Loud	Soft	—
Suffering Citizen	—	Soft	Police
Outcome	Loud ≻ Soft	Soft ≻ Police	Police ≻ Loud

$$(2.14)$$

Society in Transition

To support my claim that situations exist where, with the Theorem 2.6 interpretation, Sen's result can be viewed as capturing a societal transition stage, it is useful to examine the form Equation 2.14 would take at three different stages that reflect the differing power of individuals.

Original State. Consider changes in the table in Equation 2.14 when there are no noise abatement laws. Without any power for the suffering citizen, the de facto but unhappy outcome for the third column changes to Loud ≻ Police, which creates a transitive societal outcome reflecting an orderly, but not necessarily happy society.

Transition Stage. The second stage for our example emerges only after a law has been passed to empower citizens with the right and power to complain – and something will be done. This law has the effect of giving such a person the decisive choice in the third column to change the earlier de facto Loud ≻ Police to an outcome that reflects the citizen's preferred Police ≻ Loud. This now-permitted action leads to the Equation 2.14 cyclic behavior, which accurately captures a dysfunctional society.

Evolved State. After our Boor has received sufficient penalties to outweigh his "Loud ≻ Soft" original preferences, it is reasonable to believe that his preferences and activity will change. In practical terms, his decisive choice for the first column now reflects his newly changed preferences whereby he will select Soft ≻ Loud. By doing so, we have, again, a transitive but now tranquil societal outcome. In other words, in the Equation 2.14 setting, the Sen cycle captures the turmoil associated with the transition stage when an abused group finally obtains, and uses, retaliatory power.

It is interesting to notice that when individuals create these strong negative externalities by using their newly empowered decisive choices, the outcome carries the distinct flavor of a tit-for-tat interaction from the Prisoner's Dilemma. The importance of this observation becomes apparent when we recall how this strategic approach is used in game theory to generate cooperation. So, perhaps, as illustrated by the different stages of Equation 2.14 when Sen's formulation models a society in transition, the strong negative externalities play a positive role by injecting a societal tit-for-tat adjustment mechanism to hasten the attainment of a new state.

There is a problem. While Fine [17], among others, noted that the structure of Sen's [101] original example resembles the Prisoner's Dilemma game, it is easy to create settings illustrating Sen's result that do not have this structure [88]. Nevertheless, as Petron and I showed [88], *all examples of Sen's cycles allow a form of a tit-for-tat response; that is, all possible examples have the structure where the strong negative externalities become options for agents to exercise this retaliation strategy.*

This assertion follows from Theorem 2.6. What allows the tit-for-tat conclusion is that, if punished, a decisive person can retaliate by punishing the other person. This ability among the decisive agents in each cycle to retaliate applies to all Sen examples.

I must stress that these comments showing how Theorem 2.6 encourages interpretations of a dysfunctional society, or one in transition creating a balance between competing interests, capture only a flavor of interpretations that now can be associated with Sen's result. So much remains to be done that these options and commentary should be treated as indicating a sense of new and important directions that have not been adequately explored.

Sen's Conditions Are Everywhere

We now know why Sen's condition holds, but aspects of his negative conclusion affect us in daily life. For instance, in any setting where an "expert" makes a decision, aspects of Sen's result emerge. Additionally, the well-known Prisoner's Dilemma is central to much of what we do.

To review, the following array describes the payoffs for a Column and a Row player. For instance, if the Column player selects the second column, with the heading "Defect," and the Row player selects the first row, "Cooperate," then the outcome is (1, 15) meaning that the Row player gets only 1 (dollar, point, minute, or whatever 1 represents) and the Column player receives 15.

	Cooperate	Defect
Cooperate	(10, 10)	(1, 15)
Defect	(15, 1)	(2, 2)

$$(2.15)$$

Television mystery shows indicate why the game is called the Prisoner's Dilemma: A standard setting has two apprehended crooks. On these shows, the authorities try to extract a confession by questioning the culprits separately. If both crooks cooperate – not with the authorities but with each other – they receive a handsome reward (e.g., they may not serve jail time). To encourage one of them to defect and squeal on the other, a strong reward or inducement is offered. If both confess, or defect, both go away to prison. We know what happens; minutes before the scheduled end of the television show, one of the crooks, or maybe both, defect and confess.

In terms of the table in Equation 2.15, if the Column player plays "Cooperate," then the Row player will be better off by playing "Defect." This situation leaves the Row player with 15 and the Column player with the worse outcome of 1. A similar situation occurs in the reverse setting. Unless the players coordinate their actions, expect both to defect leading to the poor payoffs of 2 each.

An all too common example of this structure occurs during road construction season. Recall those signs warning all drivers to move into the left lane as the right one is closed a half mile ahead. If everyone would cooperate, traffic would slow down, but everyone would move along fairly smoothly. The "defector" races in the right lane until the last instant to slide ahead of traffic. If successful, this person is rewarded (15 in the matrix) at the expense of others who must slow down (1 in the matrix). If many drivers defect, as often is true, everyone suffers the resulting gridlock.

To place the Prisoner's Dilemma into Sen's framework, the following matrix assigns names for the four entries.

	Cooperate	Defect
Cooperate	A	B
Defect	C	D

Using these letters and examining who gets what awards, the Column player's preferences are $B \succ A \succ D \succ C$, and the Row player's preferences are $C \succ A \succ D \succ B$. According to the players' choices, the Column player is decisive over the pairs $\{A, B\}$ and $\{C, D\}$; the Row player is decisive over the pairs $\{A, C\}$ and $\{B, D\}$. This information leads to the following information table, which results in two cycles: $B \succ A$, $D \succ B$, $A \succ D$ and $A \succ D$, $D \succ C$, $C \succ A$.

	$\{A, B\}$	$\{B, D\}$	$\{A, D\}$	$\{C, D\}$	$\{A, C\}$
Column	$B \succ A$	—	$A \succ D$	$D \succ C$	—
Row	—	$D \succ B$	$A \succ D$	—	$C \succ A$
Outcome	$B \succ A$	$D \succ B$	$A \succ D$	$D \succ C$	$C \succ A$

The Prisoner's Dilemma, then, is a special case of Sen's framework. Because forms of the Prisoner's Dilemma are daily occurrences, Sen's result is omnipresent; his result must be taken very seriously.

2.4.3 Topological Dictators and More Effective Agents

The problem with the beach party and Theorem 2.4 is that nothing in the assumptions allow the choice rule to recognize the structure of the decision problem. If the issue is to make a choice along a flat object, such as a square piece of land free from obstacles such as holes or dismissed sites, or if we are to picnic along a straight beach, then reasonable rules exist. Problems arise when the problem involves different forms of geometry, such as a square riddled with holes or a circle. By knowing what goes wrong, we know what is needed to address the concern: We need to find ways to allow the decision rule to utilize global information about the shape of the object. The question is: How?

Insights come from unexpected sources: In this case, we find it in the commonly shared experience of driving during vacation time. What I have in mind are those road maps. Once we leave one country, or state, we need to grab another map. We then examine the overlap of the maps to

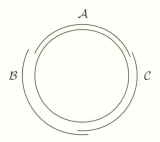

Figure 5. Using maps – and charts.

transfer the current position from one map to the other. Several maps are necessary to cover the complete region of interest when one map cannot. This overlap and completeness issue is depicted in Figure 5 where three maps, $\mathcal{A}$, $\mathcal{B}$, and $\mathcal{C}$, are used to cover the circular region.

This aside explains how to circumvent the Theorem 2.4 negative message. It is impossible for one map to capture all of the Earth, or even all of a circle; some points are missing. As indicated in Figure 5, a way to resolve this problem is with different maps covering different portions of the Earth. This description illustrates how mathematicians capture the geometric structures of manifolds, or surfaces, in higher dimensional spaces. Portions of the region are identified with a "flat" object (e.g., in the Figure 5 circle, each of the $\mathcal{A}$, $\mathcal{B}$, $\mathcal{C}$ regions can be flattened into a line interval).

As the complications confronting the decision problem are due to missing information about the geometry of the surface, a way to correct it is to use these maps, or charts. Before giving an abstract representation, let me describe the idea in terms of Figure 5.

Rather than searching for a decision rule to select a point on the circle, or beach, use maps to incorporate the geometry of the circle. Namely, each person selects a preferred point from each region and ranks the regions. A ballot, then, has the form

$$\theta_1 \in \mathcal{A}, \quad \theta_2 \in \mathcal{B}, \quad \theta_3 \in \mathcal{C}, \quad \mathcal{C} \succ \mathcal{A} \succ \mathcal{B}$$

where this voter identifies a favored position within each of the three beach regions *and* ranks the regions (e.g., this voter prefers region $\mathcal{C}$ over $\mathcal{A}$ over $\mathcal{B}$). To determine which region will host the party, use the Borda

Count. The actual position within the selected region can be the average preference over this region.

The same approach holds in general, but bear with the notation. First, cover the space $\mathcal{V}$ with a finite number, say k, of charts: This always can be done if $\mathcal{V}$, our domain and range, is a compact manifold. (For most purposes, this means $\mathcal{V}$ is bounded and closed.) Denote these charts as $\{\mathcal{C}_j\}_{j=1}^{k}$.

Instead of the Equation 2.13 expression of

$$F : \mathcal{V} \times \cdots \times \mathcal{V} \to \mathcal{V}$$

we now have

$$F : \mathcal{D} \times \cdots \times \mathcal{D} \to \mathcal{D} \qquad (2.16)$$

where $\mathcal{D} = \{\mathcal{C}_j\}_{j=1}^{k} \times \mathcal{R}(\{\mathcal{C}_j\}_{j=1}^{k})$ and where $\mathcal{R}(\{\mathcal{C}_j\}_{j=1}^{k})$ is the space of strict, complete, and transitive rankings of the $\mathcal{C}_j$ regions (i.e., $\mathcal{D}$ provides information about where a point should be selected in each region and how to rank the regions).

Some natural changes in earlier assumptions are needed. For instance, replace the $F(\theta, \ldots, \theta) = \theta$ unanimity condition with a condition that if each person has the same ranking of the regions, and each person selects the same point in each region, then that common selection is the group's outcome. The Pareto condition can be applied to each chart; continuity is over the choice of a point in a selected chart.

What Kronewetter and I proved [24] should now be obvious. In the framework of Equation 2.16, there exist many decision rules that are free from the blemish that some voter, or voters, are more effective than others.

2.5 Final Thoughts

The topics described in this chapter have played central, influential roles in our area; they have been rightfully treated as deep mysteries that have spawned numerous books and articles. Much of the puzzle disappears, however, with an understanding of the source of the problems: Explicitly specified information that we think is being used, is not. This situation reminds me of the line from the movie *Cool Hand Luke*: "What we've got here is a failure to communicate." By not communicating intent, some assumptions exclude others.

A central difficulty is the curse of dimensionality as reflected by the structure of the space of preferences. More precisely, the larger the spaces of profiles, the more we must expect outliers. The problem introduced by outliers is that, when determining the societal outcome, information we believe and intend to be used, is not. By understanding why these seminal conclusions occur, the sense of negativity spawned by these examples can be replaced with positive results.

The information needed to extract a positive conclusion is based on whatever it takes to allow a rule to determine whether or not a profile should be treated as an outlier. Answers depend on the specifics of a rule, not the profile. This comment draws support from the way I developed the structures to describe these sets of outcomes and identify their outliers; they are based on the level sets of the decision rules. For instance, there is nothing on the surface to indicate that the highly influential Condorcet triplet

$$A \succ B \succ C, \quad B \succ C \succ A, \quad C \succ A \succ B$$

is an outlier. It is not an outlier when used with positional rules, but it becomes a prominent outlier for decision rules that emphasize pairwise outcomes.

Rather than considering a profile in isolation, we must look at the properties of a decision rule that determine which profiles are mainstream (for that rule) and which ones are outliers where the outcome need not reflect what was intended. As we will see starting in the next chapter, where all voting paradoxes are examined, the same basic theme continues.

THREE

Voting Dictionaries

William Riker[1] [53] coined the term *positional election rules* to identify those voting rules where ballots are tallied by assigning specified points to candidates based on their ballot "position." These rules, and rules using them, constitute the more commonly used election methods. The first stage of a standard runoff, for instance, ranks the candidates with the plurality vote, while the second stage is a majority vote runoff between the two top-ranked candidates; two different positional rules are used.

The three-candidate vote-for-one rule is defined by the weights $(1, 0, 0)$ while the vote-for-two rule is given by $(1, 1, 0)$. The Borda Count, introduced in Chapter 1, is the sum of these choices, where the resulting $(2, 1, 0)$ means that 2, 1, and 0 points are assigned, respectively, to the first, second, and third positioned candidate on the ballot. With n candidates, a positional rule is specified by the weights $(w_1, \ldots, w_n = 0)$, where w_j points are assigned to the jth positioned candidate on a ballot, $w_j \geq w_{j+1}$ for all j, and $w_1 > 0$.

The kinds of problems that can arise with positional methods are illustrated with the next example where the preferences of 19 voters voting for a new departmental chair, Ann, Barb, or Connie, are split as follows:

Number	Preferences	Number	Preferences	
6	$A \succ B \succ C$	5	$C \succ B \succ A$	
2	$A \succ C \succ B$	4	$B \succ C \succ A$	(3.1)
2	$C \succ A \succ B$			

[1] William Riker was highly influential and one of the more important political scientists in the twentieth century. His impact continues to be felt through his papers and

With these preferences, the "winner" changes with the choice of a positional voting rule! Indeed, with the above three described rules:

Rule	Winner	Ranking	Tally
Vote-for-one	A	$A \succ C \succ B$	$8 : 7 : 4$
Vote-for-two	B	$B \succ C \succ A$	$15 : 13 : 10$
Borda	C	$C \succ B \succ A$	$20 : 19 : 18$

$$(3.2)$$

Rather than a "winner" reflecting the voters' preferences, each candidate "wins" by using an appropriate rule. Even worse, the vote-for-one and vote-for-two rules have opposite election rankings.[2] Out of frustration, these voters might seek guidance from majority votes over pairs, but this provides no help as the nondecisive outcome is the cycle $A \succ B$, $B \succ C$, $C \succ A$. With all of this conflict, who is the "correct" winner?

As this example dramatically demonstrates,

rather than capturing the "will of the voters," an election outcome may more accurately reflect the subtle peculiarities of the voting rule that just happened to be used.

This conclusion is bothersome. When we consider the impact elections can have on the direction of society, this assertion becomes frightening. As I will describe, this example only hints about what can go wrong with positional elections. The reasons for inconsistencies are described in Chapter 4.

But first it is worth illustrating how the "curse of dimensionality" plagues this simple three-candidate example. With just 19 voters, the number of possible profiles is mind-boggling; more than *60 trillion!* While the number is significantly reduced by ignoring which voter has what preferences, etc., the possibilities remain shockingly high. As these values suggest, trying to understand voting rules with a statistical analysis, or experimenting with only a few million examples, may fail to capture even the tip of the huge iceberg. Something different is required.

---

books, such as *Liberalism against Populism* [53], and through students and colleagues influenced by his development of the program at the University of Rochester.

[2] This reversal phenomenon is not an accident; it is described in Section 4.1.4.

3.1 What Goes Wrong?

A powerful intellectual magnet, which continues to attract researchers to the field of social choice, is created by the intriguing voting paradoxes such as the one outlined in the introduction to this chapter. What makes these examples surprising is that most voters probably view themselves as being semiexperts. All of us, after all, have had years upon years of voting experience starting with a show of hands to determine a kindergarten treat. We know what is going on, or do we?

Our experience suggests that several kinds of perverse voting outcomes could *never* occur. As a challenge, compile a list of election outcomes for, say, five candidates; select one ranking for each subset of candidates. Be challenging; create a list so outrageous that it clearly could never arise with the same voters. Perhaps the starting ranking is $A \succ B \succ C \succ D \succ E$, but if A drops out, we have $D \succ E \succ B \succ C$. Had B dropped out instead, we would have had $C \succ D \succ A \sim E$, and so forth. After reading this chapter, compare your list with the stated results. It will turn out that many of these "impossibility" lists *can* occur. This fact is certainly a discouraging message about the effectiveness of election rules in capturing "the will of the voters."

As shown in this chapter, surprises about election outcomes are so common that they should no longer be viewed as surprises. For instance, not only is it possible, but it is reasonably likely, for the plurality election ranking of Ann $\succ$ Barb $\succ$ Connie to be in direct conflict with majority vote outcomes where last place Connie beats both Ann and Barb, and Barb beats top-ranked Ann. Should this phenomenon occur in an election with important consequences, these starkly opposing conclusions would raise a troubling question: Is Ann, or is Connie, the top, or the bottom, choice of these voters? What else can happen? Leaning toward the wishful, wouldn't it be nice to find *everything* that could ever occur.

What makes the quest for understanding these paradoxes so consequential is that, beyond the seductively attractive mysteries generated by these voting inconsistencies, voting paradoxes serve as clarion warnings that actual election outcomes can betray the wishes of the voters. This is not a new insight: It reflects the reality that gave birth to our field a few centuries ago. As described in Chapter 1, Borda created an example to illustrate this Ann, Barb, Connie phenomenon where the pairwise majority vote rankings reverse that of the plurality vote. He used this example to demonstrate to the French Academy that using the plurality vote carried the danger of electing inferiority. (In Chapter 4, we will discuss how to create any number of profiles illustrating this and more intricate behaviors.) As Borda understood, an election outcome need not reflect the will of the voters.

3.1.1 Axiomatic Approach versus Paradoxes

Trying to determine the will of the voters, which goes hand in hand with the need to find appropriate voting rules, has been a central social choice objective starting with Borda's example. Some argue that this goal is the intent of the axiomatic approach widely used in choice theory. After all, the axiomatic approach often is promoted as able to tell us what we are really getting. If so, it would be powerful. But does it perform as advertised? As I explain in Section 3.2, in general, it does not. Indeed, I was referring to this axiomatic approach with my warning in Chapter 1 that, if misused, mathematical approaches can lead us astray.

If the axiomatic approach fails to do what we want it to do – to determine which election rules are better than others – then we must create other strategies. One approach is to find and compare properties of election rules. Here, highly skilled researchers have made fascinating but limited advances. The problem is that even though contributions are hard won, they tend to be modest because the combinatorics of profiles required to find new properties can be exceedingly difficult. This complexity, another manifestation of the curse of dimensionality, has limited what properties have been discovered.

Herein lies an obvious problem: With only a few isolated properties, how can we adequately and comfortably compare different election rules? How do we know whether a rule that performs poorly on a handful of discovered properties might excel on the thousands of properties that have yet to be discovered?

3.1.2 Dictionaries

If the cupboard is bare, try to fill it. With only a meager list of known properties for voting rules, it is reasonable to search for *all relevant properties.* To avoid an arduous search for these properties, it would be nice if we had a dictionary that listed all possible voting outcomes.

To put this goal in a historical perspective, David McGarvey [33] determined all possible lists of majority vote pairwise rankings. More precisely, with n candidates, assign a ranking to each pair; it does not matter how this is done, and ties are permitted. McGarvey proved that a profile exists where the sincere outcome for each pair is the assigned ranking. (To find all admissible three-candidate *tallies,* see my book [64].) McGarvey's result helps us understand pairwise elections, but our needs go far beyond this; we need to understand all possible election rankings that can occur with all possible positional methods over all possible subsets of candidates. The voting dictionaries are designed to achieve this objective.

My choice of the word *dictionary* is intended to invoke comparisons with that reference book sitting on the corner of your desk. This trusty, well-worn reference cannot do your writing or research; it is intended to assist and enhance your projects. You do the thinking: The "word dictionary" provides assistance by identifying what is possible. Similarly, if we had a "voting dictionary," then to analyze a specified voting rule, we could thumb through the dictionary to check the "words" – the lists of election rankings for the different subsets of candidates defined by a profile.

As an illustrating challenge, could a candidate who wins all pairwise majority votes (the Condorcet winner) be eliminated at the first stage of a runoff that uses a particular positional method? With access to a voting dictionary for this positional method, the answer follows just by checking whether there is a word with the election rankings

$$A \succ B \succ C \succ D \text{ and } D \succ A, \ D \succ B, \ D \succ C, \ldots$$

where D is the Condorcet winner but is dropped from advancing to a runoff. If such a word exists (there are many of them for most positional rules), then this perverse behavior is possible; if such a word is not in the dictionary (as is true for certain rules), then such behavior is prohibited.

Suppose we wish to understand consequences of polling information. With polling, voters may turn from one candidate to someone with a better chance of winning. Suppose that, with a specified positional voting rule, the election outcome would be $A \succ B \succ C \succ D$. If C no longer will be a viable candidate after the release of polling information, could D win? Because C would lose significant support with the released pools, it is reasonable to check whether the dictionary for the positional method has a word with the $A \succ B \succ C \succ D$ ranking and rankings for the triplet $\{A, B, D\}$ with D top-ranked. With a voting dictionary, the task reduces to a word-check.

How does this apply to strategic voting? For a motivating example, if all Nader voters in the 2000 U.S. presidential election voted for someone else, would Bush have won? By assuming that voters now will not vote for a specified candidate (Nader), insight into possible scenarios comes from checking the admissible rankings for those subsets without the candidate. For instance, if a profile defines the $A \succ B \succ C \succ D \succ E$ ranking, if voters strategically decide not to vote for E, is it possible to have a $D \succ C \succ B \succ A$ outcome where D now wins? To find out for a specified positional rule, just check whether words in its dictionary permit this flip-flop.

Recall the controversy surrounding the 1993 election to determine the host of the 2000 Summer Olympics. The decision rule is as follows: Until a candidate receives a majority support with the plurality vote, on each vote the bottom-ranked candidate is dropped. Through the early stages, Beijing appeared to be the winner:

- At the end of the first ballot, Beijing received 32 votes, Sydney 30, Manchester 11, Berlin 9, and Istanbul 7.
- On the second ballot, Beijing improved its first place standing by receiving 37 votes, Sydney 30, Manchester 13, and Berlin 9.
- On the third ballot, Beijing continued to improve with 40 votes, Sydney jumped to 37, and Manchester actually lost votes to 11; perhaps with polling information, two previous supporters of Manchester (presumably the two who originally voted for Istanbul) decided to support another city.
- China fully expected to win, but on the final ballot, Sydney *won* with 45 votes; Beijing received 43.

After the vote, several of my Chinese friends complained about strategic voting. It may have been the problem, but maybe not. For insight about this charge, we should determine whether this outcome is admissible with sincere voting. More generally, find all possible outcomes admitted by this Olympic rule. What happens should other positional rules be used? With access to a voting dictionary, this project just involves checking the admissible words.

In other words, voting dictionaries would make it possible to construct long lists of new, perhaps unexpected properties for voting rules. We could significantly extend – with less effort – research programs examining the peculiarities of election rules. With a dictionary, for instance, we could compare tournaments versus plurality elections versus runoffs – just compare how parts of a word relate to other parts of the same word.

It is reasonable to dismiss this dictionary approach as a far-fetched, wishful dream, but it exists. In Section 3.3, I will describe how I discovered and created (with a connection to chaotic dynamics) these dictionaries, what they contain, and how they can be used. For instance, remember the lists of "impossible" election outcomes I encouraged you to create? You can compare this list with the words in a voting dictionary. Beware; these dictionary results paint a frustrating portrait by showing how horribly bad most voting rules perform.

3.1.3 Aggregation Rules

Before describing the dictionaries, it is worth indicating how "voting" ties in with related interests. Doing so suggests more general ways to view the contents of this and the next chapter.

Voting is an *aggregation rule;* it aggregates voters' preferences to determine a societal ranking. While the study of voting rules can be complex, the mathematical structures tend to be elementary – most are linear functionals (positional rules) or combinations of them (e.g., runoffs, cumulative or approval voting).

Many, if not most, concerns within the social sciences involve complex aggregation rules. In economics, for instance, the price mechanism is analyzed via the supply and demand story – an aggregation rule. Anthropologists consider how individual forces cause various city-states – an aggregation analysis. Beyond the social sciences, multiscale design in engineering compares how micro behavior affects macro outcomes – an aggregation effect. Even probability and statistics are aggregation concepts.

The aggregation methods used in the social sciences, probability, statistics, and such tend to be mathematically more complex than in voting; nevertheless, it turns out that they share many characteristics. As such, expect the behaviors of voting rules to reappear elsewhere in the social sciences, statistics, and other disciplines. Indeed, it is worth exploring how any newly discovered result about voting rules predicts behavior for other aggregation processes.

This suggestion is realistic; for example, we now know that some of the dictionary results described in this chapter extend to the price mechanism from economics (e.g., see Sonnenshein [111], Mantel [30], and Debreu [14] for one kind of result, and Saari [55] for a more general one). Duncan Luce's work [29] in individual decisions is an aggregation method; its connection with voting is described in Saari [81]. In a different direction, Deanna Haunsperger [22] discovered how to transfer the voting dictionary results to create dictionaries for nonparametric statistical rules, and Laruelle and Merlin [25] were the first to develop a related approach to obtain a "dictionary of power indices." (Independently, but slightly later, Katri Sieberg and I developed a different approach [90].) Anna Bargagliotti, one of my graduate students, and I discovered results related to those in Chapter 4 to explain why many of these behaviors – and others – arise in nonparametric statistics.

3.2 Lassie and the Axiomatic Approach

It is common to justify the axiomatic method in social choice by claiming that this approach "tells us what we are getting." Axioms, after all, are the building blocks of a theory, like points and lines in geometry, so they characterize and identify what we are getting. They sound powerful.

Do I buy into the axiomatic approach? Absolutely! As a mathematician, I warmly embrace this powerful methodology. Beyond its esthetics, a pragmatic reason is that this standard mathematical technique has advanced our understanding of so many fields. It tells us what basic assumptions – the axioms – are responsible for all subsequent results. By reducing the analysis to only what is absolutely necessary – the axioms – it becomes possible to transfer and compare conclusions from one academic discipline to seemingly dissimilar areas. This is powerful stuff, but this power usually does not really happen in social choice.

A convenient way to quickly convey the inadvertent misuse of the axiomatic approach in social choice is with another slight digression. This one involves the late night TV programming that resurrects old flicks to fill the time. Most surely some of these old movies involve the legendary collie Lassie. This popular movie and TV series for children catalogued the adventures of a wonderful collie who would perform miraculous rescues often saving small children, followed by a huge helping of the loving comfort that only a patient dog can offer. The popularity among the young set of these heart-warming stories makes it is understandable why Lassie became a common name for a pet dog during the early 1950s.

This naming spree became so prevalent that it even applied to snarling monsters. It provided a valuable reality lesson for children, as they quickly discovered that naming a dog Lassie did not mean that their pet mongrel inherited the abilities to perform loving heroics. Similarly, naming a list of properties for a decision rule "axioms" does not mean they are axioms. Instead, as commonly used in social choice, most of the so-called and mislabeled axioms will never perform the heroics expected from actual axioms.

Rather than axioms, this field usually uses assumptions, or properties, or hypotheses. Often these conditions just uniquely identify a particular voting rule. "Uniquely identifying" is very different from "characterizing" or "creating the building blocks for a theory." For instance, the two properties of being of Finnish-American background and receiving my Ph.D. in mathematics from Purdue University in a certain year uniquely identify me, but they most surely do not characterize me.

A Voting Example

To illustrate this comment with voting rules, consider the "vote-for-two" rule with three candidates. A way to uniquely identify this rule is to impose certain technical properties, which ensure we are considering positional methods, and the condition that whenever a candidate is bottom-ranked by the majority of voters, she is bottom-ranked in the societal ranking. This conclusion provides a nice supporting argument for using the rule.

The same rule, however, can be uniquely identified by imposing the same technical properties plus the new property that even though almost two-thirds of the voters have her *top-ranked* – she could be just one vote away from being top-ranked by two-thirds of the voters! – she can be bottom-ranked in the election! For an example illustrating this troubling condition,

out of 3001 voters, let

- 1,000 have the Ann ≻ Barb ≻ Connie ranking
- 1,000 have the Ann ≻ Connie ≻ Barb ranking
- 1,001 have the Connie ≻ Barb≻ Ann ranking

Here, Ann receives 2,000 votes, while Barb and Connie each receives 2,001 votes. Although Ann is top-ranked by one less than two-thirds of all voters, Ann loses.

Both sets of properties uniquely identify the same rule, but neither set can be used to find the other directly. Indeed, neither set can be used to find other consequences of this voting rule or to serve as the building blocks for a theory. Instead of "axioms," these properties serve merely as assumptions that happen to identify a particular voting rule uniquely.

Who cares? Is this problem worth taking seriously, or can it be dismissed as a picky problem of semantics? Who cares whether conditions are called "assumptions," "hypotheses," or "axioms"? Actually, this difference makes an enormous difference whenever the name choice – axiom versus assumption – misleads anyone into believing that the mislabeled "axioms" really are axioms that "tell us what we are getting." This incorrect name choice can, and probably does, curb progress by discouraging an exploration of what else can happen. Rather than being a pedantic concern, this word choice can delay our understanding of what happens in this important area.

To underscore my point, let me indicate why one choice of properties makes the vote-for-two rule appear reasonable and another choice makes it worrisome. The first set relies on very special profiles where a candidate is bottom-ranked by a majority of the voters. The other choice emphasizes a different, disjoint, very special set of profiles where precisely one less than two-thirds of the voters has a candidate top-ranked while the rest have her bottom-ranked. Because these two properties reflect how this rule behaves only with highly skewed, carefully selected profiles, neither set tells us anything about what happens in general. In other words, this is another Tatjana effect, where the outcomes reflect the particular structures of special data restrictions rather than any general properties of the rule. (Also see Section 4.4.2.)

These comments further manifest how the "curse of dimensionality" permits one to find and emphasize carefully designed profiles, or outliers, with misleading outcomes. After all, neither choice reflects how the rule behaves with more general profiles of the kind that we would normally experience in actual elections. These properties should be banned by some Better Voting-Rule Bureau as constituting highly misleading advertisements.

3.3 Dictionaries

How does one find all possible properties of positional voting rules? My approach was motivated by the contributions of many people, including the thought-provoking paradoxes that Hannu Nurmi developed for his readable book [44]. Is there a unified way to explain all of Nurmi's troubling examples? I also was strongly influenced by the fascinating voting paradoxes Peter Fishburn [18, 19] discovered. One of Fishburn's paradoxes is where the sincere ranking of the plurality vote is

$$A \succ B \succ C \succ D$$

but if D should drop out of the competition, then the sincere vote of the same voters is reversed

$$C \succ B \succ A$$

What is going on? Fishburn's captivating example suggests seeking wilder, more general examples. For instance, could the plurality vote be $A \succ B \succ C \succ D$, but if *any* candidate drops out, then the outcomes reverse? For example, we would have $C \succ B \succ A$ if D drops out, and $D \succ C \succ A$ if B drops out. To add to the fun, could the outcomes reverse once more if two candidates drop out, where, say, A beats B, C, and D

in majority votes over pairs? Surprisingly, this behavior can occur; a supporting profile (from Saari [81]) is

Number	Ranking	Number	Ranking
5	$A \succ B \succ C \succ D$	9	$B \succ D \succ A \succ C$
7	$A \succ C \succ B \succ D$	8	$C \succ B \succ A \succ D$
9	$A \succ D \succ B \succ C$	11	$C \succ D \succ A \succ B$
4	$B \succ A \succ C \succ D$	8	$D \succ B \succ A \succ C$
7	$B \succ C \succ A \succ D$	10	$D \succ C \succ A \succ B$

$$(3.3)$$

This behavior is wild and counterintuitive! On the other hand, who cares? By this comment, I am referring to the natural tendency to dismiss voting paradoxes as amusing oddities. This tendency is a serious mistake! After all, these unexpected inconsistencies in election outcomes identify unanticipated properties of voting rules. Fishburn's example, for instance, proves that the plurality vote has the unexpected property where dropping the bottom-ranked candidate can cause the sincere outcome for the remaining candidates to be reversed. My example in Equation 3.3 demonstrates another unforeseen plurality vote property: If *any* candidate is dropped, the outcome can be reversed, but if *any two* candidates are dropped, the pairwise rankings can rebound to mimic the original ranking.

To find all possible properties of this kind requires finding all possible paradoxes that could occur with any positional rule over any number of candidates. Toward this objective, we need some definitions.

Definition 3.1: With $n \geq 3$ alternatives, consider all $2^n - (n+1)$ subsets with two or more alternatives. For each subset of candidates, assign a positional method. For a given profile, a *word* is the list of election rankings: The ranking assigned to a subset of candidates is the one obtained by tallying the ballots with the positional method assigned to the subset.

A *dictionary* of the specified positional methods is the collection of all possible words that can be generated with some profile. The Borda dictionary, denoted by $\mathcal{D}^n(\mathbf{B})$, contains all possible lists of rankings that can occur when the Borda Count is used over all subsets of candidates. Similarly, the plurality dictionary, denoted by $\mathcal{D}^n(\mathbf{P})$, contains all possible lists of election rankings when all subset of candidates are ranked with the plurality vote-for-one positional rule.

As an illustration, the *plurality word* (i.e., all subsets are tallied with the plurality vote) defined by the Equation 3.3 profile is

$$(A \succ B \succ C \succ D, C \succ B \succ A, D \succ B \succ A, D \succ C \succ A,$$
$$D \succ C \succ B, A \succ B, A \succ C, A \succ D, B \succ C, B \succ D, C \succ D)$$

For comparison, the "plurality-Borda" word – where the plurality vote is used to tally the outcome for the set of all four alternatives, the Borda Count for all subsets of three alternatives, and the majority vote for pairs – is

$$(A \succ B \succ C \succ D, A \succ B \succ C, A \succ B \succ D, A \succ C \succ D,$$
$$B \succ C \succ D, A \succ B, A \succ C, A \succ D, B \succ C, B \succ D, C \succ D)$$

With this mixture of voting rules, the election outcomes (for this profile) over the different subsets of candidates now are in complete agreement.

3.3.1 A Little Chaos

Forget trying to find all entries for positional voting dictionaries $\mathcal{D}^n(\mathbf{W})$ by using a direct, combinatorial approach; the project could not be completed in any number of lifetimes. To offer a taste of the complexity of the task, let me assure you that the list of rankings, where the five candidates are ranked as $A \succ B \succ C \succ D \succ E$, where the rankings mimic the *reversal* of this ranking when any one candidate is removed, where all triplet rankings mimic the mixture $C \succ B \succ D \succ A \succ E$, and where all pairs mimic the original ranking, is a vote-for-two word (namely, for each set of candidates, other than pairs, use the vote-for-two rule). Can you prove this statement directly? Finding a supporting profile involves an investment of time and effort. Once done, the work has just started because the next step is to prove whether some other list of rankings can, or cannot, occur. This is difficult stuff! For five candidates alone, this could be the source of thousands of Ph.D. theses. (As indicated later, this estimate of "thousands" is exceedingly optimistic.)

Knowing that the stated list is a vote-for-two word and that other words of unexpected types can be found leaves us with a distinct sense

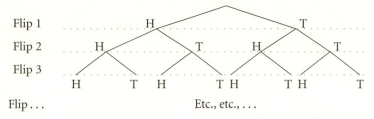

Figure 6. Flipping a coin – and explaining chaos.

that election outcomes can be highly chaotic. This "chaotic" observation is precisely what is needed to find answers. To explain where I am headed along with a hint about how all of this was discovered, *chaotic dynamics* is a mathematical tool that I commonly use in my research in mathematical astronomy. (The interested reader can browse, for instance, my book [80] on the Newtonian *N*-body problem.) One form of chaos, called *symbolic dynamics*, seeks to determine *everything* that can happen.

This "everything that can happen" phrase coincides with the goal of finding all possible words in a positional voting dictionary (i.e., finding everything that can happen with positional voting rules). Maybe, just maybe, the mathematics central to these advances in chaotic and symbolic dynamics can be modified in a manner to allow us to find *all possible entries* in positional voting dictionaries for any number of candidates. This is what I did. To explain the connection, the following section provides an intuitive explanation of chaotic dynamics.

Flip the Coin, Roll the Die!

Start with something that is accepted as being highly random – maybe flipping a fair coin or rolling a die. To keep everything simple, consider the standard decision method of Heads or Tails. A convenient way to list all possible repeated events is with a tree, where what happens on each flip, either Heads or Tails, is followed by what happens on the next flip. Flipping the coin *n* times leads to 2^n possible lists describing what can occur. Flipping forever defines an infinite number of lists that differ from one another.

With Figure 6, for instance, there are eight possibilities; (H, H, H), (H, H, T), (H, T, H), (H, T, T), which occur when the first flip is a Head, and (T, H, H), (T, H, T), (T, T, H), (T, T, T) when the first flip

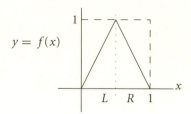

$y = f(x)$

Figure 7. A simple dynamic.

is a Tail. To find the different sequences of possibilities, just follow the different branches downward.

The "ét ceteras" at the bottom of the figure indicate that the number of flips goes on forever, so Figure 6 characterizes a highly random event. Think of *chaotic dynamics* as occurring where the complexity associated with such a random event, as depicted by all of the branches of the tree, can transpire with a deterministic process. Rather than chance determining what happens next, the apparent randomness is a consequence of a deterministic change.

For an example of such complexity, a specified function, $f(x)$, defines a deterministic dynamic

$$x_{n+1} = f(x_n), \quad n = 0, 1, 2, \ldots \quad (3.4)$$

of the kind commonly used throughout the social sciences. Here, function f models the individual or societal behavior, which describes how what happens today, x_n, will translate into what will happen tomorrow, x_{n+1}, as determined by Equation 3.4. Figure 7 is the graph of a particularly simple choice of f. Because the graph remains within the unit square (given by the dashed lines), all motion remains in the unit interval $0 \le x \le 1$.

The vertical dotted line passing through the peak of the graph of $y = f(x)$ divides the unit interval into a Left and a Right side. In earlier years, the traditional way to analyze the dynamic was to experiment. With experience, for instance, we might be able to *guess* what can happen; the task was to find a supporting initial condition. One approach was to choose an initial condition x_0 and then precisely compute the iterates given by $(x_0, x_1, x_2, \ldots)$. The next step would be to examine this sequence to see whether what we hoped would occur, did occur: Maybe something else happened.

To develop insight, replace the x_j iterates with the symbol that indicates whether each iterate is in the left or the right side of the interval. If doing so defined the sequence $(R, R, L, \ldots)$, it meant that the initial iterates x_0 and x_1 are on the right; the next iterate x_2 is to the left, ... Clearly, analyzing the dynamic in a traditional manner of carefully computing each iterate involved considerable effort and skill, yet only limited results and conclusions resulted. Surely we can do better.

We can do better, much better. Using modern techniques of symbolic dynamics, rather than finding only a bit of what can happen with the Equation 3.4 dynamic, we can find everything that can happen! To state the result, first equate this dynamic to the coin flip by associating L with H and R with T. It can be proved that *for any infinitely long sequence* of Hs and Ts, an initial condition x_0 can be found so that, after renaming the entries in the selected sequence with Rs and Ls, the Figure 7 dynamic will have precisely that future! This means, for instance, that because it is possible to have a coin flip sequence of the

$$(H, T, T, T, H, T, H, H, \ldots)$$

type, there is an initial position so that the Equation 3.4 iterates satisfy a

$$(L, R, R, R, L, R, L, L, \ldots)$$

future. Namely, because the first letter is L, the starting x_0 is to the left of the dividing line. The next three letters are Rs, so the next three iterates – x_1, x_2, x_3 – all are to the right of the dividing line. The next letter is an L, so the next iterate, x_4, is to the left. The point to be made – and this is where the notion of deterministic chaos arises – is that the deterministic dynamic of even seemingly simple systems can be equated with the complexity of random events.

An uncountable number of sequences can be constructed with two letters, so there are an uncountable number of different futures for the iterates of this simple dynamic. Moreover, each sequence consists of an infinite number of iterates, where iterates can suddenly veer off at unexpected times to assume a different, wild behavior, which makes it impossible to fully appreciate the dynamic of even the simple Figure 7 dynamic in a direct, traditional, computational fashion.

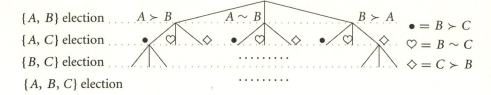

{A, B} election

{A, C} election

{B, C} election

{A, B, C} election

$\bullet = B \succ C$

$\heartsuit = B \sim C$

$\diamond = C \succ B$

Figure 8. Relating chaos to election outcomes.

Instead of a direct analysis, an indirect approach, which emphasizes the locations where bifurcations arise (as determined by the peak of the function in Figure 7), was created. The power of this mathematics is captured by the fact that we now can prove that *any sequence* is supported by at least one initial condition. (A brief description, with references, is in Saari [65].)

3.3.2 Chaos within Voting Theory

To relate the description of dynamics to traditional voting theory approaches, recall that ever since Jean-Charles de Borda, researchers tend to promote one voting rule over another by creating examples where the researcher's favored system delivers a reasonable result and the competing system does not. Even more, a way to discover new properties about voting rules is to guess what kind of anomalistic outcomes might occur over different subsets of candidates and then search for a supporting profile **p**.

This traditional approach toward voting theory closely mimics my story about dynamics: In dynamics, the standard approach involved searching for an initial x_0 that does what we suspect might occur. In voting, we search for a profile **p** that does what we suspect might happen. As is true with dynamics, the traditional approach in voting theory can be very difficult with only limited results and conclusions. Surely we can do better.

We can do better, much better. To do so, I modified the mathematics used in dynamics to create useful tools for voting theory. Doing so exposes an unexpected relationship between chaotic dynamics and voting outcomes.

The explanation starts with Figure 8, which represents all $3 \times 3 \times 3 \times 13 = 351$ lists of rankings. The diagram starts with the three possible majority vote elections for each of the three pairs. The first level, for instance, lists the three $A \succ B$, $A \sim B$, $B \succ A$ possible outcomes. Attached to each $\{A, B\}$ outcome is another tripod listing the three possible $\{A, C\}$ conclusions, and each of these nine branches is connected to a third tripod of the three $\{B, C\}$ possibilities. The tree then moves on to attach to each of these twenty-seven legs of possible binary rankings the thirteen possible election outcomes that can occur over the triplets: For the triplets, there are six rankings with no ties, six with one tie, and one with a complete tie.

This same 351-legged graph can also list outcomes resulting from the highly random events of first rolling a three-sided die three times and then a thirteen-sided die once. This comparison with rolling dice indicates that if lists of admissible election outcomes can be identified with all legs of this graph, then the complexity of random events and chaotic dynamics is connected with admissible elections outcomes. That we will do. (For obvious reasons, I did not draw this 351-legged graph.)

3.3.3 Dictionary Listings for Positional Rules

To carry out this program, we need to find the voting rules where all possible legs represent actual outcomes. For each of the 351 legs, we need to determine whether a profile exists so that the sincere election ranking for each of the four subsets of candidates is as specified in the leg.

The power of the symbolic dynamic example of Figure 7 is that the object was *not* to find an initial iterate x_0 that fulfilled a specified future but to prove that such an initial iterate *existed*. A similar situation exists with voting; the object is *not* to find a supporting profile **p** causing the specified election rankings to occur, but to prove that such profiles exist. A mathematical approach, borrowing heavily from dynamics (an exposition is in Saari [65]), was created to accomplish this objective. The next result provides the answer for three alternatives.

Theorem 3.1 (Saari [56]): For three alternatives, if the positional election rule $(w_1, w_2, 0)$ is not the Borda Count (i.e., $w_1 \neq 2w_2$), then for each of the 351 lists of possible rankings in Figure 8, a profile can be found where each ranking specified in the leg is the sincere one; each list is a word. The Borda Count is the only positional method that cannot realize all of the lists. For instance, any list with a Condorcet winner and a Condorcet loser must Borda rank the Condorcet winner strictly above the Condorcet loser; any leg where the pairwise votes end in ties must have a completely tied Borda ranking. Branches without these properties are not admitted. However, all such legs do occur with any other positional rule.

Restating this result in terms of a dictionary (Definition 3.1), Theorem 3.1 asserts that the three-alternative dictionary for all non-Borda positional methods includes as words all 351 lists of rankings. Only $\mathcal{D}^3(\mathbf{B})$, the Borda dictionary, excludes certain lists. These excluded lists cannot be Borda words, so they define Borda consistency properties; some are described in Section 3.4.1.

Now that we know what happens with three candidates, the next step is to determine what happens with $n \geq 3$ candidates. Even though trees of potential outcomes now are unmanageable, they still provide a nice way to envision the outcomes. For instance, with just four alternatives, the number of possible legs jumps from $3^3 \times 13 = 351$ for three alternatives to $3^6 \times 13^4 \times 69 = 1{,}436{,}646{,}861$, or almost a *one and a half billion* different four-candidate possibilities! Surprisingly, all of these ways to list the rankings of pairs, triplets, and the set of four are admissible plurality election outcomes! With five, six, or seven alternatives, the variety of words escalates so rapidly that the description involves numbers without common names.[3]

Theorem 3.2 (Saari [56]): For $n \geq 3$ alternatives, select any ranking for the set of all n candidates, any ranking for each of the n sets of $(n-1)$ candidates, any ranking for each of the $\binom{n}{n-2}$ sets of $(n-2)$ candidates, ... ,

---

[3] With five alternatives, the number of tree legs jumps to 5.4874×10^{27} – a number much larger than a million times the number of seconds that have elapsed since the Big Bang. With more alternatives, we encounter *really* big numbers; for example, with six alternatives there are 4.815×10^{75} words, a number so large that if a trillion of the world's fastest computers were used to divide up the counting chore, and all of them started counting at the Big Bang, they would not have made even a dent into this number. These gee-whiz results are sobering manifestations of the curse of dimensionality.

any ranking for each of the $\binom{n}{2}$ sets of pairs. There exists a profile so that the sincere plurality election ranking for each of the specified subsets of candidates is the selected one.[4] The same conclusion holds if, for each subset of candidates, either the plurality vote-for-one election rule is used, or it is replaced with any of the admissible vote-for-k election rules. (The value of k is less than the number of candidates in the subset.) Thus, the dictionaries for each of these combinations of positional voting rules contains all possible lists of rankings over all possible subsets of candidates.

So those vote-for-k rules, which are commonly used in academic and other elections, admit election outcomes that can be as chaotic as desired. Remember that list of "impossible" election rankings you were asked to construct? If the assigned voting method was a vote-for-k rule, then your list *does* represent actual election outcomes! For a gee-whiz comparison, if election outcomes behaved as some people naively believe, where the outcome for the five candidates determines the outcomes for all subsets, then (by including all possible ties, etc.) there would be precisely 431 different five-candidate election outcomes. Instead, by Theorem 3.2, these rules admit around a billion times a billion times a billion different, convoluted lists of sincere election outcomes! Thus, mind-boggling "dimensionality-curse" numbers already occur with only five candidates!

Good News?

That's the bad news; For partially positive results, concatenate the positional voting rules specified for each subset to define a "system voting vector." This system voting vector specifies which positional rule is used with which subset of candidates.

As all voting vectors assign zero points to a last place candidate, drop the last zero. For instance, with four candidates, if $(1, 0, 0)$ is used to tally the $\{A, B, C\}$ election, $(6, 5, 0)$ the $\{A, B, D\}$ election, $(1, 1, 0)$ the $\{A, C, D\}$ election, $(7, 1, 0)$ the $\{B, C, D\}$ election, and $(3, 2, 1, 0)$ the

---

[4] If the specified rankings do not involve ties, there is an open set of supporting profiles; the outcome is, in this sense, robust.

election for all four candidates, the system voting vector is

$$[(1, 0); (6, 5); (1, 1); (7, 1); (3, 2, 1)]$$

The majority vote over pairs always uses $(1, 0)$, so ignore all of them. This list is the *system voting vector*; it is a vector in $\mathbb{R}^\beta$ where the actual $\beta = 2^{n-1}(n-2) + 1 - \binom{n}{2}$ value is not important for the discussion.

Theorem 3.3 (Saari [56, 58]): For any integer $n \geq 3$, there exists a lower dimensional algebraic variety $\mathcal{V}^n$ in $\mathbb{R}^\beta$ with the following property. If a system voting vector is not in $\mathcal{V}^n$, then its dictionary contains all possible lists of rankings (e.g., the dictionary is as described in Theorem 3.2). If the system vector is in $\mathcal{V}^n$, then some lists of rankings over the different subsets of candidates are not words (i.e., these lists are not in the dictionary).

If **W** is a system voting vector, where at least one subset of three or more candidates is not ranked with the Borda Count, then

$$\mathcal{D}^n(\mathbf{B}) \subsetneqq \mathcal{D}^n(\mathbf{W}) \qquad\qquad (3.5)$$

That's a mathematical mouthful! To translate Theorem 3.3 into real-world words, the algebraic variety assertion means that the combination of voting rules that avoid the Theorem 3.2 difficulties – where anything you can imagine, and even worse, can occur – are very rare. It also means that if you do have a collection of voting rules that do not permit all possible outcomes, even the slightest change in the weights of any of the voting rules can readmit problems, serious problems!

To interpret Equation 3.5, take any example demonstrating an inconsistency in Borda election outcomes. It is not difficult, for instance, to create one where the Borda outcome for four candidates is $A \succ B \succ C \succ D$, but if D is dropped, the outcome switches to $C \succ B \succ A$. Equation 3.5 asserts that the same phenomenon, whatever it may be, *must occur with all positional methods* – namely, a Borda word also is a word for all choices of positional methods! This surprising statement imposes a new perspective on how to interpret the examples that have been created in this field.

So, any and all inconsistencies in election outcomes over subsets of candidates experienced by the Borda Count *must* occur with every other positional method. The inequality symbol, however, means that by not using the Borda Count with every subset of candidates, the resulting system of voting vectors admits words exhibiting pathological behavior over the subsets of candidates that can never occur with the Borda Count!

Whatever measure one might adopt – the number or kinds of inconsistent election outcomes – the Borda Count is significantly more consistent than any possible combination of positional rules. As this assertion is based on the dictionaries whereby everything that can happen is identified, it constitutes a significant advance over what can be discovered by constructing examples. Instead, the constructive approach must be expected to provide isolated results that, in general, fail to identify typical behavior.

Any Real Benefit?

Skeptical readers should question whether there are any meaningful differences between Borda and plurality dictionaries. To explore this question, let $|\mathcal{D}^7(\mathbf{B})|$ and $|\mathcal{D}^7(\mathbf{P})|$ represent, respectively, the number of words in the Borda and plurality dictionaries for seven candidates. If, for instance,

$$|\mathcal{D}^7(\mathbf{B})| + 1,000 \leq |\mathcal{D}^7(\mathbf{P})|$$

which means that the plurality dictionary has *more than a thousand more words* than the Borda dictionary, we might be momentarily impressed. But this difference of at least a thousand words quickly loses interest by recalling those gee-whiz values comparing the number of words in a dictionary with multiples of the time elapsed since the Big Bang. Avoiding a thousand, or even a million, words of election inconsistencies has the significance of changes in the shoreline caused by tossing a bucket of water into Lake Superior.

Larger differences are needed to impress. It would be interesting, for instance, if rather than a difference of a thousand words, the plurality dictionary had a thousand *times* more entries than the Borda dictionary.

What makes the inequality

$$10^3 |\mathcal{D}^7(\mathbf{B})| \leq |\mathcal{D}^7(\mathbf{P})|$$

which is true, impressive is that *each Borda word* can be converted into at least *a thousand different words of inconsistencies* admitted by the plurality rule! This is a more impressive assertion.

The actual result is so stunning that it is almost unbelievable: The difference in the number of words in these dictionaries satisfies

$$10^{50} |\mathcal{D}^7(\mathbf{B})| \leq |\mathcal{D}^7(\mathbf{P})|$$

Thus, the size of the plurality dictionary relative to the Borda dictionary is far more extreme than a billion times the number of water droplets in all oceans in the world.[5] To characterize the differences with my favorite, overused comparison, if even a *billion* of the world's fastest computers starting counting at the Big Bang, they would be nowhere near counting – forget computing! – all ways a *single* seven-candidate Borda word can be converted into different plurality words! Arrow's theorem identified problems of this field; as this inequality shows, his result represents not even a tiny needle smothered in a very huge hay pile.

3.4 Using the Dictionaries

Dictionaries identify new and different properties of positional rules. Indeed, Fishburn's example demonstrating that the plurality ranking of four alternatives can be the opposite of the plurality outcome when the bottom-ranked candidate is dropped motivated my development of the dictionaries. From the dictionaries (and an earlier result by Saari [54] that led to the creation of the dictionaries), we now know that *all positional voting rules share this reversal property*. Beyond my extension of

---

[5] The volume of water in all of the oceans is estimated [15] to be 1.37×10^9 km^3, or 1.37×10^{24} cm^3. Assuming there are a billion droplets in a cubic centimeter, there would be 10^{33} droplets of water in all of the oceans. Thus, the true "multiple," 10^{17} or a hundred million "billions," is another gee-whiz value.

Fishburn's example (Equation 3.3[6]), we now know that almost all combinations of positional voting rules have the property that any conceivable lists of election rankings over the different subsets of candidates can occur.

Practical Tools for Analysis

To convert these results into useful tools, consider those election methods used in practice, or theoretically examined, that use positional rules with different subsets of candidates. A standard runoff, for example, ranks the n candidates with the plurality vote and reranks the two top candidates with the majority vote. There are other kinds of runoffs. For instance, to drop candidates that most voters have bottom-ranked, *Coombs rule* uses the "vote-for-$(n-1)$ candidates" rule to rank the n candidates; one version advances the top two to a majority vote. *Nanson's rule* (Nanson [42]) uses the Borda Count: At each stage, one version drops all candidates not receiving an average number of votes, and the remaining candidates are reranked with the Borda Count; this process continues until a single candidate remains. Nanson's rule, then, involves the Borda rankings of several sets of candidates. *Black's rule* [7] uses majority votes over pairs; with a cycle, it uses the Borda Count over all n candidates.

Analyzing rules defined over several subsets of candidates is difficult. Does Nanson's method always give the same outcome as the version that drops only the bottom candidate at each stage? What happens by using Nanson's approach with a non–Borda Count positional method? How wild can outcomes differ for different kinds of runoffs? These questions can be quickly answered by using the dictionaries. Indeed, the fact that dictionaries can significantly simplify the analysis is nicely illustrated with the work of Merlin et al. [41] where they used the dictionaries (results from Section 3.5) to answer quickly several concerns that have been raised in this field.

An efficient way to illustrate these dictionaries is with a challenge problem of the kind often considered in this field. (Nurmi [44, 45] provides fascinating examples.) Here is a far-fetched question that is

---

[6] This Equation 3.3 behavior holds for most, but not all, positional rules (e.g., it never occurs with the Borda Count).

worse than the usual challenge and that would seem to be difficult to answer. Is there a five-candidate profile such that

- A is the plurality winner;
- B is the plurality runoff winner, where the two top-ranked plurality candidates are advanced to a majority vote runoff;
- C wins with the unusual runoff voting rule whereby after the plurality bottom-ranked candidate is dropped, the remaining four candidates are ranked with a vote-for-two rule;
- D wins with a rule where the vote-for-two winner of $\{A, B, C\}$ is advanced to compete with D and E; the plurality winner of this triplet is selected; and
- E is the Condorcet winner?

That's quite a question! This challenge would be difficult to handle using standard approaches, but with dictionaries, the immediate answer is yes; many supporting profiles exist. Consider the following explanations:

- The first two conditions are satisfied with the plurality and majority vote rankings of, respectively, $A \succ B \succ C \succ D \succ E$ and $B \succ A$.
- The third condition is satisfied with a vote-for-two ranking of $C \succ B \succ D \succ A$.
- The fourth condition is satisfied with a vote-for-two outcome of $A \succ B \sim C$ and a plurality outcome of $D \succ A \succ E$.
- The last condition is satisfied by letting E be the winner in the four pairwise elections that involve E.

The challenge involves nine subsets of candidates, so the specified rankings identify nine of the twenty-six entries in a word. Theorem 3.3 ensures that many words have these entries (i.e., a large number of profiles produces the specified outcomes when using the specified positional voting rules). As rankings for only nine of the twenty-six subsets of candidates are specified, the seventeen extra rankings can be chosen in any imaginable way to create wilder examples.

In general, then, whenever different voting rules determine their outcome with positional rankings over disjoint subsets of candidates, expect the outcomes to vary as wildly as desired. I encourage you to construct other examples (e.g., find the properties of a voting rule that combine the positional rankings over different subsets).

3.4.1 Variety Coming from Varieties

The message coming from Theorems 3.2 and 3.3 is that any list of rankings that could be assembled – one ranking for each subset of candidates – is an actual election ranking for some profile. This result holds for almost all choices of positional election rules assigned to the different subsets of candidates. In simpler terms, expect negative things to happen.

That's enough of the negative! To find some good news, focus attention on that mysterious set V^n. My paper with Sieberg [89] explains why this set is of interest. We showed that not only do pairs lose information but so do "parts," whether triplets or quadruples or whatever. Indeed, the dictionary results state that, in general, no consistency exists among the positional rankings of candidates in subsets and the full set. All positional methods that allow partial relations reside in V^n. In the following discussion, I sample results about V^n developed in Saari [59]. In doing so, I will discuss a candidate who wins all of her plurality elections, a condition that resembles the definition of a Condorcet winner – the candidate who wins all of her pairwise majority votes. So, let me coin a term for general elections.

Definition 3.2: For n candidates and $k < n$, a candidate is a k-tuple $\mathbf{w}^k$ Condorcet winner if she wins all k-candidate elections tallied with $\mathbf{w}^k$. A $\mathbf{w}^k$ Condorcet loser is bottom-ranked in all $\mathbf{w}^k$ elections.

Returning to V^n, while words in a voting dictionary describe properties of positional voting rules, those lists *not* in a dictionary probably define more interesting properties. For an example, suppose the $(3, 1, 0, 0)$ positional rule is used with four candidates, and the plurality vote is used with all triplets. As will be shown, any list with a three-candidate plurality Condorcet winner who is bottom-ranked by the $(3, 1, 0, 0)$ rule *cannot be a word* (i.e., this combination never occurs). Even more, a list where the three-candidate plurality Condorcet winner is ranked below the plurality Condorcet loser *cannot* be a $(3, 1, 0, 0)$ outcome. As these lists cannot be words, they constitute *consistency properties* shared by the $(3, 1, 0, 0)$ and plurality vote systems.

The issue is to find which combinations of positional methods are in the variety $\mathcal{V}^n$ and their properties. The only three-candidate voting rule in $\mathcal{V}^3$ is the Borda Count. Among its properties, it never ranks a Condorcet winner equal to, or below, a Condorcet loser, or if all pairs end in ties, the Borda ranking must be a complete tie. These properties occur because a candidate's Borda tally is the sum of the points she receives in her two majority vote pairwise elections. To explain this connection between the Borda and pairwise outcomes, start with a voter with the $A \succ B \succ C$ preference ranking and determine whom he would vote for over the three possible pairs. This listing is given by

Subset	A	B	C
$\{A, B\}$	1	0	—
$\{A, C\}$	1	—	0
$\{B, C\}$	—	1	0
Total	2	1	0

$$(3.6)$$

The sum of points this voter assigns to a candidate equals the number of points he assigns to her with the Borda Count. In a real sense, then, the Borda Count is the natural extension of the pairwise majority vote.

As positional methods satisfy the mathematical symmetries of anonymity (names of the voters do not matter) and neutrality (names of the alternatives do not matter) and are summations, it follows from Equation 3.6 that a way to obtain a candidate's Borda tally is to add the number of points she receives over all majority vote elections. As a consequence, if all majority votes over pairs end in ties, then the Borda outcome must also be a complete tie. If A is the Condorcet winner, she receives over half of the votes in each of her two pairwise comparisons, so her Borda tally must be more than the average Borda score – she cannot be Borda bottom-ranked. Similarly, a Condorcet loser must be Borda-ranked below a Condorcet winner. All basic Borda properties derive from this simple connection. This is the source of the surprising fact that *only Borda Count rankings* always are related to pairwise rankings. This means that any modification of the Borda Count, no matter how slight, destroys this relationship and allows, for instance, electing the Condorcet loser.

Four and More Candidates

Other combinations of positional rules in $\mathcal{V}^4$, beyond the Borda Count, are found in the manner suggested by Equation 3.6. Select any three-candidate positional rule, say the vote-for-two rule. Four candidates define four sets of three candidates, so determine, as indicated in Equation 3.7, the number of points a voter with $A \succ B \succ C \succ D$ preferences assigns to each candidate over these triplets.

Using the same argument about the Borda Count, it follows that a candidate's (3, 3, 2, 0) election tally equals the number of points she receives in all vote-for-two three-candidate elections. As with the Borda Count, this summation generates strong consistency properties. For instance, the (3, 3, 2, 0) voting system always ranks the Condorcet (1, 1, 0) winner strictly above the Condorcet (1, 1, 0) loser. If all vote-for-two three-candidate elections are ties, then so is the (3, 3, 2, 0) four-candidate outcome. These properties resemble the Borda Count properties with respect to Condorcet winners and losers because the conclusions are obtained in precisely the same manner.

Subset	A	B	C	D
$\{A, B, C\}$	1	1	0	—
$\{A, B, D\}$	1	1	—	0
$\{A, C, D\}$	1	—	1	0
$\{B, C, D\}$	—	1	1	0
Total	3	3	2	0

$$(3.7)$$

To find other $\mathcal{V}^4$ entries, take any $(w_1, w_2, 0)$ rule and do the same as with Equation 3.7 to obtain

Subset	A	B	C	D
$\{A, B, C\}$	w_1	w_2	0	—
$\{A, B, D\}$	w_1	w_2	—	0
$\{A, C, D\}$	w_1	—	w_2	0
$\{B, C, D\}$	—	w_1	w_2	0
Total	$3w_1$	$w_1 + 2w_2$	$2w_2$	0

$$(3.8)$$

The table in Equation 3.8 means that a candidate's tally in a $(3w_1, w_1 + 2w_2, 2w_2, 0)$ positional election agrees with the sum of her tallies over all triplets tallied with $(w_1, w_2, 0)$. Therefore, the $(3w_1, w_1 + 2w_2, 2w_2, 0)$ positional rule always ranks the $(w_1, w_2, 0)$ Condorcet winner over the Condorcet loser; if all $(w_1, w_2, 0)$ elections end in ties, then so will the $(3w_1, w_1 + 2w_2, 2w_2, 0)$ positional election, and so on. The comments regarding Definition 3.2 follow by using Equation 3.8 with the plurality vote $(1, 0, 0)$, which yields $(3, 1, 0, 0)$.

Interestingly, applying Equation 3.8 to the $(2, 1, 0)$ Borda Count yields the Borda Count. In other words, the Borda Count enjoys consistency properties with the majority votes of pairs *and* with the Borda Count outcomes of all triplets of candidates. To illustrate, suppose A is the Borda winner over four candidates but loses in a particular three-candidate Borda election. (In Chapter 4, I show how to construct all possible examples of this type.) Because A's Borda tally for four candidates is the sum of her Borda tallies for the three three-candidate elections, we immediately know that A does reasonably well in her other two three-candidate Borda elections!

How Wild Can It Get?

This approach continues for any number of candidates. A major result is that the Borda Count, and only the Borda Count, ensures consistencies over the election outcomes of all possible subsets of candidates. It is the only rule with some consistency among pairwise rankings, one of a few that has consistency with triplets and the like. The next step is to find other rules that relate the election outcomes of a many-candidate subset with the outcomes for subsets of these candidates. To do so, use the Equation 3.8 approach (e.g., in the obvious manner, a six-candidate positional rule can be found that relates five-candidate plurality election rankings, or four-candidate vote-for-two outcomes, or ...).

Even though this description is surprisingly simple, it is complete. If the positional rules in a system voting vector cannot be described with this summing manner, the system is *not* in $\mathcal{V}^n$, which means it allows anything to happen. Beware; even systems in $\mathcal{V}^n$ have surprises. For instance, using a mix-and-match version of the Equation 3.8 computation, we can find positional rules that favor the Condorcet *losers* over the winners. Indeed, wild examples can be created (see Saari [60]).

To illustrate the unexpected, notice that over all pairs, a voter with $A \succ B \succ C \succ D$ preferences votes three times for A, twice for B, once for C, but never for D. If $(w_1, w_2, 0)$ points are used in all three-candidate elections and $(\lambda, 0)$ for pairs, then over all pairs and triplets (Equation 3.8), our voter would cast $3w_1 + 3\lambda$ points for A, $w_1 + 2w_2 + 2\lambda$ points for B, $2w_2 + \lambda$ points for C, and none for D. As we now know from the preceding discussion, the rankings for four-candidate positional systems with these features must be related to the appropriate three-candidate and pairwise outcomes.

Theorem 3.4: Consider a four-candidate positional method where

$$\mathbf{w}^4 = (3w_1 + 3\lambda, w_1 + 2w_2 + 2\lambda, 2w_2 + \lambda, 0) \qquad (3.9)$$

is a voting vector for $w_1 \geq w_2 \geq 0$, $w_1 \neq 0$, and scalar λ. If $\lambda = 0$, then relationships exist among the election rankings for $\mathbf{w}^4$ and the three-candidate rankings obtained by $\mathbf{w}^3 = (w_1, w_2, 0)$. For example, a Condorcet $\mathbf{w}^3$ winner cannot be bottom-ranked in the $\mathbf{w}^4$ election; she is strictly $\mathbf{w}^4$ ranked over a Condorcet $\mathbf{w}^3$ loser. If all $\mathbf{w}^3$ elections end in ties, so does the $\mathbf{w}^4$ election.

If $\lambda \neq 0$, then the relationships between $\mathbf{w}^4$ and $\mathbf{w}^3$ elections also involve majority votes over pairs. For example, if all $\mathbf{w}^3$ *and* majority votes over pairs end in ties, so must the $\mathbf{w}^4$ outcome. If $\lambda > 0$ and a candidate is both a Condorcet $\mathbf{w}^3$ winner and Condorcet winner over pairs, then she is $\mathbf{w}^4$ strictly ranked over someone who is both a Condorcet $\mathbf{w}^3$ loser and the Condorcet loser over pairs. With $\lambda < 0$, the situation changes; a Condorcet $\mathbf{w}^3$ winner and the Condorcet loser over pairs is strictly ranked over a Condorcet $\mathbf{w}^3$ loser and Condorcet winner over pairs.

As an illustrating example, with $w_1 = 3$, $w_2 = 1$, and $\lambda = -1$, the voting vector in Equation 3.9 is $(6, 3, 1, 0)$. Because λ is negative, the pair $(6, 3, 1, 0)$ and $(3, 1, 0)$ favor the Condorcet *loser* over the Condorcet winner. The reason is clear; the negative λ value promotes losing candidates in pairwise elections over winning ones.

A similar conclusion holds by using negative values for w_1 and w_2. For instance, by using $w_1 = -2$, $w_2 = -\frac{1}{2}$, $\lambda = 3$, we have that the $(3, 3, 1, 0)$ system along with the majority vote results favors $(2, \frac{1}{2}, 0)$ Condorcet losers over winners.[7] Also, using nothing more than elementary algebra, you can analyze your favorite positional rule to determine whether it admits election relations and, if so, with what rules. For instance, to determine whether the positional rule $(12, 7, 3, 0)$ admits election relationships, solve the system (from Equation 3.9)

$$12 = 3w_1 + 3\lambda, \quad 7 = w_1 + 2w_2 + 2\lambda, \quad 3 = 2w_2 + \lambda \quad (3.10)$$

to obtain the unique solution $w_1 = 3$, $w_2 = 1$, $\lambda = 1$. This means that the $(12, 7, 3, 0)$ election outcomes are related to those of $(3, 1, 0)$ over triplets and the majority vote pairwise outcomes. On the other hand, $(1, 1, 0, 0)$ does *not* admit solutions in an Equation 3.10 format, so it does *not* admit election relationships with three- and two-candidate outcomes.

These examples make it clear how to create surprising results involving any number of candidates. If you are intrigued by these assertions, you will enjoy the related arguments in my papers [60, 66].

3.4.2 Other Dictionaries

This dictionary approach applies to other voting rules such as the Kemeny and Copeland rules. For instance, athletic supporters among the readers will recognize that teams are ranked in certain sports using the Copeland rule [13]. This is where a team receives one point for a victory, zero points for a loss, and a half point for a tie (in sports such as hockey). Thus, sports that rank teams according to the number of their victories use the Copeland rule.[8] For elections, replace sport victories with majority vote victories; the Copeland rule awards one point to the winning candidate,

---

[7] When emphasizing results describing winners and losers, not tallies, these comments hold when $(2, \frac{1}{2}, 0)$ is replaced with, say, $(4, 1, 0)$.

[8] Arthur Copeland (1898–1970) was a professor of mathematics at the University of Michigan. In mathematics, he is better known for, among other things, the Copeland-Erdös constant.

zero to the loser, and each receives a half a point with a tie. The candidates are ranked according to the sum of assigned points.

Because the Copeland rule offers an interesting approach to determine societal rankings, it is reasonable to find its basic properties (i.e., to find the Copeland dictionary). Vincent Merlin[9] and I did this in [86]. In another paper [39], we showed how to find all possible ways to be strategic with the Copeland rule, how to handle the myriad of Copeland rule problems that arise when new voters arrive, or voters change preferences, or . . . this list goes on.

Kemeny's rule [23] was invented by the mathematician John Kemeny[10] to introduce reason into the cyclic behavior that can accompany pairwise majority vote rankings. Some researchers, such as Peyton Young [120], suspect that Kemeny's method is what Condorcet had in mind when he proposed ways to extract a winner out of majority vote cycles.

Kemeny wanted to straighten out the cycles. For instance, the cycle $A \succ B$, $B \succ C$, $C \succ A$ can be converted into a transitive ranking by interchanging the ranking of any one pair. However, which pair should be used? We could select the pair that affects the fewest number of voters. For instance, suppose the tallies for the three pairs are, respectively, 40 to 20, 35 to 25, and 32 to 28. As the $\{A, C\}$ election is the tightest, seemingly the fewest voters would be affected by interchanging the $\{A, C\}$ ranking to obtain the transitive $A \succ B \succ C$ ranking.

To motive Kemeny's more involved definition, reversing the $C \succ A$ binary ranking to attain a transitive one might be acceptable to voters with $B \succ C \succ A$ preferences, but not to those with $C \succ B \succ A$ preferences who have the stalemate of a cycle replaced by crowning as winner their least liked candidate! Somehow, more consideration should be attached to the second voter's more extreme $\{A, C\}$ ranking than the first.

---

[9] Vincent Merlin, a frequent coauthor, is a member the French national research group, CNRS; he is located at the Université de Caen. His excellent 1996 Ph.D. thesis on social choice won the award for being the best 1996 Ph.D. thesis in economics for the country of France – a very nice recognition!

[10] Older readers who suffered through FORTRAN with those punched cards recall being rescued by the Basic program; John Kemeny was the inventor. He also was the chair of the Dartmouth Department of Mathematics and later the president of the university.

Kemeny cleverly addressed these concerns by introducing a "distance" between rankings. To explain with $A \succ B \succ C$ and $B \succ A \succ C$, decompose both into pairs and count the number of differences. In the listing

Ranking	$\{A, B\}$	$\{A, C\}$	$\{B, C\}$
$A \succ B \succ C$	$A \succ B$	$A \succ C$	$B \succ C$
$B \succ A \succ C$	$B \succ A$	$A \succ C$	$B \succ C$

the only difference is in the $\{A, B\}$ column, so the Kemeny distance between these two rankings is one. Now compare the designated $A \succ B \succ C$ with the $C \succ B \succ A$ preferences of the disappointed voters. Here the decomposition

Ranking	$\{A, B\}$	$\{A, C\}$	$\{B, C\}$
$A \succ B \succ C$	$A \succ B$	$A \succ C$	$B \succ C$
$C \succ B \succ A$	$B \succ A$	$C \succ A$	$C \succ B$

displays the Kemeny distance of three!

With this definition, we can compute the distance between a specified ranking $\mathcal{P}$ and each voter's preference ranking. The sum of these distances measures the distance of $\mathcal{P}$ from the aggregate wishes of the voters. The Kemeny outcome is a transitive ranking $\mathcal{P}$ that minimizes this distance. By minimizing the distance, where large differences in rankings increase the sum, Kemeny's rule accommodates voters with strong disagreements.

To discover properties of Kemeny's rule, Vincent Merlin and I determined the Kemeny dictionary [87]; some of our results extended to earlier ones discovered by Le Breton and Truchon [26] and Young and Levenglick [120]. For instance, our conclusions include the phenomena that the Kemeny rule always ranks the Borda winner above the Borda loser, and, to repeat the favor, the Borda Count always ranks the Kemeny winner over the Kemeny loser. Also, with the correct geometry, the Kemeny rule is a projection from the election tallies of pairwise votes to election tallies of transitive rankings – a description that makes it easier to handle previously complicated computations.

As with the Copeland rule, we then characterized all ways to vote strategically with Kemeny's rule as well as described voting phenomena that arise when new voters arrive, or voters change votes, or anything imaginable [40]. For instance, if a voter forgets to vote, can he be rewarded with a better election outcome? These notions extend to other voting rules.

While dictionaries for other voting rules would provide valuable insights, I know of no others. Hopefully, others will correct this literacy problem.

3.5 Comparing Outcomes over a Set of Candidates

Dictionaries capture how election outcomes can vary over the different subsets of candidates. The next quesion, as illustrated with Equation 3.1, is to determine what happens for a fixed subset of candidates when the choice of the positional rule changes. What happens if each voter can choose the positional rule to tally his or her ballot? (This happens!) The conclusions are surprising and worrisome!

3.5.1 General Results

The general results will be described at two levels. The first is directed toward the reader interested in an overview. Then, for the reader seeking deeper insights, I provide a geometric description to explain what happens and why.

The main result, Theorem 3.5, asserts that, with the same candidates and voter preferences, there can be a stunning number of different election rankings caused by changing how the ballots are tallied. Remember, each voter marks his or her ballot; their preferences remain fixed. Only the choice of a positional method varies. For clarity, I worded the theorem to assert that "a profile" exists with the specified property. In fact, the conclusion is robust because it holds for many profiles.

Theorem 3.5 (Saari [62]): For $n \geq 2$ alternatives and any integer k satisfying

$$1 \leq k \leq (n-1)((n-1)!) \tag{3.11}$$

a profile exists with precisely k different strict (no ties) election rankings caused by changing the positional method. No profile exists with more strict positional rankings.

With $n = 2$, Equation 3.11 describes the obvious: Each profile defines precisely one election ranking. With $n = 3$, there can be $(3 - 1)(3 - 1)! = 4$ strict rankings; an illustrating example is the table in Equation 3.1. Equation 3.12 provides a sense of how rapidly the numbers of possibilities escalate with changes in the number of candidates. Had I included election outcomes with ties, the numbers would have been significantly larger multiples.

The numbers of candidates in this table, which range from three to twelve, are the numbers of candidates one can expect to start a U.S. presidential primary election season. That a ten-candidate primary could allow millions of different outcomes depending on how the ballots are tallied might frustrate a losing candidate who would have won with a different rule. The numbers of outcomes are large; however, a surprising "dimensionality curse" consequence is that examples can be created using an unexpectedly small number of voters. For instance, creating an n-candidate example where candidate c_i wins with the vote-for-i rule, $i = 1, \ldots, n - 1$, and c_n is the Borda winner takes no more than a few handfuls more voters than candidates![11]

Candidates	Rankings	Candidates	Rankings
3	4	8	5,047
4	18	9	322,560
5	96	10	3,265,920
6	600	11	36,288,000
7	4,320	12	439,084,800

$$(3.12)$$

[11] It is easy, for instance, to construct a fourteen-voter ten-candidate example. Write down tallies so that with the vote-for-i rule, c_i receives $i + 5$ votes, c_{10} receives $i + 4$, and all other candidates receive no more than $i + 4$, with a little fiddling so that for all $i > 3$, the *sum* of votes cast over the vote-for-i rules for c_{10} is larger than any other candidate. The increased dimensionality makes it easy to find preferences creating the tallies. For instance, $c_{10} \succ c_5 \succ c_9 \succ c_8 \succ c_6 \succ c_1 \succ c_7 \succ c_2 \succ c_4 \succ c_3, c_{10} \succ c_6 \succ c_5 \succ c_9 \succ c_7 \succ c_2 \succ c_8 \succ c_3 \succ c_1 \succ c_4, c_{10} \succ c_7 \succ c_6 \succ c_5 \succ c_8 \succ c_9 \succ c_1 \succ c_4 \succ c_2 \succ c_3, c_{10} \succ c_8 \succ c_7 \succ c_6 \succ c_9 \succ c_4 \succ c_5 \succ c_2 \succ c_3 \succ c_1, c_{10} \succ c_9 \succ c_8 \succ c_7 \succ c_6 \succ c_3 \succ c_4 \succ c_5 \succ c_1 \succ c_2, c_1 \succ c_2 \succ c_3 \succ c_4 \succ c_5 \succ c_6 \succ c_7 \succ c_8 \succ c_9 \succ c_{10}, c_1 \succ c_2 \succ c_3 \succ c_4 \succ c_5 \succ c_6 \succ c_9 \succ c_8 \succ c_{10} \succ c_7, c_1 \succ c_2 \succ c_3 \succ c_4 \succ c_5 \succ c_6 \succ c_7 \succ c_{10} \succ c_9 \succ c_8, c_1 \succ c_2 \succ c_3 \succ c_4 \succ c_5 \succ c_6 \succ c_{10} \succ c_8 \succ c_9 \succ c_7, c_1 \succ c_2 \succ c_3 \succ c_4 \succ c_5 \succ c_{10} \succ c_7 \succ c_8 \succ c_9 \succ c_6, c_1 \succ c_2 \succ c_3 \succ c_4 \succ c_{10} \succ c_6 \succ c_7 \succ c_8 \succ c_9 \succ c_5, c_2 \succ c_3 \succ c_4 \succ c_{10} \succ c_5 \succ c_6 \succ c_7 \succ c_8 \succ c_9 \succ c_1, c_3 \succ c_4 \succ c_{10} \succ c_1 \succ c_7 \succ c_8 \succ c_9 \succ c_6 \succ c_5 \succ c_2, c_4 \succ c_{10} \succ c_5 \succ c_2 \succ c_8 \succ c_7 \succ c_3 \succ c_9 \succ c_6 \succ c_1$.

In France, it is reasonable to expect up to sixteen or more candidates during a presidential election. But with sixteen candidates, profiles can be created with $(16 - 1)((16 - 1)!) = 19{,}615{,}115{,}520{,}000$ different strict rankings. For instance, some profiles allow about 19.5 *trillion* different strict election rankings; the rankings change with how the ballots are tallied! So, which rule best represents the views of the voters? Without good reasons to have confidence in our voting rule, all we can say is "What a mess!" Rather than an election, a sense of a lottery emerges.

That's disturbing, but the actual assertion is much worse. With enough candidates (four or more), not only can all of the phenomena in the table in Equation 3.12 occur, but examples can be constructed so that *each candidate is top-ranked with some voting rule, second-ranked with another one, . . . , and bottom-ranked with still another rule.* This conclusion suggests a real mess; it underscores the need to find voting rules with outcomes that best reflect the views of the voters. Progress in this direction is described in the next chapter.

3.5.2 Let Elementary Geometry Do the Work

I discovered Theorem 3.5 by first normalizing the weights for any three-candidate positional rule into a $(1, s, 0)$ form where s, $0 \leq s \leq 1$, is a specified weight for a second-ranked candidate. As an illustration, the Borda Count uses the weights $(2, 1, 0)$. To find its normalized form, divide each weight by 2 to obtain $(1, \frac{1}{2}, 0)$, so $s = \frac{1}{2}$; the standard Borda tallies are recovered by multiplying each normalized tally by 2. Similarly, the normalized form of $(9, 7, 0)$ is $(1, \frac{7}{9}, 0)$ so $s = \frac{7}{9}$. To obtain the regular tally, multiply each candidate's normalized tally by 9.

The normalized form reduces the complexity of the analysis. This feature, for instance, immediately leads to the expression

$$(1 - s)(1, 0, 0) + s(1, 1, 0) = (1, s, 0) \quad \text{for } 0 \leq s \leq 1 \quad (3.13)$$

which describes each election rule as a point on the straight line connecting the plurality and the vote-for-two election rules. The vote-for-two rule also is called the antiplurality rule because, in effect, it requires a voter to vote against one person. In turn, because the mathematics of tallying election ballots is linear, it follows that *all positional outcomes are on the straight line connecting the plurality and the vote-for-two election tallies.* The election tally expression I developed is

$$(1 - s)(\text{Plurality tallies}) + s(\text{Antiplurality tallies}) = (1, s, 0) \text{ tallies}$$

$$(3.14)$$

To convert Equation 3.14 into a working tool, I assigned the election tallies for A, B, and C, respectively, to the x-, y-, and z-axes of the standard three-dimensional space. Illustrating with the table in Equation 3.1, when listed in the (A, B, C) ordering, the plurality and antiplurality tallies are, respectively, $(8, 4, 7)$ and $(10, 15, 13)$.

According to Equation 3.14, the $(1, s, 0)$ tallies for Equation 3.1 are

$$(1 - s)(8, 4, 7) + s(10, 15, 13) = (8 + 2s, 4 + 11s, 7 + 6s) \quad (3.15)$$

To check with the Borda Count $(s = \frac{1}{2})$, the normalized tallies become

$$\left(8 + 2\left(\frac{1}{2}\right) = 9, \ 4 + 11\left(\frac{1}{2}\right) = 9\frac{1}{2}, \ 7 + 6\left(\frac{1}{2}\right) = 10\right)$$

To recover the usual $(2, 1, 0)$ Borda Count tallies, I doubled each candidate's normalized tally to obtain the $(18, 19, 20)$ scores, which agree with the Borda values in Equation 3.2.

Plotting Points

To find all possible positional outcomes defined by a profile, plot the plurality and antiplurality points, draw the connecting line, and determine which regions include portions of this *procedure line* (Saari [64]). Each point on the line is the normalized tally of some positional rule.

The procedure sounds nice, but in a three-dimensional space drawing a line that can be envisioned is difficult. Try it; you won't like it. To simplify the story, normalize the tallies so that a candidate's tally specifies her fraction of the total vote; this is what the press does when reporting that "Sue received two-thirds of all votes." The previous plurality tally of $(8, 4, 7)$ has a normalized form of $(\frac{8}{19}, \frac{4}{19}, \frac{7}{19})$, while the antiplurality tally of $(10, 15, 13)$ assumes the normalized form of $(\frac{10}{38}, \frac{15}{38}, \frac{13}{38})$.

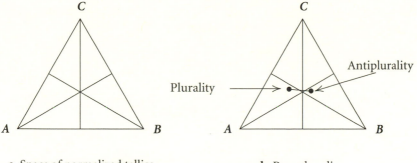

a. Space of normalized tallies   **b.** Procedure line

Figure 9. Finding all positional outcomes.

The sum of normalized tallies equals unity, so the tallies are in the simplex

$$\mathbb{S} = \{ (x, y, z) \,|\, x + y + z = 1, \ x, y, z \geq 0 \}$$

which is found by connecting the points at a unit distance on each of the three positive axes. The resulting equilateral triangle is similar to the one in Figure 9a. A point at a vertex means that that candidate received all possible votes, and the other candidates received none. The three lines indicate ties (e.g., the vertical one is where the A and B tallies are tied, and the line moving in the upward direction is where $B \sim C$). The six small triangles are *ranking regions*; they represent where the election outcome is a strict outcome. The one in the lower left bottom, for instance, is closest to the A vertex, next closest to the B vertex, and farthest from the C vertex, so all points in this ranking region have the $A \succ B \succ C$ election ranking.

3.5.3 Procedure Lines

So, plot the normalized plurality and antiplurality outcomes in the triangle, draw a line, and check which ranking regions are crossed by the procedure line. To plot the points, use an equilateral triangle where $u = 0, v = 0$ is the A vertex; $u = 2, v = 0$ is the B vertex; and

$u = 1, v = \sqrt{3}$ is the C vertex. To plot a (x, y, z) normalized tally, use

$$u = 2y + z, \quad v = \sqrt{3}z \qquad (3.16)$$

With Equation 3.16, the plurality tally of $(\frac{8}{19}, \frac{4}{19}, \frac{7}{19})$ is plotted on the Figure 9b triangle as the (u, v) point $(\frac{15}{19}, \frac{7}{19}\sqrt{3})$. The $(\frac{10}{38}, \frac{15}{38}, \frac{13}{38})$ normalized antiplurality tally is plotted as $(\frac{43}{38}, \frac{13}{38}\sqrt{3})$. Connecting these two points, as in Figure 9b, determines the procedure line.

The Figure 9b procedure line meets four open triangles. Each point on the line represents the normalized tally for a particular positional rule; the associated election ranking is that assigned to the small triangle. These four different strict election outcomes are the four promised by Theorem 3.5 for three candidates.

The procedure line also crosses three line segments where an election rule has an outcome with a tie. The Equation 3.1 profile, then, creates *seven* different election rankings with different positional rules. Although the rankings are difficult to see because the line is near the indifference point, which means that all elections are close, starting with the plurality ranking, the rankings are

$$A \succ C \succ B, \quad A \sim C \succ B, \quad C \succ A \succ B, \quad C \sim A \sim B,$$
$$C \succ B \succ A, \quad C \sim B \succ A, \quad B \succ C \succ A$$

An alternative way to compute these rankings is to use elementary algebra with Equation 3.15. For instance, this profile creates an $A \sim C$ tie when $8 + 2s = 7 + 6s$, or for the $s = \frac{1}{4}$ rule. As B's tally of $4 + 11(\frac{1}{4})$ is less than the tied outcome, the $(1, \frac{1}{4}, 0)$ outcome is $A \sim C \succ B$.

More Candidates

Analyzing what happens with more candidates requires venturing into higher dimensional spaces (e.g., tallies for four candidates define a point in a four-dimensional space). The normalized tallies live in a three-dimensional simplex – an equilateral tetrahedron – the four faces are equilateral triangles. For five or more candidates, the normalized outcomes reside in a simplex with a dimension too large to analyze with pictures. Yet, the ideas remain the same.

To find all possible positional outcomes, compute the election outcome for each "vote-for-k-candidates" voting rule (e.g., with ten candidates, the ballots are tallied with each of nine different election rules). Then, similar to a grade school project of "connect the dots," the *procedure hull* is the convex hull defined by these points. It can be difficult to envision this hull, but the properties are fairly immediate. For instance, the Borda Count outcome always is at the midpoint of the procedure hull.

3.5.4 Other Rules, Such As Approval Voting

It is worth digressing to describe what happens with voting systems such as Approval Voting. When Jill Van Newenhizen,[12] a former graduate student of mine, and I analyzed systems such as Approval Voting [93, 94], we coined the name "multiple voting systems" to represent rules whereby, in reality, each voter is permitted to select one of multiple choices of positional rules to tally his or her ballot. Here are some of our examples:

- *Approval Voting:* In this system, which is promoted by Brams and Fishburn [9],[13] a voter votes "approval" for as many candidates as desired. In practical terms, then, a voter can choose to have his or her ballot tallied with any of the vote-for-k-candidates voting systems. For instance, a voter with preferences $A \succ B \succ C \succ D$ could give one point only to A, or a point to each of A and B, and the possibilities go on.
- *Truncated Ballots:* Although asked to rank all of the candidates, some voters, for strategic reasons or just out of crankiness, might rank only some of them. If such ballots are not disqualified, then, by truncating the ballot, the voter effectively selects a different voting

---

[12] Jill Van Newenhizen is an Associate Professor of Mathematics at Lake Forest College in Lake Forest, Illinois.

[13] Steven Brams, a Professor of Political Science at New York University, is one of the more creative researchers in the areas of game theory, political science, and "fairness" in understanding what can go wrong with standard, widely used systems. His frequent coauthor, Peter Fishburn, is a well-known researcher who spent a large portion of his career at Bell Laboratories. His seminal work is widely recognized in areas as diverse as combinatorics, probabilistic voting, individual decision making, and voting theory, among others. One of Fishburn's many examples is mentioned in Section 3.3.

rule to tally the ballot. For instance, if the (3, 1, 1, 0) system is used
to tally a four-candidate election but, instead of registering my full
preference ranking of $A \succ B \succ C \succ D$, I only list $A \succ B$, I am
selecting the rule (3, 1, 0, 0) to tally my ballot.

- *Cumulative Voting:* This system, which was used in the state of
Illinois for several years, assigns a voter a certain number of votes;
for discussion, suppose it is two. The voter could cast both votes for
one candidate (called *bullet voting*) or one vote each to two different
candidates. In practical terms, the voter selects between having his
ballot tallied with (2, 0, 0, 0) or (1, 1, 0, 0).

- *Divide a Fixed Number of Points:* A frequently proposed method
gives a voter a specified number of points, say 10; the voter can
divide them among the candidates in any desired manner. This rule
differs from cumulative voting in that the selected values need not
be integers. The voter, then, selects any desired positional method to
tally his ballot as long as the sum of the weights equals the specified
number.

Multiple voting systems are based on positional methods; the difference is that the voters are divided into groups according to the positional
method selected to tally his or her ballot. What stymied the analysis of
multiple systems was an inability to determine all outcomes coming from
a single profile – another dimensionality curse. I developed a geometric
solution for this problem in [64]. To illustrate the ideas, I will find all Approval Voting (AV) outcomes allowed by the preferences in Equation 3.1:
This same "extreme votes" approach can be used with other multiple
voting systems.

A candidate's extreme AV tallies are given by her plurality (only voters
who have top-ranked the candidate vote for her) and antiplurality (all
voters who have not bottom-ranked the candidate vote for her) tallies;
this is the only needed information.

	A	B	C
Antiplurality	10	15	13
Plurality	8	4	7
SPT	2	11	6

$$(3.17)$$

The bottom line is the difference between each candidate's antiplurality and plurality tallies; call these entries, which describe how many second place votes a candidate can receive in an AV election, the candidates' *second-place tallies* (SPT).[14] For instance, *A* has the SPT value of 2. Because she may receive zero second-place votes, she has the three possible AV tallies of 8, 9, or 10. Likewise, *B*'s SPT value of 11 means she has twelve different AV tallies, and *C* has six. This one profile, then, admits $3 \times 12 \times 7 = 252$ different AV tallies! For each of them, we can construct scenarios showing why it could be a sincere outcome or, maybe, a strategic one. With so many AV outcomes, only readers with masochistic tendencies would plot all 252 points!

There is an alternative approach; as the AV tally for each candidate is between the extremes, only the eight extreme tallies in the table in Equation 3.17 need to be plotted. After connecting these plotted points, all AV outcomes are in the hull. These eight extreme points are

$$(8, 4, 7), \quad (10, 4, 7), \quad (8, 4, 13), \quad (8, 15, 7),$$
$$(8, 15, 13), \quad (10, 15, 7), \quad (10, 4, 13), \quad (10, 15, 13)$$

with the normalized tallies of

$$\left(\tfrac{8}{19}, \tfrac{4}{19}, \tfrac{7}{19}\right), \quad \left(\tfrac{10}{21}, \tfrac{4}{21}, \tfrac{7}{21}\right), \quad \left(\tfrac{8}{25}, \tfrac{4}{25}, \tfrac{13}{25}\right), \quad \left(\tfrac{8}{30}, \tfrac{15}{30}, \tfrac{7}{30}\right),$$
$$\left(\tfrac{8}{36}, \tfrac{15}{36}, \tfrac{13}{36}\right), \quad \left(\tfrac{10}{32}, \tfrac{15}{32}, \tfrac{7}{32}\right), \quad \left(\tfrac{10}{27}, \tfrac{4}{27}, \tfrac{13}{27}\right), \quad \left(\tfrac{10}{38}, \tfrac{15}{38}, \tfrac{13}{38}\right)$$

These eight points are plotted in Figure 10 using the data from Equation 3.16. The 252 different AV tallies are located in the shaded region. For a first estimate, treat them as being essentially equally spaced within the region.

The shaded region covers all thirteen ranking regions, which means that, with this profile, *any of the thirteen ways to rank three alternatives* can be the AV election ranking. This indeterminacy phenomenon where

---

[14] Steve Barney and I introduced this SPT term in our paper [85], which analyzed what happens when each voter's preference is reversed. One would expect the societal outcome also to be reversed, but this is false in general. We characterized which voting rules had this reversal property and which ones did not. Barney, who lives in Wisconsin, has been analyzing voting rules for many years; he is an activist promoting changes in our voting rule to one with outcomes that more accurately reflect the views of the voters.

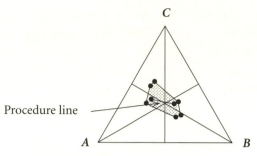

Figure 10. Approval Vote hull.

a single profile can admit many different election outcomes is a general characteristic of multiple voting systems (Saari and Van Newenhizen [93, 94]). With AV, *all possible profiles admit multiple possibilities for the societal ranking.*

Clearly, this indeterminacy makes it impossible to use standard comparisons such as asserting that the AV winner always is the Borda or Condorcet winner. Some theorists, such as Brams and Fishburn, treat indeterminacy as a positive aspect. Others, including me, view it as a danger whereby the actual election outcome resembles a lottery or dice roll outcome, rather than the aggregated views of the voters.[15]

The Figure 10 procedure line is in the interior of the AV hull. This must always happen because the plurality and antiplurality outcomes are two of the eight points determining the AV hull. Consequently, each sincere positional voting outcome is an Approval Voting outcome, but most AV outcomes can never be positional outcomes. The extra AV election rankings come from ranking regions that include the AV hull but not the procedure line; Figure 10 has nine such rankings with many different tallies. Reasons justifying these extra rankings must be developed.

3.5.5 A Working Tool for Actual Elections

Who can avoid the temptation to check whether the outcome for a close election would have changed had a different election method been used?

---

[15] A comment in Section 2.5 explains why AV, which sounds good, has so many serious problems. Giving more options to voters creates a *much* larger space of profiles, which, as we now know, spawns many, many outliers with questionable outcomes.

In the past, the required effort limited investigating only a few voting rules. The procedure line removes this limitation. If we can determine the plurality and antiplurality outcomes, we can find all possible positional outcomes. Just compute the procedure line, which is easy to do, and the outcomes for all possible positional rules follow.

I was invited to use this approach (Saari [76]) to analyze the AV election for president of the Society for Social Choice and Welfare. As the analysis proved, and as we now must expect, the AV outcome failed to satisfy earlier assertions that it always elects the Condorcet or Borda winner. An interesting phenomenon occurred, which must be expected in any closely contested election (as explained later in this chapter) – most voters voted for only one candidate. In other words, the AV election reduced to the flawed plurality vote, which AV was explicitly designed to replace.

Tabarrok's Analysis

Alex Tabarrok used my procedure line to analyze the closely contested 1992 presidential election among Bill Clinton, George H. W. Bush, and Ross Perot. As Clinton received less than 50 percent of the popular vote, it was natural to investigate whether the outcome would have changed had a different voting rule been used. One of Tabarrok's surprising results [114] was that Clinton would have won no matter what positional rule had been in effect! Rather than a close election, the consistency over all voting outcomes indicate a decisive Clinton victory.[16] Tabarrok then used the procedure line to create a new way to analyze the strength of an election outcome. You can check the details in his paper, but his idea, in general, is that should a candidate be the winner with all possible positional methods, then the victory is a solid one.

Tabarrok[17] also proved that had Approval Voting been used in this 1992 election, then, as suggested by the multiple AV outcomes in Figure 10, *any of the thirteen possible ways to rank the three candidates could have been the 1992 election ranking;* in particular, Clinton, Bush, or Perot could have emerged victorious. Which AV outcome could we have expected?

---

[16] For more about this, see the material in Section 4.2.2 after Theorem 4.5.

[17] Alex Tabarrok is an economist at George Mason University and director of the university's Center for Study of Public Choice. His widespread interests range from economics, analyzing voting behavior, to questions in empirical law. Along with a colleague, he has the popular blog http://www.MarginalRevolution.com.

A natural scenario of voter behavior for the 1992 election borrows from the Brams and Fishburn persuasive argument that a rational voter would never vote for all candidates. After all, voting for everyone fails to distinguish among them, so it has the effect of not voting at all. Similarly, if either of a voter's top two choices could win, a rational voter would vote for only one of them – voting for both drops any distinction, which pragmatically has the effect of not voting for either. (This voting behavior occurred in the mentioned Society for Social Choice and Welfare election; with three excellent candidates, most voters voted for only one choice.) Thus, rational 1992 voters with Bush and Clinton as their top two choices would vote only for one candidate. Similarly, voters with Perot top-ranked would support only Perot to improve his chances. Consequently, the only rational voters who would vote for two candidates are those with Perot second-ranked. Had they done so in an AV election, we would have had *President Perot.*[18]

I also recommend the interesting Tabarrok and Spector paper [115], which is partially described in my book [74]; it analyzes the 1860 four-candidate presidential election won by Abraham Lincoln. This election had been widely studied, but previous comparisons used only a few positional rules. By using my procedure hull (described previously), Tabarrok and Spector determined the outcomes *for all possible positional rules.* As they discovered, the choice of the election rule could have made a significant difference in who would have been elected, and maybe in what would have happened in the United States during those tumultuous years.

3.5.6 Back to the Original Problem: Creating Examples

We have just seen how to find all possible positional election rankings for a specified profile. At this point, I wish to reverse direction by showing how to create examples that exhibit any possible behavior. Namely, start with a line, or hull – perhaps one that crosses several desired ranking regions – and determine whether it is the procedure hull for some profile. Doing so requires finding properties of the endpoints.

---

[18] Because of this tendency for AV to revert to a plurality vote in closely contested elections, Brams and Sanver are exploring "modified" AV systems that incorporate the spirit of the Borda Count.

With three candidates, a procedure line's endpoints are determined by the plurality and antiplurality tallies. A convenient way to describe these endpoints is with the SPT (table in Equation 3.17) where

$$\text{Plurality tallies} + \text{SPT} = \text{Antiplurality tallies} \qquad (3.18)$$

Using Equation 3.18 and the fact that the number of voters equals the sum of plurality tallies equals the sum of SPT tallies, the basic properties of a procedure line's endpoints are as follows:

- Each SPT entry is nonnegative, so a candidate's antiplurality vote is at least as large as her plurality vote.
- If a voter votes for one candidate in a plurality election, he also votes for a different candidate in the antiplurality vote – these are the SPT entries. Thus, each candidate's antiplurality vote is bounded above by half the number of votes cast.

To describe these properties in terms of normalized tallies, let c_P and c_A represent, respectively, candidate c's normalized plurality and antiplurality tallies. To find c_P, divide the candidate's integer plurality tally by the number of voters; c_A is found by dividing the candidate's antiplurality integer tally by twice this number; candidate c's normalized SPT component is $2c_A - c_P$. A necessary condition for normalized tallies to come from a profile is that

$$0 \le \frac{1}{2}c_P \le c_A \le \frac{1}{2} \qquad (3.19)$$

Surprisingly, with the added condition that the c_A and c_P values are fractions, this also is a sufficient condition. *Any line with endpoints satisfying the Equation 3.19 is a procedure line!*

Finding Properties
Finding how profiles can change the outcomes of positional methods now is as easy as dropping straight sticks on an equilateral triangle. The endpoints just need to satisfy the Equation 3.19 constraints as indicated in Figure 11a. The normalized antiplurality endpoint, for instance, must be in the larger dashed triangle where all coordinates are bounded above by a half.

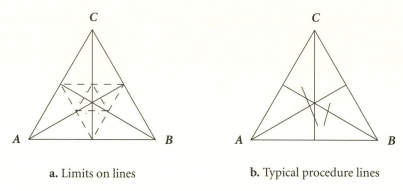

a. Limits on lines   b. Typical procedure lines

Figure 11. Finding procedure lines.

Also, the normalized plurality tally must not be more than twice the normalized antiplurality value. For instance, if A's normalized plurality tally equals unity – she is the unanimous plurality winner – then A's normalized antiplurality score is on the nearest leg of the largest dashed triangle. This makes sense; by receiving all first place votes, A receives half of all antiplurality votes, so the procedure line must have an end on this dashed line (meaning A wins with all positional methods).

An interesting setting has the procedure line crossing several regions; the supporting profile allows election rankings to change with positional rules. As an example, suppose the plurality outcome is in the larger dashed triangle where candidates receive at most half of the votes. The corresponding antiplurality vote is at least half the plurality vote, so all candidates receive at least one-fourth of the normalized antiplurality vote. Thus, if the plurality endpoint is in the larger dashed triangle and the antiplurality is in the smaller one, then the line is supported by a profile.

Even though a line length might need to be modified, any line with rational endpoints drawn close enough to the midpoint is a procedure line for some profile. As examples, the short line to the right in Figure 11b meets two strict ranking regions and one with a tie, so a profile exists with these outcomes. As the slanted line to the left in Figure 11b indicates, there are profiles with four different strict election rankings; with this line they are $C \succ A \succ B$, $A \succ C \succ B$, $A \succ B \succ C$, and $B \succ A \succ C$. This is the Theorem 3.5 assertion for three candidates. The full theorem for any number of candidates is proved in a similar geometric way by using procedure hulls rather than the lines.

Proof of Theorem 3.5: Use the fact that the n-candidate hull has $n - 1$ corners. These corners correspond to vote-for-k-candidates rules; the properties are found by adding third-place tallies, fourth-place tallies, and more to Equation 3.18. The proof uses the fact that if the corners of a hull are given by fractions and are close enough to the completely tied point, it is a procedure hull for some profile.

It remains to be determine how many regions a hull can cross. This geometric argument involves determining where to place the "corners" of the hull. Carrying out the details for four candidates is instructive and indicates how to do this in general. I leave the details to you; impatient readers can check my paper [62].

Creating Profiles from Procedure Lines

To conclude this chapter, I use an example to show how to find supporting profiles for any specified procedure line. Let $(\frac{1}{2}, \frac{1}{6}, \frac{1}{3})$ and $(\frac{1}{4}, \frac{5}{12}, \frac{1}{3})$ be, respectively, proposed normalized plurality and antiplurality tallies; they satisfy Equation 3.19. This procedure line passes through the midpoint where $A \sim B \sim C$ (e.g., the plurality ranking is $A \succ C \succ B$, the antiplurality ranking is the reversed $B \succ C \succ A$, and the Borda ranking is $A \sim B \sim C$). Thus, all positional outcomes are one of two opposite rankings, or the Borda complete tie.

To find a supporting profile, start with the normalized SPT $2(\frac{1}{4}, \frac{5}{12}, \frac{1}{3}) - (\frac{1}{2}, \frac{1}{6}, \frac{1}{3}) = (0, \frac{4}{6}, \frac{1}{3})$. Multiplying the plurality and SPT vectors by the common denominator of 6 leads to $(3, 1, 2)$ and $(0, 4, 2)$. The SPT values mean that nobody has second-ranked A and that B and C are second-ranked, respectively, four and two times. This information makes it easy to find a supporting profile: One voter has $A \succ B \succ C$ preferences, two have $A \succ C \succ B$, one has $B \succ C \succ A$, and the last two have $C \succ B \succ A$.

To create an example where *all positional outcomes have the same normalized outcome*, the plurality and antiplurality normalized outcomes must agree so the procedure line becomes a point. Take any point where each candidate's normalized tally is not more than a half (to satisfy Equation 3.19), such as $(\frac{1}{2}, \frac{1}{6}, \frac{1}{3})$. Here the normalized SPT vector agrees with the normalized plurality vector: $2(\frac{1}{2}, \frac{1}{6}, \frac{1}{3}) - (\frac{1}{2}, \frac{1}{6}, \frac{1}{3}) = (\frac{1}{2}, \frac{1}{6}, \frac{1}{3})$. Multiplying the plurality and SPT vectors by the common denominator of 6 yields the common $(3, 1, 2)$ for the plurality and SPT outcomes. These numbers mean, for instance, that A has three first- and three second-place votes. Finding a supporting profile is easy; one choice has two voters with $A \succ B \succ C$ preferences, one with $A \succ C \succ B$, one with $B \succ A \succ C$, and two with $C \succ A \succ B$.

By using procedure hulls, a similar approach applies for any number of candidates. Try it; surprises are easy to find.

FOUR

Explaining All Voting Paradoxes

To find a medical cure, we first must understand what causes the problem. Similarly, to find good news for voting rules, we first must understand *why* all of the election inconsistencies occur. Doing so has several advantages; it identifies how to handle the dreaded curse of dimensionality, and it suggests how to discover which voting rules best represent the "will of the voters." The latter goal, of course, requires establishing a reasonable definition for the elusive "will of the voters."

To motivate my approach, let me repeat a description (e.g., Saari [74]) about my nonexistent consulting business.

For a price, I will come to your organization before your next election. You tell me who you want to win. After talking with each member of your group, I will design a "fair" election rule (i.e., all candidates will be considered, and it will be acceptable to the voters). The candidate you want to win will win.

To illustrate this boast, let me pose a challenge concerning an election for a new chair. Of the fifteen members in a department, suppose

- Five prefer Ann ≻ Barb ≻ Connie ≻ Deanna ≻ Elaine ≻ **Fred**
- Five prefer Barb ≻ Connie ≻ Deanna ≻ Elaine ≻ **Fred** ≻ Ann
- Five prefer Connie ≻ Deanna ≻ Elaine ≻ **Fred** ≻ Ann ≻ Barb

It is easy to find ways to elect Connie; use the Borda Count or the vote-for-three rule. But how would you elect **Fred**? The complexity of this task is exacerbated by the fact that *everyone* prefers Connie to

Deanna to Elaine to Fred! An approach to accomplish this seemingly impossible task is described in Section 4.1.6. Before looking at it, you should try to find a "fair voting rule" to elect Fred for this Fred-Challenge profile.

4.1 Profile Coordinates

Voting and social choice are among the many victims of the curse of dimensionality. What makes two-candidate elections so well understood is that they offer only two choices: Vote for or against a particular candidate. The resulting two-dimensional profile space is devoid of those "if this happens, then . . . " complexities associated with more candidates, so the analysis is manageable. There is no dimensionality curse here.

With three candidates, however, profile space jumps to $3! = 6$ dimensions: Each of the six ways to rank the three candidates defines a new direction. The principal difficulty is to understand how to manage this dimensionality curse. As it is not clear how to do so, let's take a break to reflect about these complexities over a cup of coffee.

4.1.1 Coffee Reflections

Nothing is better than starting the day with a steaming cup of that strong morning brew. As is true with politics, economics, and sports, anyone with minimal knowledge about the topic instantly becomes a self-appointed expert. In terms of coffee, each of us has an authoritative opinion about what makes an excellent cup of coffee.

Start with the basic and neutral element of water. As long as the water is clean, free from heavy metals and purifying chemicals, the water does not contribute to the coffee's taste, but it makes the coffee possible. The strength of the coffee is determined by the kind and amount of coffee grounds that are added to the water in the brewing pot. After the steaming coffee is poured into a cup, embellishments, such as cream and sugar, are added according to personal taste. A person's preferred choice, then, is described in terms of the specified proportions of

$$\text{(Water, Coffee, Cream, Sugar)} \tag{4.1}$$

Water, coffee, cream, and sugar

Equation 4.1 describes a coordinate system. The choice of coordinates, which is determined by our objective – a good, strong cup of coffee – is important for our discussion. After all, we could use a coordinate system emphasizing, say, the chemical composition of the final cup of coffee. A chemist might embrace this system, but it would be useless, even counterproductive, to us early in the morning when, with sleepy eyes, we *want* the coffee to be ready. Rather than a listing of the chemical components, we want to know how the coffee tastes and if it is strong enough. In other words, a useful coordinate system is tailored to quickly and accurately meet specific needs.

Maybe these reflections over a cup of coffee can provide useful insights about voting theory. This coffee episode suggests that when certain ingredients affect something of interest, we should catalogue these inputs in terms of an appropriately designed coordinate system. Not just *any* coordinate system will do; it must be a carefully tailored system where each coordinate captures a specific aspect of our objectives. With morning coffee, the appropriate coordinates involve water, coffee grounds, cream, and sugar because each identifies different impacts on our morning needs. For a sweeter taste, we add sugar, not more cream. Rather than chemical compositions, the Equation 4.1 coordinates more pragmatically address our desperate morning needs.

The same principle applies to choice theory. To analyze voting problems and behavior, I will design an appropriate coordinate system for profile space. As with the coffee story, "appropriate coordinates" are those where an increase or decrease in any specified profile direction creates expected and specified changes in the outcomes of voting rules. The profile coordinates developed here do this for positional and pairwise voting outcomes – the rules described in this and the previous chapter. For other choice rules, appropriate coordinate systems can and should be developed.

To indicate where I am headed, equate the usual voting coordinate system, which specifies how many voters have each preference ranking, with the coordinate system specifying the chemical composition of a cup of coffee. With coffee or voting, adding a specified component makes a change, but it is not clear what it is (e.g., I have no idea how the taste of the coffee would change by increasing a particular chemical component). Similarly, even though adding a voter with $A \succ B \succ C$ preferences might change the outcome for some voting rule, it is not clear in advance what it will be. Just as with coffee reflections, the new goal is to discover appropriate configurations of voter preferences whereby we know *in advance* what will happen by adding more of that profile configuration to the mix.

As an added benefit, the resulting profile coordinate system is a powerful way to tame and control the dimensionality curse manifested by those "if she changes her preferences..." opportunities causing surprising changes in election rankings. Much of the mystery disappears by discovering which configurations of voter preferences have different *specified* effects on voting rules. Just as the sugar direction affects the sweetness of the coffee but not its strength, we will find appropriate configurations of voter preferences that affect, say, majority, but not positional, rankings.

A caveat: To avoid notation contamination, I emphasize three-candidate elections with occasional comments indicating what happens in general. As much of the literature emphasizes three candidates, this description should suffice for many readers. Proofs and a more complete description are in Saari [70]. A description for any number of candidates is in my papers [71, 72]. Unfortunately, these references proved to be difficult to read, so I have developed a more intuitive approach to handle the general setting and will describe it elsewhere. I do offer hints about what to expect.

4.1.2 The "Water" for Voting Rules

Water is the neutral but crucial element in making a cup of coffee. What takes the place of water with positional rules are those configurations of voter preferences where *all* positional and majority vote outcomes end in a complete tie. An obvious choice for three candidates is where one voter is assigned to each of the six possible rankings: Call this the *standard kernel vector*. The name is borrowed from the mathematical *kernel*, which consists of points with a neutral (usually a zero) outcome. As we should expect, any three-candidate configuration with this "everything is completely tied" property is a multiple of the standard kernel; that is,

for three candidates, if a profile yields a completely tied outcome for all possible positional rules and for all majority votes over pairs, then the profile has an equal number of voters assigned to each of the the six ways there are to rank the alternatives.

The *kernel configurations* define a one-dimensional space in the six-dimensional space of preferences.

A surprise occurs with four or more candidates: The kernel is much richer. There is, of course, the standard four candidate kernel element where the same number of voters is assigned to each of the 4! = 24 rankings. But other configurations of preferences cause complete ties of all positional rules over the four candidates, the four sets of three candidates, and all majority votes over the six pairs. Adding any of these kernel configurations to an existing profile has absolutely no effect on the rankings.

A way to describe these new vectors is to explain how to alter *any* given profile without causing any ranking or tally changes. Any two alternatives, say A and C, define four rankings where these alternatives are in first and second place:

Row	Number	Rankings		
Row 1	(+1)	$A \succ C \succ B \succ D,$	$C \succ A \succ D \succ B$	(4.2)
Row 2	(−1)	$A \succ C \succ D \succ B,$	$C \succ A \succ B \succ D$	

Separate these rankings into rows: In each row, the rankings for two pairs are reversed (e.g., in the first row, one ranking has $A \succ C$ and $B \succ D$; the next ranking reverses each pair's ranking). Between rows, the ranking of only one pair is reversed (e.g., row 1 has $(A \succ C) \succ (B \succ D)$; row 2 has $(A \succ C) \succ (D \succ B)$). The meaning of those $+1$ and -1 terms will become apparent in the next example.

An Illustration

To illustrate the Equation 4.2 configuration, consider this fairly complicated profile.

Number	Ranking	Number	Ranking	
3	$A \succ C \succ B \succ D$	4	$C \succ A \succ D \succ B$	(4.3)
2	$A \succ C \succ D \succ B$	2	$C \succ A \succ B \succ D$	
2	$A \succ B \succ C \succ D$	7	$D \succ A \succ C \succ B$	

It would be nice if we could simplify the profile without affecting any positional ranking over the set of all four candidates, any positional ranking over the four triplets, and any majority vote ranking over the six pairs. This goal mimics lessons learned from coffee reflections: Find appropriate configurations of preferences where we know in advance what will happen when adding the configuration to *any four-candidate profile*. Our immediate objective is to find configurations where, when added to Equation 4.3 or any other profile, *nothing happens to the ranking of any set of candidates*.

Toward this objective, notice that the second row of Equation 4.3 has two units of the second row of Equation 4.2. So replace the entries of the second row of Equation 4.3 with two units of the first row of Equation 4.2 to obtain the simpler but "election ranking equivalent" profile as shown.

Number	Ranking	Number	Ranking
5	$A \succ C \succ B \succ D$	6	$C \succ A \succ D \succ B$
2	$A \succ B \succ C \succ D$	7	$D \succ A \succ C \succ B$

Namely, one row of Equation 4.2 is *added* to the Equation 4.3 profile, and rankings from the other row are *subtracted;* this explains the $+1$ and -1 signs. Whatever the original profile, the two profiles have precisely the same positional and majority vote rankings over all sets. Just as with three candidates where adding one voter to each of the six possible rankings will change the tallies but not the differences or rankings, the tallies over sets of candidates can differ, but the differences between tallies never change.

As another illustration, the first row of Equation 4.3 has three units of the first row of Equation 4.2, so the replacement could go in the opposite direction creating a third profile, where again, all positional and majority vote rankings all agree. Here is this third profile.

Number	Ranking	Number	Ranking
0	$A \succ C \succ B \succ D$	1	$C \succ A \succ D \succ B$
5	$A \succ C \succ D \succ B$	5	$C \succ A \succ B \succ D$
2	$A \succ B \succ C \succ D$	7	$D \succ A \succ C \succ B$

The point is that the Equation 4.2 configuration – where one row has a (-1) assigned to it and the other has a $(+1)$ to indicate that, in any given profile, certain preferences are replaced with other preferences – is in the kernel. These configurations never change any positional ranking for any set of candidates or any majority vote ranking.

To prove that the Equation 4.2 element is in the kernel, tally all positional and pairwise ballots: Use the negative numbers of voters in the obvious way. For the pairwise votes, notice that each row of Equation 4.2 reverses the $\{A, C\}$ and $\{B, D\}$ rankings, which causes ties for these pairs. For the other pairs, a ranking in one row is countered by the same ranking, but with a negative number of voters, in the second row. To handle the positional outcomes, recall from Section 3.5.3 that only the "vote-for-k-candidates" outcomes need to be computed, and this is immediate.

Dimension Count and the Dimensionality Curse

The kernel for four candidates, then, includes the *standard kernel vector* where a voter is assigned to each of the twenty-four ways to rank the four candidates, and the Equation 4.2 choice. These two vectors create a two-dimensional space of other combinations. For instance, adding them means that the four-candidate kernel includes the profile where one voter is assigned to each of the twenty-four possible rankings except those in Equation 4.2. For these four rankings, two voters are assigned to each ranking in the top row of Equation 4.2, and zero voters, for each ranking in the second row.

There is nothing special about which candidates are used to construct the Equation 4.2 profile, so other choices create new kernel elements. The six ways to do this are linearly independent, so the kernel for the four-candidate profile space is *seven-dimensional.* An orthogonal basis for this space is given by the standard kernel vector and the six different ways to create an Equation 4.2 example. All possible combinations of these seven vectors create profiles with a voting behavior similar to that of water for coffee; while crucial, it plays a neutral role.

To indicate some kernel implications, consider the Equation 3.1 four-candidate example. By adding elements from the four-candidate kernel to this example, it follows that there are an infinite number of other profiles that have the exact same election behavior. Thus, rather than an isolated phenomenon, the Equation 3.1 behavior, where election rankings can reverse depending on how many candidates are in a set, is supported by at least a *seven-dimensional space of profiles.*

This kernel occupies *seven* of the twenty-four dimensions of profile space. These profiles, which inhabit almost a third of the available dimensions of the four-candidate profile space, merely pad the election tallies without ever affecting any positional or majority vote ranking! With five or more candidates, these neutral profiles now *assume more than half of the available dimensions* (e.g., with five candidates, the kernel space consists of 71 of the available 120 dimensions). This comment is a special case of the following theorem.

Theorem 4.1 (Saari [71]): For $n \geq 2$, the kernel in the $n!$ dimensional n-candidate profile space has dimension $[n! - 2^{n-1}(n-2) - 1]$.[1] For five candidates, the kernel occupies about 59 percent of the dimensions of profile space; for six candidates, the kernel consists of more than 90 percent of the profile space dimensions; and for seven candidates, the kernel takes up about 95 percent of the available dimensions. As the number of candidates approaches infinity, the ratio of the dimensions of the kernel to profile space rapidly approaches unity.

Tempering That Dimensionality Curse
Theorem 4.1 essentially states that with five or more candidates, most of the dimensions of profile space are consumed by profiles with no

---

[1] Theorem 2 of my paper [71] uses the $[n! - 2^{n-1}(n-2) - 2]$ value. This dimension is for the portion of the kernel that is orthogonal to the standard kernel vector. As the kernel given here includes the standard kernel vector, the dimension increases by one.

electoral teeth; they just cause tied elections with all possible positional elections and so on. This comment has interesting implications.

Some consequences reflect the fact that these kernel profiles pad other kinds of election behavior. So, with enough candidates, any particular election ranking behavior is supported by huge dimensional sets of profiles. To prove this, just mimic the preceding comments describing how the Equation 3.1 plurality election behavior is supported by a seven-dimensional set of profiles. By using the same arguments with Theorem 4.1, we can assert that *any seven-candidate election ranking behavior is supported by at least a 4,719-dimensional set of profiles within the 5,040-dimensional profile space.* What tempers this stunning and troubling statement is that the lion's share of these dimensions, 4,719, come from the kernel.

The statement holds for whatever behavior is considered. Consider, for instance, profiles causing majority vote cycles. As is described later in this section with n candidates, a profile subspace of dimension $\frac{(n-1)!}{2}$ causes all pairwise cyclic behavior (Saari [71]). Adding anything from the kernel to such a profile yields the same pairwise rankings, so according to Theorem 4.1, the set of profiles causing cyclic behavior has dimension $[n! - 2^{n-1}(n-2) - 1] + \frac{(n-1)!}{2}$. This impressive statement appears to mean that cyclic behavior eventually takes over; this kind of assertion can be found in the literature.

Care must be exercised in making such interpretations because, as is also described later, there is an $(n-1)$-dimensional subspace where nothing ever goes wrong with voting rules; these profiles ensure complete consistency with all positional outcomes over all subsets of candidates. This subspace has a smaller dimension than the one causing cyclic behavior; however, using Theorem 4.1 leads to the impressive, but misleading, comment that the set of profiles where nothing goes wrong has the huge dimension of $[n! - 2^{n-1}(n-2) - 1] + (n-1)$. This assertion falsely suggests that nothing goes wrong with elections as the number of candidates increases.

To appreciate what is happening, compare this discussion with the coffee story. Placing a teaspoon of sugar into a huge container of water creates a lot of sugar water. But most of the volume consists of the neutral component of water, not the small amount of sugar. The same is true with voting, With large numbers of candidates, the dominating portion of the profiles supporting a particular election behavior represents the kernel rather than the actual cause of the effect. After all, as asserted in Theorem 4.1, with an increase in the number of candidates, the kernel rapidly overwhelms profile space.

Now consider the usual profile coordinate system that specifies how many voters have each preference ranking. This standard system does not, and cannot, recognize the role of the kernel. If, for instance, we wish to examine all possible six-candidate cyclic behavior, we must confront a 651-dimensional set of profiles that resides within the 720-dimensional space! These frightening numbers capture the dimensionality curse; the resulting analysis could be compared to taking on a ferocious tiger! However, 591 of these dimensions involve neutral kernel elements, so *only* a 60-dimensional subspace, rather than the tenfold larger 651-dimensional set, must be explored. Even though the problem is difficult, it becomes more manageable.

As these numbers make clear, the profile coordinate system being developed here makes any analysis more realistic (i.e., the system tames the dimensionality curse). By ignoring the dominating kernel and concentrating on those coordinate directions that do make a difference, the analysis becomes much easier. Admittedly, this coordinate system will not simplify the analysis from that of a ferocious tiger to a calm pussycat, but it does allow comparisons of dealing with an angry alley cat.

The kernel is sufficiently important that it must be fully understood. As described earlier, we understand kernels for three and four candidates, but nobody has systematically examined even the five-candidate kernel, let alone the structure for any number of candidates. Some results are immediate; for example, extensions of the Equation 4.2 construction hold for any number of candidates, but they fail to complete the $n \geq 5$ candidates analysis.

A valued research contribution would be to fully characterize all n-candidate kernels. This goal probably can be accomplished by examining the symmetry structures of voting rules, which is how I discovered the Equation 4.2 profiles. However, as of this writing, nobody has carefully examined the kernel structures for even five candidates.

4.1.3 Nothing Goes Wrong

You know the saying, one person's heaven could be another person's hell. One could jest that, within choice theory, this dichotomy would occur if, suddenly, nothing could ever go wrong with any profile. Such a world would admit no difficulties of any kind: There would be no problems such as those reflected by Arrow's and Sen's theorems. Such a setting would be heaven for concerned voters, but it would be abhorrent for voting theorists who now would need to find another research area.

Voting theorists need not worry; their jobs are secure. As demonstrated by the introductory example of Chapter 3 (Equation 3.1) and the dictionary results of that chapter, voting rules admit so many difficulties that the true surprise occurs if complete consistency arises. As the introductory example in Equation 3.1 demonstrates, different positional rules can elect different "winners," and the majority votes may be of no help by defining a cycle. Consistency in general cannot be expected, but maybe certain kinds of profiles do exhibit this "heavenly" behavior.

In other words, can configurations of profiles be found where *nothing goes wrong* because all election rankings agree? This condition is *not* satisfied by unanimity; if everyone prefers $A \succ B \succ C$, the plurality $A \succ B \sim C$ ranking disagrees with the Borda $A \succ B \succ C$ and the antiplurality $A \sim B \succ C$ rankings. Let's seek much more than even unanimity can deliver; how about recklessly throwing all reserve to the wind by searching for profile configurations where, by knowing the tallies of, say, the plurality vote, *we know the tallies of all positional and majority rules*. Such profiles would be at an opposite extreme from the Equation 3.1 choice where the plurality vote tells us very little about what else can happen.

Basic Profiles, the Coffee Grounds for Voting
Surprisingly, configurations of profiles where nothing goes wrong exist. They are so basic for voting theory that, well, I call them *basic profiles* (an imaginative word choice made by a mathematician). By "basic," I mean that, because all positional rules have the same outcome with these profiles, they determine the "basic strength" of election outcomes; they are the "coffee grounds" for voting theory. As a corollary, *all* possible

differences among election outcomes must be created by adding other kinds of configurations of profiles into the mix; these other configurations will correspond to the sugar and cream that are added to that cup of coffee. Stated mathematically, only basic profiles deliver what is absolutely consistent among all rules, so an orthogonal configuration of preferences either resides in the kernel or forces differences in election tallies for some rules.

Start with the A-Basic profiles. As we will discover, adding multiples of this configuration of preferences to any profile will enhance candidate A's standing with *all positional and majority vote rules*. As is true with Equation 4.2, the same number of rankings are associated with a $+1$ as with a -1. The A-Basic adjustment profile is

Row	Number	Rankings		
Row 1	$+1$	$A \succ B \succ C$	$A \succ C \succ B$	(4.4)
Row 2	-1	$B \succ C \succ A$	$C \succ B \succ A$	

The top row has the only two rankings where A is top-ranked; the second row has the only two rankings where A is bottom-ranked. The B-Basic and C-Basic adjustment profiles are similarly defined (e.g., the B-Basic profile is

Row	Number	Rankings		
Row 1	$+1$	$B \succ A \succ C$	$B \succ C \succ A$	(4.5)
Row 2	-1	$A \succ C \succ B$	$C \succ A \succ B$	

where B is top-ranked with the first-row rankings and bottom-ranked with the second-row rankings).

The importance of these profiles derives from their tallies. First, normalize the positional rules in the manner introduced in Section 3.5.2, where the top-ranked candidate receives one point. Carrying out the tallies, where -1 counts as a negative number of voters, it follows that

with *any* $(1, s, 0)$ positional election used with the A-Basic profile, A receives 2 points, and B and C each receive -1 points. Thus, as advertised, with basic profiles, all positional tallies agree. With pairwise tallies, the $\{A, B\}$ and $\{A, C\}$ tallies are $2 : -2$, and the $\{B, C\}$ outcome is a tie with a $0 : 0$ tally.

The tallies for B- and C-Basic profiles are obtained with a name change.

What do *negative* numbers of voters mean? This choice just reflects how profiles are, in fact, designed; we move voters with one kind of ranking (the −1 term) to another kind of ranking (the +1) similar to how the Equation 4.2 kernel elements are used. Namely, if a given profile includes elements from one row, then those elements can be replaced with elements from the second row taking the signs into consideration. (Otherwise, the preceding tallies reverse.) Adding multiples of these particular basic profiles changes all positional and majority vote tallies in the same way.

Moving voter preferences requires the same number of +1s and −1s. For a different explanation, add the standard kernel vector to the Equation 4.4 adjustment profile to remove the negative terms and obtain

Row	Number	Rankings
Row 1	2	$A \succ B \succ C$ $A \succ C \succ B$
Row 2	1	$B \succ A \succ C$ $C \succ A \succ B$

where the first row has all rankings with A top-ranked and the second has all rankings with A middle-ranked. Here the outcomes with the $(1, s, 0)$ tallies assign $4 + 2s$ points to A, and B and C are tied with $-(1 + 2s)$ points each. These tallies now depend on the positional rules, and the added terms merely reflect the kernel element, which adds $2 + 2s$ points to each candidate's tally. Thus, to avoid "kernel contamination," Equation 4.4 includes negative numbers of voters so that the basic profiles are orthogonal to the standard kernel vector; it creates a profile configuration with complete consistency.

The following theorem summarizes the basic profiles; more details and results are in Saari [70].

Theorem 4.2 (Saari [70]): For three candidates, the sum of the three basic profiles has zero voters for each ranking. Because any two basic vectors are independent, the basic profiles define a two-dimensional subspace of the six-dimensional profile space. Any two of these profiles serve as a basis for the basic profile subspace.

For any profile in the basic subspace, the tallies for all positional rules are the same. For a specified candidate, this tally is two times the number of that candidate's basic profiles minus the number of basic profiles for the other candidates.

The majority vote rankings for pairs always define a transitive ranking that agrees with the common ranking for the positional methods. In a pair, the majority vote tally for a particular candidate is two times the number of that candidate's basic profiles minus two times the number of basic profiles for the opposition candidate in the pair.

By knowing the basic profile tally of the candidates for any positional method, or for the majority vote pairwise tallies, the tallies for all other of these rules can be determined.

Examples with Basic Profiles

A way to illustrate why the basic profiles serve as the coffee grounds of voting is to create an example where all rules have the same outcome. Later, when configurations representing the sugar and cream of voting are introduced, they will be added to this basic example to change the flavor of the election tallies.

Suppose we want an example where all voting rules have the $A \succ B \succ C$ outcome. To do so with basic profiles, start with, say, three units of an A-Basic profile and two units of a B-Basic profile. Adding everything together yields the profile

Number	Ranking	Number	Ranking
3	$A \succ B \succ C$	1	$A \succ C \succ B$
-2	$C \succ A \succ B$	-3	$C \succ B \succ A$
-1	$B \succ C \succ A$	2	$B \succ A \succ C$

$$(4.6)$$

There is no need to tally ballots. According to Theorem 4.2, A receives $2 \times 3 = 6$ votes from the A-Basic terms and $2 \times (-1) = -2$ votes from the B-Basic for a total of 4, B receives $2 \times 2 = 4$ votes from the B-Basic term and -3 from the A-Basic for a total of 1, and poor C receives -5 votes. These numbers provide each candidate's tally for all positional rules. According to the theorem, the majority vote tallies for $A : B$ are $(3 \times 2) - (2 \times 2) = 2 : (2 \times 2) - (3 \times 2) = -2$; for $B : C$ it is $2 \times 2 = 4 : 2 \times (-2) = -4$; and for $A : C$ we have $3 \times 2 = 6 : -(3 \times 2) = -6$.

To convert Equation 4.6 into a profile with a nonnegative number of voters, notice that the most negative Equation 4.6 value is -3. By adding three units of the standard kernel profile to Equation 4.6, which adds three more voters to each ranking, we obtain a desired

Number	Ranking	Number	Ranking	
6	$A \succ B \succ C$	4	$A \succ C \succ B$	(4.7)
1	$C \succ A \succ B$	0	$C \succ B \succ A$	
2	$B \succ C \succ A$	5	$B \succ A \succ C$	

All differences between the tallies in Equations 4.6 and 4.7 reflect the kernel element: It adds $3(2 + 2s) = 6 + 6s$ points to each candidate's tally to make the A, B, C positional tallies, respectively, $10 + 6s$, $7 + 6s$, and $1 + 6s$. For majority votes over pairs, add $3 \times 3 = 9$ points to each candidate's tally leading to the tallies of $A : B$ being $11 : 7$, of $B : C$ being $13 : 5$, and of $A : C$ being $15 : 3$.

More Candidates, Another Basic Subspace

The basic subspace for any number of candidates is much the same. For a specified candidate, say A, the basic profile attaches one voter to each of the $(n - 1)!$ rankings where A is top-ranked and -1 voters to each of the $(n - 1)!$ rankings where A is bottom-ranked. An easy computation proves that with any profile from this space, the tallies for any number of candidates for any positional method uniquely determine the tallies for the same candidates over all possible subsets of candidates and all positional rules.

This result means, for instance, that the majority vote tallies over all pairs of six candidates uniquely determine the plurality tallies over all sets of three candidates and the vote-for-two tallies over the set of all six candidates. Such a strong relationship fails to hold in general. This profile subspace where nothing goes wrong is an $(n - 1)$-dimensional subspace of the $n!$-dimensional profile space. Proving that size need not matter, even though the dimension of this space is minimal, these profiles – the coffee grounds of voting – have a significant impact on election outcomes.

Let me expand on this last paragraph in a way that will provide insight into the highly chaotic, paradoxical settings catalogued in Chapter 3.

Recall that this is where the kinds and numbers of possible election in-consistencies rapidly grow with the number of candidates. Some number counting helps to explain why this can happen.

Start by ignoring the one-dimensional kernel for three candidates. With what remains, the basic profile subspace fills two of the remaining five dimensions of profile space. Namely, the basic profiles are dominated by the three-dimensional subspace of profiles that mix up election out-comes. So, with three candidates, there are more dimensions of cream and sugar than of coffee. Nevertheless, with more dimensions of profiles that change outcomes rather than contribute to consistency, we can un-derstand why it is rare to encounter profiles where everything, including tallies, is consistent.

To appreciate the skyrocketing nature of the problem, consider four candidates. Ignoring the seven-dimensional kernel, the profiles that determine the election outcomes reside in a $24 - 7 = 17$-dimensional space. In this seventeen-dimensional space, *only three of the dimensions are the basic profiles*, so $17 - 4 = 13$ dimensions contain all of those trouble-making profiles that mix up and modify election rankings. Thus, the contributions being made by basic profiles can be swamped by all of those "paradoxical" outcomes!

With five candidates, the problem becomes even more overwhelming; ignoring the seventy-one-dimensional kernel, the subspace of profiles that affect election rankings is forty-nine-dimensional. *Of these forty-nine dimensions, only four of them constitute the basic profiles*, so there is a tenfold larger, forty-five-dimensional, subspace of profiles that mix up and modify election outcomes! Indeed, with five candidates, the basic profiles constitute only about 8 percent of the dimensions of the effective part of profile space, and this percentage rapidly approaches zero as the number of candidates approaches infinity.

Notice how quickly basic profiles become lost within profile space while those profiles that cause inconsistencies in election tallies and rank-ings quickly take over. Using the coffee simile, with enough candidates the voting analysis quickly resembles the composition of a young child's cup of coffee – a teaspoon of coffee accompanied by lots of sugar and milk.

4.1.4 A Creamy Addition: Positional Differences

As described, most of the effective dimensions of profile space contain profiles that change the election rankings. So, to understand what happens with positional voting rules, we must find them. The search starts here.

If we are to find a coordinate system for profile space, it is critical that we find appropriate configurations of profiles that affect positional, but never majority vote, rankings. Let me see; if the profile cannot affect majority vote rankings, then, for each pair, the configuration must have the same number of voters assigned to both ways the pair can be ranked. An easy way to satisfy this condition is with a pair of reversals (e.g., with the $A \succ B \succ C$ ranking include its reversal of $C \succ B \succ A$).[2]

It is easy to create stories suggesting what should happen with a pair of reversal rankings. My favorite is that even though I love my wife, we do have opposing opinions. If I prefer $A \succ B \succ C$, she may prefer $C \succ B \succ A$. Adopting the "make lemonade out of lemons" philosophy, this conflict creates opportunities. For instance, if election day is on a delightful beach day, then, with clear consciences, we can skip voting because her ballot will only cancel mine.

Will it? The ballots cancel with the pairwise vote because the two of us rank each pair in an opposite manner. But something very different occurs with the $(1, s, 0)$ positional rules. Here the tallies are

Ranking	A	B	C
$A \succ B \succ C$	1	s	0
$C \succ B \succ A$	0	s	1
Total	1	$2s$	1

(4.8)

Rather than a tie, a positional rule with $s < \frac{1}{2}$, such as the plurality vote where $s = 0$, has the $A \sim C \succ B$ election outcome identifying B as the "loser." On the other hand, all positional rules where $s > \frac{1}{2}$, such as the antiplurality rule where $s = 1$, deliver the *opposite* $B \succ A \sim C$ election ranking where B is the "winner." Recall that earlier we encountered

---

[2] Mathematically, this is a $\mathbb{Z}_2$ orbit of a ranking.

opposing plurality and antiplurality rankings with the Equation 3.1 profile; soon I will explain this behavior.

As this example demonstrates, a ranking and its reversal never affect majority vote pairwise rankings, but a ranking can affect positional
rankings. Aha! This is precisely the kind of configuration we have been
seeking. To express this behavior in a coordinate format, the *A-Reversal*
profile adjustment is where

Row	Number	Rankings	
Row 1	+1	$A \succ B \succ C$	$A \succ C \succ B$
Row 2	+1	$C \succ B \succ A$	$B \succ C \succ A$
Row 3	−2	$B \succ A \succ C$	$C \succ A \succ B$

$$(4.9)$$

Notice how the reversal of a row 1 ranking is immediately below in
row 2. It is interesting to examine this profile with respect to the effect
it has on positional outcomes. Adding the first row, which consists of all
rankings where A is top-ranked, to any profile will enhance A's tally with
all positional rules. Balance is provided by the second row, which consists
of all rankings where A is bottom-ranked. To appreciate the second row's
role, recall that the vote-for-two rule is equivalent to voting against a
candidate. Adding the second row to a profile, then, hurts A's standing
with the antiplurality and all positional rules that recognize second-
place rankings (i.e., all rules except the plurality vote). This yin–yang
balance provides distinctions among the positional methods by affecting
A's positional tallies in different ways. Row 3 is introduced to convert
this configuration of profiles into a coordinate direction by eliminating
kernel effects.

The power of these profiles, and support for the assertion that they
distinguish among positional rules, comes from their election tallies.

The majority vote tallies for any pair with an A-Reversal profile assign zero
points to each candidate. With $(1, s, 0)$ positional methods, A receives $2 - 4s$
points, while B and C each receive $2s - 1$ points.

So, the only positional method agreeing with the pairwise outcomes, by
having a complete $A \sim B \sim C$ tie, is the Borda Count (where $s = \frac{1}{2}$).
The rankings of all other positional rules flip from $A \succ B \sim C$ when
$s < \frac{1}{2}$ to $B \sim C \succ A$ when $s > \frac{1}{2}$. At this point we should (accurately)

expect that these reversal profiles completely explain why the plurality and antiplurality rankings can be directly opposite each other, as with the profile in Equation 3.1. This is the case; reversals are not accidents.

As these tallies correctly suggest, only the Borda Count ranking enjoys relationships with pairwise rankings. Indeed, to create an example where any other positional ranking differs as radically as we wish from the pairwise rankings, just add appropriate reversal components to a profile.

The B- and C-Reversal configurations are defined in the same manner and have similar election tallies. For instance, the B-Reversal profile, which follows, assigns a positive number to all rankings where B is top-ranked and all rankings where B is bottom-ranked; it assigns a negative number to all rankings where B is middle-ranked.

Row	Number	Rankings	
Row 1	$+1$	$B \succ A \succ C$	$B \succ C \succ A$
Row 2	$+1$	$C \succ A \succ B$	$A \succ C \succ B$
Row 3	-2	$A \succ B \succ C$	$C \succ B \succ A$

$$(4.10)$$

The next theorem summarizes the behavior and properties of reversal vectors.

Theorem 4.3 (Saari [70]): For three candidates, the sum of the A-, B-, and C-Reversal profiles is the null profile with zero voters assigned to each ranking. As such, the reversal profiles define a two-dimensional subspace of profile space: Any two of these profiles serve as a basis.

For any profile in the reversal subspace, the majority vote tallies for all pairs are ties; each candidate receives zero votes. The same completely tied election outcome occurs with the Borda Count.

With the $(1, s, 0)$ positional method, a candidate's election tally is $2 - 2s$ times the number of that candidate's reversal profiles minus $(1 - s)$ times the number of reversal profiles for the other two candidates.

All possible differences in three-candidate positional elections, in rankings and tallies, are caused by reversal profiles.

The last sentence is surprising; it asserts that "all possible differences among positional methods are based on, and can be completely understood in terms of, reversal profiles." It means, for instance, that the reversal terms are totally responsible for all differences between plurality and antiplurality rankings, such as reversing each other. It means that with all properties or axiomatic[3] characterizations of three-candidate positional rules, a critical juncture in the analysis must involve reversal profiles.

Using Reversal Profiles

The basic profiles serve as the coffee grounds for voting by determining the basic strength of all positional outcomes. Think of the reversal profiles as representing the cream of voting theory. Just as adding various amounts of cream can vary the taste from essentially straight coffee to café au lait to even a setting of straight cream having a hint of a coffee taste, adding various levels of the reversal profiles can significantly change the behavior of different positional rules.

This comment can be illustrated by adding reversal components to the profile in Equation 4.6 to change the outcome. As the common outcome in Equation 4.6 is $A \succ B \succ C$, add enough reversal terms to have, say, a $C \succ A \succ B$ plurality outcome. (Any plurality ranking can be selected.) This requires adding reversal terms that assist C and B. Using elementary algebra and adding x and y units, respectively, of C- and B-Reversal profiles to Equation 4.6 leads to the profile

Number	Ranking	Number	Ranking
$3 + x - 2y$	$A \succ B \succ C$	$1 - 2x + y$	$A \succ C \succ B$
$-2 + y + x$	$C \succ A \succ B$	$-3 + x - 2y$	$C \succ B \succ A$
$-1 - 2x + y$	$B \succ C \succ A$	$2 + x + y$	$B \succ A \succ C$

$$(4.11)$$

where the A, B, C positional tallies are, respectively,

$$4 - x - y + 2(x + y)s, \ 1 - x + 2y + 2(x - 2y)s,$$
$$-5 + 2x - y + 2(y - 2x)s \tag{4.12}$$

The desired plurality ranking (where $s = 0$) of $C \succ A \succ B$ requires satisfying the inequalities

$$-5 + 2x - y > 4 - x - y > 1 - x + 2$$

---

[3] Recall that this is an incorrect use of "axiom." See Section 3.2.

or $x > 3$ and $2 > y$. The choices of $y = 0$ and $x = 4$ suffice: The profile is

Number	Ranking	Number	Ranking
7	$A \succ B \succ C$	-7	$A \succ C \succ B$
2	$C \succ A \succ B$	1	$C \succ B \succ A$
-5	$B \succ C \succ A$	7	$B \succ A \succ C$

$$(4.13)$$

with A, B, C tallies of

$$0 + 8s, \quad -3 + 8s, \quad 3 - 16s \qquad (4.14)$$

Of course, to convert the profile into one with nonnegative entries, just add seven times the standard kernel to Equation 4.13; this contributes $7(2 + 2s)$ points to each candidate's tally.

The tallies in Equation 4.14 have a $C \succ B \succ A$ plurality ranking, and the SPT values are the coefficients of the s terms. These coefficients force the antiplurality ranking ($s = 1$) to reverse the plurality ranking. Indeed, this reversal phenomenon occurs whenever a strong enough dosage of reversal components is added to the brew.

As required by Theorem 4.3, the Borda, $s = \frac{1}{2}$, tally for this example agrees with the original tally in Equation 4.6 because the Borda Count is the only positional rule that is immune to reversal terms. By using the procedure line methods (see Section 3.5.2), it follows that this profile defines seven different positional election outcomes. Indeed, there always are seven different outcomes when the reversal terms force opposite plurality and antiplurality strict rankings and the Borda ranking is not a complete tie.

To appreciate what happens by pouring even more cream into our coffee cup, notice from Equation 4.14 that the $s = \frac{1}{4}$, or the $(4, 1, 0)$ rule, has the $A \succ B \sim C$ outcome. So, could pouring more of a reversal profile into the Equation 4.6 mix create a $(4, 1, 0)$ $C \succ A \succ B$ outcome? To find the correct amount, use $s = \frac{1}{4}$ with Equation 4.12 to obtain the necessary inequalities

$$-5 + x - \frac{1}{2}y > 1 - \frac{1}{2}x + y > 4 - \frac{1}{2}x - \frac{1}{2}y,$$

or $x > \frac{8}{3} + y$ and $y > 2$, where adding the stronger reversal dosage of $y = 3$ and $x = 6$ suffices.

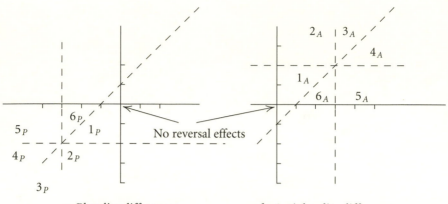

a. Plurality differences   **b.** Antiplurality differences

Figure 12. Reversal effects.

4.1.5 Anything Can Happen

One might think that reversal profiles allow anything to happen. That's not quite true, but it is close. To indicate what can occur (in general), add x units of A-Reversal and y units of B-Reversal profiles to Equation 4.6 to obtain the profile

Number	Ranking	Number	Ranking
$3 + x - 2y$	$A \succ B \succ C$	$1 + x + y$	$A \succ C \succ B$
$-2 - 2x + y$	$C \succ A \succ B$	$-3 + x - 2y$	$C \succ B \succ A$
$-1 + x + y$	$B \succ C \succ A$	$2 - 2x + y$	$B \succ A \succ C$

(4.15)

The x and y values define the different plurality and antiplurality election rankings depicted in Figure 12. (The dashed lines are where one pair is tied; e.g., the long diagonal on the left is where the plurality ranking has $A \sim B$. Using the profile in Equation 4.15, it is where $(3 + x - 2y) + (1 + x + y) = (-1 + x + y) + (2 - 2x + y)$.) To make the diagram readable, rankings are replaced with numbers according to the following code

Code	Ranking	Code	Ranking
1	$A \succ B \succ C$	4	$C \succ B \succ A$
2	$A \succ C \succ B$	5	$B \succ C \succ A$
3	$C \succ A \succ B$	6	$B \succ A \succ C$

(4.16)

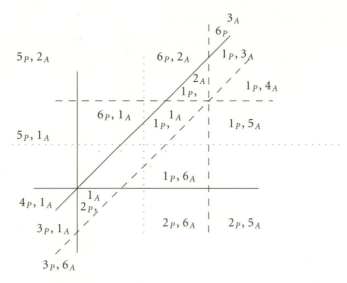

Figure 13. Comparison between plurality and antiplurality rankings.

For instance, 2_P represents the plurality ranking of $A \succ C \succ B$, and a 3_A region represents x and y values with the $C \succ A \succ B$ antiplurality ranking.

Point $x = 0$, $y = 0$ is where there are no reversal terms; with only basic terms, all positional outcomes agree. But notice how even reasonably small x and y values can alter the plurality and/or antiplurality ranking. Even more, the procedure line arguments (Section 3.5.2) require these changes to alter the rankings of other positional rules. Indeed, the region of x, y values where reversal terms do not affect positional rankings is much smaller than where these terms have an influence.

Also notice how changes in plurality and the antiplurality rankings spiral in a clockwise direction about their centers, while the centers of $x = -3$, $y = -2$ and $x = 3$, $y = 2$ have opposite signs. This diametrically opposite positioning of the centers (which always happens if the Borda ranking is not a complete tie) ensures there are regions where the two rankings differ. To capture this comparison in Figure 13, I essentially suppress the x- and y-axes by using dots. I do so to emphasize those x and y values that change the plurality (solid lines) and antiplurality (dashed lines) rankings.

Start with the x and y values in Figure 13 where the plurality ranking agrees with the Borda ranking; this is the wide, solid-line 1_P wedge that includes $(0, 0)$, where there are no reversal terms. In this 1_P region, x and y values *can be selected to force the antiplurality ranking to assume any of the thirteen possibilities*. (The wedge representing the 1_P ranking includes the center for the antiplurality choices.) Such a statement holds for any nonzero choice of basic profiles (e.g., whenever the Borda ranking is not a complete tie).

Similarly, thirteen different plurality rankings can accompany one antiplurality ranking for (x, y) points in the 1_A wedge; this is where the antiplurality ranking agrees with the Borda outcome. All together and not counting ties, seventeen different pairs of plurality and antiplurality rankings emerge by changing the reversal components. Thus, some consistency is retained because $36 - 17 = 19$ possible pairs of plurality and antiplurality outcomes can never occur. For instance, if the Borda ranking is $A \succ B \succ C$, it is impossible for the plurality and antiplurality ranking to both be $C \succ B \succ A$.[4]

In particular, adding enough of a reversal term to the mix forces the plurality and antiplurality rankings to reverse each other. It is easy to find this behavior in Figure 13 because the numbers representing opposite rankings differ by three (e.g., a $(2_P, 5_A)$ region has reversed rankings). The extremes regions of Figure 13 include all six pairs with numbers differing by three; these x and y values reverse the plurality and antiplurality rankings.

4.1.6 Sugar and Spice, and All Those Nice Cycles

That's enough cream; let's add some sugar. This spicier effect involves majority vote cycles of pairs. Here we have top cycles, bottom cycles, and most surely other cycles sporting fancier names. Cycles are interesting because they cause fundamental problems ranging from Arrow's and Sen's theorems (Chapter 2) to the inability to make majority vote decisions.

---

[4] This result can also be obtained by using the procedure line (Section 3.5.2); fix the Borda ranking and vary the plurality endpoint.

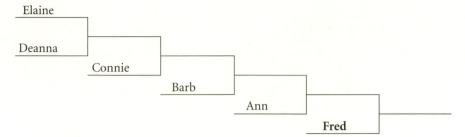

Figure 14. Electing Fred.

Indeed, finding ways to cope with cycles is what motivated Kemeny's, Dodgson's, and Copeland's rules; studies of tournaments; agendas; and on and on. In this section, I will explain what causes all possible majority vote cycles. However, first, let's take care of some unfinished business.

Electing Fred

The challenge at the beginning of this chapter of finding an election rule to elect Fred is difficult because Fred is not appreciated: *All voters prefer Connie to Deanna to Elaine to Fred.* But by showing how easy it is to elect poorly regarded Fred, some readers may become uncomfortable by recognizing how certain decisions of personal interest were decided with the same rule. The approach is to use the commonly employed agenda, which is just an ordered sequence of pairwise comparisons of the kind often used in departmental and other discussions. After all, a way to maintain order is to require the discussion to concentrate on two alternatives at a time; after one is dismissed, the remaining one may be compared with a different choice.

The trick is to carefully schedule the order in which candidates are compared. As the consultant hired to elect Fred, I would propose the Figure 14 "tournament-style" agenda that starts by matching Deanna and Elaine. Everyone prefers Deanna, so she advances to be compared with Connie. Connie unanimously beats Deanna to move on to meet Barb. But Barb beats Connie with a two-thirds landslide vote, so she now meets Ann. As Ann easily defeats Barb with a two-thirds vote, Ann progresses to the final comparison with Fred. *Fred wins with a landslide two-thirds vote.*

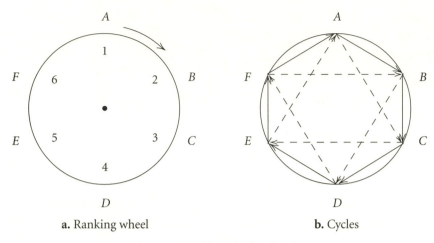

a. Ranking wheel   **b.** Cycles

Figure 15. Ranking wheel and cycles.

Each majority vote is decided unanimously or by a two-thirds land-slide, so it is unlikely for anyone to question the outcome – even though we, in a privileged position of knowing everyone's preferences, recognize that Fred is the voters' bottom choice. Even though the outcome is dis-appointing, it most surely would be accepted as decisively "reflecting the views of the voters."

Fred can be elected because the preferences define a majority vote cycle. Everyone prefers Elaine to Fred, so these rankings define the cycle

> Elaine ≻ Fred,   Fred ≻ Ann,   Ann ≻ Barb,
> Barb ≻ Connie,   Connie ≻ Deanna,   Deanna ≻ Elaine

With a cycle, anyone can be elected: The idea is to start at an appropriate juncture and then compare candidates in a direction counter to the cycle. In practical terms, as illustrated with the selection of Fred, let the top-ranked contenders eliminate each other before introducing your preferred choice.

Ranking Wheel

To create Fred-Challenge preferences for any number of candidates, use what I call a ranking wheel. As illustrated in Figure 15a, the wheel, which freely rotates about its center, is attached to a surface. With *n* candidates, evenly place the ranking numbers from 1 to n near the edge. Next, select any n-candidate ranking; the one chosen for Figure 15a is $A \succ B \succ C \succ D \succ E \succ F$. Place each candidate's name on the surface next to the appropriate ranking position (e.g., in Figure 15a, A is positioned next to the ranking number 1, B is next to 2, and so forth).

The purpose of the n-candidate ranking wheel is to create an n-voter profile that generates a majority vote cycle. After the initial ranking of

$$A \succ B \succ C \succ D \succ E \succ F$$

rotate the wheel so that the ranking number 1 is by the next candidate; read off the new ranking. In Figure 15a, by rotating the wheel so 1 is next to B, the ranking numbers generate the ranking

$$B \succ C \succ D \succ E \succ F \succ A$$

Continue until the ranking number 1 has been adjacent to each candidate once. The complete Figure 15a six-voter profile is

$$
\begin{aligned}
&A \succ B \succ C \succ D \succ E \succ F, \quad B \succ C \succ D \succ E \succ F \succ A, \\
&C \succ D \succ E \succ F \succ A \succ B, \quad D \succ E \succ F \succ A \succ B \succ C, \quad (4.17) \\
&E \succ F \succ A \succ B \succ C \succ D, \quad F \succ A \succ B \succ C \succ D \succ E
\end{aligned}
$$

where, by construction, each candidate is in each position precisely once. Call such a profile the *Condorcet n-tuple* generated by the specified starting ranking; for example, the Equation 4.17 profile is the "Condorcet six-tuple generated by $A \succ B \succ C \succ D \succ E \succ F$." In mathematical terms, this profile is the $\mathbb{Z}_6$ orbit generated by $A \succ B \succ C \succ D \succ E \succ F$.

Because each candidate is in each position precisely once, all positional rankings are complete ties. But the cyclic way in which the profile was generated suggests that it is accompanied by majority vote cycles. In other words, as it distinguishes between positional and pairwise rankings, this profile configuration is the kind for which we have been searching!

Actually, this profile defines several cycles; all can be extracted from Figure 15b. The solid arrows pointing to adjacent candidates define the *primary cycle*. The candidate at the arrow's base beats the one at the arrow's tip by a $6 - 1 = 5$ to 1 vote. The dashed arrows, which connect every other candidate (so they are removed by two), define two *secondary cycles* where each majority vote tally is $6 - 2 = 4$ to 2. Each point has a solid and a dashed arrowhead pointing toward it, and a dashed and solid arrow leaving it. So, by following arrows around the circle and sliding from solid to dashed arrows, all possible cycles generated by this profile are found. Examples include the cycle

$$A \succ B, \ B \succ D, \ D \succ E, \ E \succ A, \ A \succ C, \ C \succ D, \ D \succ F, \ F \succ A$$

and the cycle

$$A \succ C, \ C \succ E, \ E \succ F, \ F \succ B, \ B \succ D, \ D \succ E, \ E \succ A$$

To create a Figure 15b diagram for any Condorcet n-tuple, place the candidate's names about a circle in the order specified by the ranking wheel. All pairwise votes for adjacently positioned candidates – the primary cycle – are $(n - 1) : 1$. The secondary cycles are where the candidates are not adjacent; for candidates that are two removed, the election tallies are $(n - 2) : 2$, and for candidates that are j positions separated on the circle, where $j < \frac{n}{2}$, the outcomes are $(n - j) : j$. All cycles allowed by this Condorcet n-tuple are created by following the various arrows.

From Arrow to Tournaments to Engineering

The Fred-Challenge profile is fascinating because by using only three of the Condorcet six-tuple rankings, Fred becomes the voters' bottom-ranked choice. This is a general phenomenon; cycles arise with any three adjacent rankings from a Condorcet n-tuple. The message accompanying this behavior is that when using pairwise rankings, even portions of a Condorcet n-tuple can cause inferior choices and introduce other complexities.

Another interesting feature of the Condorcet n-profile is that, arguably, its outcome should be a complete tie. After all, each candidate is in each position precisely once. Moreover, suppose an argument is advanced to select A. A simple name change where B replaces A, C replaces B, and so on yields precisely the same profile where the argument now implies that B, rather than A, should be selected. Using the argument repeatedly leads to the conclusion that everyone should be selected; there should be a complete tie. With pairwise comparisons, however, this is not the case.

The explanation for the cycles is immediate; as described in Chapter 2, the myopic nature of the pairwise vote prevents the rule from recognizing the full symmetry of a profile. By failing to use all information from the profile, cycles, rather than a complete tie, arise. Indeed, adopting a higher dimensional version of the Chapter 2 outlier argument, the majority vote rule confuses the actual Condorcet n-tuple with a class of supporting profiles that is heavily dominated by cyclic preferences from a statistical point of view. As argued in Chapter 2, *we* might require transitive preferences, but this insistence is useless until the rule is structured and trained to respect our assumption.[5]

More generally, we must anticipate that decision difficulties will occur *anywhere* where pairwise or partwise comparisons are used. This includes Arrow's and Sen's theorems, issues concerning the seeding of tournaments, and, to introduce concerns from another discipline, engineering decisions. The complexity of engineering problems suggests using rules based on pairwise comparisons. As we now know, however, using such rules becomes a "penny-wise, pound-foolish" proposition. (For more about pairwise and partwise decision rules in engineering, see my paper with Katri Sieberg [91].)

Ad Hoc Construction, or General Behavior?

We want to find *all profile configurations* that affect majority vote pairwise rankings but not positional rankings. Even though the Condorcet n-tuples satisfy this condition, is this construction complete? Can other configurations be found with this property? Surprisingly, there are no more; the Condorcet n-tuples and their various combinations complete the story.

To convert these configurations into basis vectors for profile space, we need to introduce a structure similar to that of Equation 4.2, where $+1$ is assigned to some preferences and -1 is assigned to the same number of

---

[5] As shown in Chapter 2, precisely five profiles have the pairwise tallies of the Condorcet triplet; only the Condorcet triplet has transitive preferences because the four other profiles involve cyclic preferences. These other profiles come from the geometry of the cube. A similar geometric argument with n candidates identifies at least $2^{\binom{n}{2}-1}$ profiles other than the Condorcet profile with identical tallies, and each involves cyclic preferences (Saari [71]). Accompanying the six-candidate profile in Equation 4.17, for instance, are at least 16,384 other profiles with cyclic preferences and the same pairwise tallies. As the pairwise vote cannot distinguish among them, the Chapter 2 outlier argument and those in my paper with Sieberg [89] explain why this rule reflects the nonexistent cyclic profiles.

other preferences. These different signs are used just as with Equations 4.2 and 4.4: Preferences from one row can be replaced with preferences from the second row. The same mathematical explanation holds: These negative terms are needed to create an orthogonal coordinate system, which separates the effects of profiles on pairwise rules from others.

For three candidates, the basis vector is

$$
\begin{array}{c|c|ccc}
\textbf{Row 1} & +1 & A \succ B \succ C, & B \succ C \succ A, & C \succ A \succ B \\
\hline
\textbf{Row 2} & -1 & C \succ B \succ A, & B \succ A \succ C, & A \succ C \succ B
\end{array} \tag{4.18}
$$

With n candidates, the basis vectors have the similar form given by

$$
\begin{array}{c|c|c}
\textbf{Row 1} & +1 & \text{Condorcet } n\text{-tuple generated by ranking } r \\
\hline
\textbf{Row 2} & -1 & \text{Condorcet } n\text{-tuple generated by the reversal of } r
\end{array}
$$

$$\tag{4.19}$$

Denote these profiles by $\mathbf{C}_j^n$; they are orthogonal vectors, so call the space generated by these profiles the *Condorcet space*. With n candidates, of course, any ranking from the $\mathbf{C}_j^n$ vector generates either $\mathbf{C}_j^n$ or $-\mathbf{C}_j^n$, so the Condorcet subspace has $\frac{n!}{2n} = \frac{1}{2}(n-1)!$ basis vectors. With three candidates, a single-dimensional Condorcet subspace causes all of those pairwise differences and problems. With $n = 4$, the difficulties escalate by being created by a three-dimensional space, and when $n = 6$, the complexities come from a sixty-dimensional space, and the placid basic profiles live in a comparatively miniscule five-dimensional subspace. As the dimensional differences become more extreme with more candidates, in any setting with heterogeneity in voter preferences and an increase in the number of serious candidates, we must expect pairwise voting problems to occur with rules that are based on pairwise majority votes.

Theorem 4.4 (Saari [71]): For n candidates, the Condorcet subspace has dimension $\frac{1}{2}(n-1)!$. An orthogonal basis is given by Equation 4.19. This space is orthogonal to the basic and reversal subspaces.

For a given profile and each pair of candidates, compute the difference between the candidates' majority vote tallies. If for all pairs of candidates this difference is the same positive constant multiple of the differences between the same two candidates' Borda scores, then the profile does not have a Condorcet component. If for even one pair the differences do not agree, then the profile has a component in the Condorcet space.

Let me illustrate the last paragraph of this result with three candidates. Using the representation in Equation 4.16, the three-alternative Condorcet direction is given by $\mathbf{C} = (1, -1, 1, -1, 1, -1)$, so a profile has no terms in the Condorcet direction if and only if the scalar product of the profile with $\mathbf{C}$ is zero. One example is

$$(6, 5, 2, 0, 1, 4) \tag{4.20}$$

where the dot product is

$$\begin{aligned}
(6, 5, 2, 0, 1, 4) &\cdot (1, -1, 1, -1, 1, -1) \\
&= (6 \times 1) + (5 \times -1) + (2 \times 1) + (0 \times -1) + (1 \times 1) + (4 \times -1) \\
&= 6 - 5 + 2 - 0 + 1 - 4 = 0
\end{aligned}$$

For this example, the pairwise outcomes are $A : B$ by $13 : 5$, $B : C$ by $11 : 7$, and $A : C$ by $15 : 3$; the Borda outcome (computed with $(2, 1, 0)$) is $A > B > C$ by $28 : 16 : 10$. Now the difference in Borda tallies for A and B is $28 - 16 = 12$, and for the $\{A, B\}$ pair it is $13 - 5 = 8$. The ratio of the Borda tally difference of this $\{A, B\}$ pair to the majority tally difference is $12/8 = 3/2$. Similarly, as Theorem 4.4 requires, the ratio for the $\{B, C\}$ pair is the same $(16 - 10)/(11 - 7) = 6/4 = 3/2$, and for $\{A, C\}$ we have $(28 - 10)/(15 - 3) = 18/12 = 3/2$. As the theorem asserts, this is no accident; for three alternatives, this occurs if and only if the dot product is zero. The generalization to any number of alternatives holds, but now the dot product condition must hold for all of the Condorcet terms.

An even nicer result of mine [71] is that if this dot product condition holds, and only if this condition holds, then differences between pairwise tallies behave as a naive person might expect them to behave. Namely,

the difference between A's and B's pairwise tallies plus the difference between B's and C's pairwise tallies equals the difference between A's and C's pairwise tallies. This holds for any number of alternatives and any change in the names of the alternatives.

To illustrate this assertion with the profile in Equation 4.20, the difference in A's and B's pairwise tallies is 8, the difference between B's and C's tallies is 4, and the difference between A's and C's tallies is 12 leading to the desired $8 + 4 = 12$. In contrast, select any profile that does not satisfy this dot product condition and compute these ratios and differences; the conditions will not be satisfied.

Returning to the theorem, even though the properties are desirable, nobody really expects to encounter a profile satisfying the extreme consistency of the last part of the theorem. This fact underscores the pervasive effects of the Condorcet components. Even the unanimity profile fails this consistency test. For instance, with five voters sharing the same $A \succ B \succ C$ preferences, the $A \succ B \succ C$ Borda outcome has a $10 : 5 : 0$ tally. As both $A \succ B$ and $A \succ C$ majority vote tallies are $5 : 0$, this common difference of five is not the *same multiple* of the $10 - 0 = 10$ Borda difference between A and C and the $10 - 5 = 5$ difference for A and B. As such, even the unanimity profile is flavored with a sprinkle of the Condorcet term.

An Example

Just as the amount of sugar added to a cup of coffee varies the taste from only a hint of sweetness to a setting of damp sugar, adding various levels of Condorcet terms to a profile varies the pairwise tallies from essentially no noticeable effect to highly dominant majority vote cycles spiraling in one or the other direction.

To illustrate, by adding α units of the Equation 4.18 Condorcet triplet to the basic profile in Equation 4.6, the resulting profile is

Number	Ranking	Number	Ranking	
$3 + \alpha$	$A \succ B \succ C$	$1 - \alpha$	$A \succ C \succ B$	(4.21)
$-2 + \alpha$	$C \succ A \succ B$	$-3 - \alpha$	$C \succ B \succ A$	
$-1 + \alpha$	$B \succ C \succ A$	$2 - \alpha$	$B \succ A \succ C$	

with pairwise tallies $A : B$ being $2 + \alpha : -2 - \alpha$, $B : C$ being $4 + \alpha : -4 - \alpha$, and $A : C$ being $6 - \alpha : -6 + \alpha$. Figure 16 shows how the pairwise majority vote rankings change with the α value.

The extremes ends of the Figure 16 line verify my comment that a strong enough Condorcet term will overwhelm the basic components and cause a cycle. A small dosage of Condorcet, where $-2 < \alpha < 6$, affects the

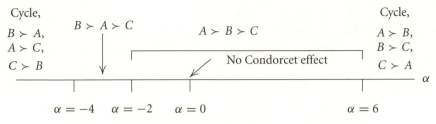

Figure 16. Effect of Condorcet terms.

pairwise tallies but not enough to change the pairwise rankings; they still agree with the Borda ranking. For this example, differences between the Borda and pairwise rankings require pouring in more of the Condorcet term as given by $\alpha \leq -2$ and $\alpha \geq 6$. Adding different strengths of the Condorcet term, given by $-4 < \alpha < -2$, keeps the ranking transitive, but notice how the identity of the Condorcet winner changed. This is discussed later.

First, let me offer a challenge that, with the developed structure, is not overly difficult to prove (a proof is in Saari [76]). Figure 16 shows that the Condorcet and Borda winners can differ, but this need not always happen. For three candidates, prove that if the difference between the Borda tallies of the Borda top- and second-ranked candidates is larger than the tally difference between the Borda second- and third-ranked candidates, then the Borda and Condorcet winners always agree. As the Equation 4.20 profile satisfies this condition, when a Condorcet winner exists, it agrees with the Borda winner. But the Equation 4.6 profile flunks this difference test, so, with enough of a Condorcet term, the Condorcet and Borda winners disagree.

All Possible Problems with the Borda Count
To fulfill my promise to show how to create all possible profiles with inconsistent Borda outcomes, start with the Condorcet four-tuple

$$A \succ B \succ C \succ D, \quad B \succ C \succ D \succ A,$$
$$C \succ D \succ A \succ B, \quad D \succ A \succ B \succ C$$

This profile, of course, forces a complete tie for all positional methods. Dropping a candidate, say D, defines the Condorcet triplet

$$A \succ B \succ C, \quad B \succ C \succ A, \quad C \succ A \succ B$$

plus the extra ranking of $A \succ B \succ C$! This extra ranking creates inconsistency problems. After all, all positional methods deliver a complete tie for the first three rankings, but by addressing that extra ranking, *all positional rules, including the Borda Count, have a nontied outcome.*

Adding this Condorcet four-tuple to any profile creates no ranking changes with the set of four, but we must anticipate inconsistencies to arise when considering the triplets. To illustrate, start with the profile where one person has the $C \succ B \succ A \succ D$ ranking; the election outcomes are obvious. Adding two units of the Condorcet four-tuple does not change any positional ranking of the four candidates, but it does change ranking for all triplets. Indeed, all positional methods ignore the Condorcet term, so the four-candidate plurality and Borda rankings for this nine-voter profile remain, respectively, $C \succ A \sim B \sim D$ and $C \succ B \succ A \succ D$.

Dropping last-place D unleashes what I call the *Condorcet effect*. To explain, the profile for $\{A, B, C\}$ starts with a ranking $C \succ B \succ A$ from the initial person. The Condorcet four-tuple yields two Condorcet triplets, which can be ignored when computing the positional outcomes, plus *two $A \succ B \succ C$ rankings* that cannot be ignored as they favor A. The Condorcet effect, then, bars the former winner C from winning with any positional rule over this triplet; for example, the plurality, Borda, and antiplurality rankings are, respectively, $A \succ C \succ B$, $A \succ B \succ C$, and $B \succ A \succ C$.

The Condorcet *n*-tuples create an interesting new species of cyclic voting structures. To introduce them, return to Figure 15b where the primary cycle is depicted with an arrow from A to B, then one from B to C, and so forth. *A similar cyclic effect occurs with triplets, or with four-tuples, or. . . . As with the pairwise cycle, these more general cycles are created by the rankings that remain by dropping different candidates from a Condorcet n-tuple.*

To see this behavior, list the extra rankings that result when D is dropped from the Condorcet four-tuple, then, instead of D, drop A, then B, then C. In the resulting structure, illustrated in Figure 17, the circular arrow encompasses three candidates rather than using an arrow to an adjacent candidate. The implied ranking has the top candidate at

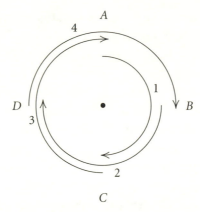

Figure 17. New kinds of cycles using triplets.

the base of the arrow with declining popularity by moving to the arrow head. These rankings define the Figure 17 "triplet cycle" of

$$A \succ B \succ C, \quad B \succ C \succ D, \quad C \succ D \succ A, \quad D \succ A \succ B \quad (4.22)$$

These cycles play an interesting role later in this chapter, but already we know they affect positional outcomes over triplets much as Condorcet triplets affect pairwise rankings. A similar effect, found in the same way, holds for all k-tuples in a Condorcet n-tuple where $2 \leq k < n$. The $k = 2$ case is, of course, the standard majority vote cycle.

These extra terms affect *all* positional outcomes over triplets, and, for $n > 4$, all k-tuples (i.e., they create inconsistencies in election rankings). Still other profile configurations affect all other positional methods, but only the Condorcet effect can influence Borda rankings (Saari [71]). As such, *all possible inconsistencies in Borda rankings over the subsets of candidates are strictly due to Condorcet terms,* nothing else affects the Borda rankings (i.e., any example illustrating Borda inconsistencies must include portions of Condorcet terms). Even though the Condorcet effect affects all positional rules, all other rules remain susceptible to still other kinds of profile properties.

4.1.7 Differences between Borda and Condorcet

As we now know, the Condorcet terms, and only the Condorcet terms, cause inconsistencies in Borda rankings. This reality suggests placing faith in the Borda ranking over all n legitimate candidates rather than in Borda rankings over any subsets of candidates. The argument is simple: All disagreements between two Borda rankings are due to Condorcet terms, so accepting the ranking of a subset has the effect of accepting a nontied outcome for the Condorcet n-tuple. For instance, accepting A over C in the example at the end of Section 4.1.8 has the effect of accepting a nontied outcome for the Condorcet four-tuple. I have yet to find a convincing reason to do so.

This argument holds for any k-tuple where $2 \leq k < n$. Thus, it holds for the special case of $k = 2$ where the Borda ranking for n candidates is compared with the majority vote rankings over pairs. Indeed, as illustrated in Figure 16 with α values in $-4 < \alpha < -2$, all possible differences between Condorcet and Borda winners are due to Condorcet terms. Think about this in terms of ways to tally ballots. An alternative to tallying ballots in the usual manner is to first count all natural ties; the winner is then determined by any remaining ballots. For instance, if Anni had twenty-two votes and Adrian has twenty, then tally ballots in pairs: one for Anni and one for Adrian. After twenty pairs of ties, Anni has two remaining ballots of support, so she wins.

To carry this count-tied-configurations-first approach to n candidates, if the reader agrees that the Condorcet n-tuples should be ties, then a natural way to tally the ballots is to replace the Anni–Adrian tied pairs with "Condorcet n-tuples." As this tallying removes all Condorcet terms (and this can be fractional terms), the Condorcet and Borda winners will agree with the left over ballots. This argument means that to justify the Condorcet winner over the Borda winner, we must justify a nontied outcome for the Condorcet n-tuples. Even though I know of no convincing argument to do so, it is possible that someday someone might find one, but I doubt it.

4.1.8 Kemeny, Dodgson, and Other Systems; Who Cares?

Let me be contentious. The Kemeny, Dodgson, and other systems were designed to introduce structure into the societal pairwise rankings when cyclic effects arise. Because we understand what causes all pairwise voting problems, it may be time to reevaluate whether anyone should trust the outcomes coming from these rules.

In Section 2.3, I expressed doubts as to whether anyone should use these rules. Exploring these systems is similar to including a discussion about nineteenth-century medical practices in a modern course in medical school, they are valuable topics in the introduction of a topic. But whenever the discussion turns to what is good for actual voting, these rules appear to be useless antiques.

The argument is simple. As argued in Chapter 2 and (Saari [82]), voting rules that rely totally on pairwise rankings ignore crucial information. For instance, we usually require rankings to come from transitive preferences. As argued several times in this book, however, by using pairwise comparisons, the voting rule cannot use this reality. The crucial information lost by using pairwise voting is that the voters have transitive preferences.

This reality, which has been examined in a few ways in this book, leads to two options.

1. If the transitivity of individual preferences is a valued criterion, then we should never use methods that are based on pairwise outcomes. After all, the myopic tendency of the rule dismisses this assumption.
2. If the transitivity of individual preferences is not that valued, then we should not include it in basic assumptions and never use methods, such as Kemeny's rule, that artificially impose transitivity on the outcome.

In other words, insisting that voters have transitive preferences, and then using voting rules that negate this assumption, is a contradiction. If it is not assumed that voters have transitive preferences, expect cyclic behavior. Similarly, if individual rationality is assumed but the adopted rules do not use this assumption, then expect outcomes with cyclic behavior. Tying to straighten out cycles is an artificial goal; it does nothing for determining the voters' choice. The only rational conclusion appears to be to abandon interest in voting rules based on pairwise comparisons where the transitivity of individual preferences is lost.

There is another consequence. We know (Chapter 2) that the myopic nature of the pairwise vote effectively replaces the transitive preferences of the Condorcet n-tuple with the preferences of nonexistent cyclic voters. (See, for example, the discussion starting in Section 2.2.2.) Thus, by accepting pairwise rankings, we jeopardize the assumption that the voters are rational.

4.2 All Possible Three-Candidate Outcomes

We are done – at least for three candidates! For three candidates, the preceding discussion completes the analysis; no new coordinate directions are needed.

Proving this assertion is simple. Profile space for three candidates is six-dimensional, so we just need to prove that these coordinates span the six-dimensional space. To carry out the dimension count, recall that

- The kernel vector, which just adds to the tallies of all rules but has absolutely no influence on differences between tallies for any of the rules, is one-dimensional
- The basic profiles, which provide a common election outcome and tally for all rules, define a two-dimensional space
- The reversal vectors, which change positional tallies but have absolutely no influence on Borda and pairwise rankings or differences in tallies, form a two-dimensional subspace
- The final, sixth dimension comes from the Condorcet direction, which changes pairwise tallies but has no effect on positional rankings or differences in tallies between candidates

As this count proves, these profile coordinates account for everything. Thus, any other configuration of profiles that impacts on election outcomes must be a combination of these points. But if other choices constitute a different profile coordinate system, this can be useful.

Other Coordinate Systems

My invitation to create new profile coordinates extends my comments motivating the search for profile coordinates. The comparison involved morning coffee: We prefer to use coordinates – coffee, cream, and sugar – that simplify and assist our objective of having an appropriate tasting cup of coffee. Similarly, with profile space, the "appropriate" coordinate system depends on what we wish to achieve. These coordinates explain all possible inconsistencies that could occur in pairwise and positional outcomes, but other coordinate systems may be more useful with other concerns.

Suppose, for instance, we want to analyze the plurality vote. We could use this system, but it might be easier to create an alternative profile coordinate system that emphasizes plurality outcomes (Saari [77]). As another example, we may want to have a coordinate system that is sensitive to specified conditions. An example is the set of axioms Luce [29] created to characterize individual decisions. In Luce's formulation, a profile does not describe how many people have a particular ranking preference; it looks at the likelihood that an individual has each particular ranking. This similarity allows using "voting theory" to obtain new conclusions for this branch of psychology. To do so, a convenient approach is to design a profile coordinate system that reflects Luce's axioms (e.g., see Saari [81]).

The number of fascinating issues in social choice should suggest other choices of coordinate systems that can, and should be, investigated. Using the profile coordinates described previously, these other systems can be determined by using standard tools from linear algebra.

4.2.1 Creating Examples

By using the profile coordinate, all possible examples illustrating all possible three-candidate behavior for positional and pairwise rules can be created. To illustrate, let's create an example where the Borda outcome is $A \succ B \succ C$, the Condorcet winner is B, the plurality outcome is $C \succ A \succ B$, and the antiplurality outcome is $B \succ A \succ C$.

With the profile coordinates, this is simple. Start with the earlier choice (see Eq. 4.6) of 3 units of A-Basic and 2 of B-Basic; this coffee grounds start ensures that the Borda ranking will be $A \succ B \succ C$. To ensure that B is the Condorcet winner, it follows from Figure 16 that we should add -3 units of the Condorcet term, the sugar effect. Next, to have the plurality $C \succ A \succ B$ and antiplurality $B \succ A \succ C$ rankings, just examine Figure 13 to find the $(3_P, 6_A)$ region; this determines how much cream to add to the mix. As this region is in the lower left-hand corner, x and y must have negative values, the values $x = -4$, $y = -6$ suffice. All together, we have

Number	Ranking	Number	Ranking
8	$A \succ B \succ C$	-6	$A \succ C \succ B$
-3	$C \succ A \succ B$	8	$C \succ B \succ A$
-14	$B \succ C \succ A$	7	$B \succ A \succ C$

$$(4.23)$$

It remains to add the water, or the neutral kernel. The most negative value is -14, so by adding 14 units of the standard kernel, we obtain the profile

Number	Ranking	Number	Ranking
22	$A \succ B \succ C$	8	$A \succ C \succ B$
11	$C \succ A \succ B$	22	$C \succ B \succ A$
0	$B \succ C \succ A$	21	$B \succ A \succ C$

$$(4.24)$$

that does everything that was requested.

4.2.2 Converting Molecules into Coffee, Sugar, and Cream Coordinates

As illustrated by the preceding example, by describing a profile in terms of the profile coordinates, we immediately know how many voters have each preference. To illustrate, let $\mathbf{B}_A$, $\mathbf{B}_B$, $\mathbf{R}_A$, $\mathbf{R}_B$, $\mathbf{C}^3$, $\mathbf{K}$ denote, respectively, the A-Basic, B-Basic, A-Reversal, B-Reversal, Condorcet, and Kernel vectors. The example created in Section 4.2.1 can be expressed as

$$\mathbf{p} = 3\mathbf{B}_A + 2\mathbf{B}_B - 4\mathbf{R}_A - 6\mathbf{R}_B - 3\mathbf{C}^3 + 14\mathbf{K}$$

and the standard "chemical decomposition" is given in Equation 4.24. In other words, going from the coffee, cream, and sugar expression into the chemical description is simple.

To analyze a given profile, we need to go in the opposite direction. Namely, for a profile expressed in the Equation 4.24 format, we want to find its decomposition in the form

$$\mathbf{p} = a_B \mathbf{B}_A + b_B \mathbf{B}_B + a_R \mathbf{R}_A + b_R \mathbf{R}_B + \gamma \mathbf{C}^3 + k\mathbf{K} \qquad (4.25)$$

In terms of our analogy, we must learn how to go from the chemical decomposition into the coffee, sugar, and cream expression.

By doing so, the relative sizes of the coefficients explain what different effects are illustrated by the profile. Large $|a_R|$ and $|b_R|$ values relative to the $|a_B|$, $|b_B|$ values, for instance, indicate a strong reversal influence that tends to be manifested by the plurality and antiplurality outcomes reversing each other. A large $|\gamma|$ value indicates a strong Condorcet term, which in turn suggests a disarray among the pairwise outcomes.

The decomposition of a standard three-candidate profile into a profile coordinate representation is given by Theorem 4.5. In this statement, a profile is expressed according to the Equation 4.16 code. So, p_4 is the number of voters with the ranking coded by 4, or $C \succ B \succ A$. Thus, the Equation 4.24 profile is

$$\mathbf{p} = (22, 8, 11, 22, 0, 21)$$

Theorem 4.5 (Saari [70]): Any three-alternative profile $\mathbf{p}$ can be expressed in the Equation 4.25 format according to the matrix equation

$$
\begin{pmatrix} a_B \\ b_B \\ a_R \\ b_R \\ \gamma \\ k \end{pmatrix}
= \frac{1}{6}
\begin{pmatrix}
2 & 1 & -1 & -2 & -1 & 1 \\
1 & -1 & -2 & -1 & 1 & 2 \\
0 & 1 & -1 & 0 & 1 & -1 \\
-1 & 1 & 0 & -1 & 1 & 0 \\
1 & -1 & 1 & -1 & 1 & -1 \\
1 & 1 & 1 & 1 & 1 & 1
\end{pmatrix}
\begin{pmatrix} p_1 \\ p_2 \\ p_3 \\ p_4 \\ p_5 \\ p_6 \end{pmatrix}
\tag{4.26}
$$

This is it. To find the profile decomposition representation of a profile in standard form, just carry out a simple matrix multiplication. In the following description, the matrix is represented by $\mathcal{T}$.

Certain subtleties can be immediately captured. Consider, for instance, a unanimity profile where everyone prefers $A \succ B \succ C$, so $\mathbf{p}$ is given by $p_1 = 1$ and $p_j = 0$ for $j = 2, \ldots, 6$. The matrix multiplication of $\mathcal{T}(\mathbf{p}^t)$ (the superscript t on $\mathbf{p}$ means we are using the column, rather than row, representation of the vector) results in each entry of the first column of $\mathcal{T}$ being multiplied by $\frac{1}{6}$. Here we observe strong basic components of $a_B = \frac{2}{6}$ and $b_B = \frac{1}{6}$ resulting in the Borda ranking of $A \succ B \succ C$. However, the weak reversal value of $a_R = -\frac{1}{6}$ causes the plurality and antiplurality rankings to be, respectively, $A \succ B \sim C$ and $A \sim B \succ C$ rather than $A \succ B \succ C$. Consequences of the Condorcet term, $\gamma = \frac{1}{6}$ are manifested in the pairwise tallies where the A-C difference agrees with the A-B difference, rather than reflecting the reality that B has a higher status than C.

For a real-world example, use the profile Alex Tabarrok [114] computed for the 1992 U.S. presidential election among Bush, Clinton, and Perot. Let alternatives A, B, C represent, respectively, Clinton, Bush, and Perot. Tabarrok found that $\mathbf{p}_{1992} = (20.85, 22.10, 13.5, 6.15, 16.35, 21.05)$, where each value is a percentage, is a reasonable profile for the 1992 election. A computation shows that

$$\mathcal{T}(\mathbf{p}^t_{1992}) = (7.1167, 0.500, 0.6500, 1.9083, 2.333, 16.6667)$$

As described earlier in Section 3.5.5, although no candidate received a majority vote, Tabarrok proved that Clinton enjoyed surprisingly strong support. In other words, the closeness of the actual plurality outcomes reflects the peculiarities of the plurality voting rule rather than the voters' preferences. For a sharper conclusion, notice from the profile decomposition that $a_B = 7.1167$ and $b_B = 0.500$, which mean that $c_B = -7.6167$ (the sum of coefficients for the three basic components equals zero). As these values indicate, Clinton (candidate A) received significantly stronger support, and Perot had a weaker appeal than previously recognized.

The misrepresentation of the plurality outcome becomes apparent from the reversal term $b_R = 1.9083$, which ensures a distortion of the plurality outcome in favor of candidate B, or Bush. Notice the $\gamma = 2.3333$ value indicating a "twist" in the pairwise majority vote outcomes that would help Clinton over Bush, Bush over Perot, and Perot over Clinton. While this particular twist would not change the majority vote rankings of Clinton $\succ$ Bush $\succ$ Perot, it would enhance certain tallies making, for instance, Clinton's pairwise victory over Bush somewhat larger.

As demonstrated, the decomposition provides a subtle tool to more accurately analyze and interpret actual election outcomes.

4.3 The Will of the Voters

We have all been in a restaurant and not sure of what to order. The same effect occurs in voting; when standing in the voting booth, we may have trouble identifying our own "will" when voting. Thus, trying to establish the aggregate "will of the voters" is a daunting challenge; however, there are natural and pragmatic ways to tackle the question, such as the one described next.

Armed with a cup of coffee amidst a group of friends, we may put forth notions about what the voters really want. In fact, such commentary tends to bombard us after many elections with politicians and pundits trying to convince us as to what the election outcome actually meant.

Here is a radical idea: To determine what the voters want, why not examine what they say they want. Rather than scrutinizing election outcomes, or the characteristics of voting rules, why not examine the properties of a profile? After all, a profile is intended to specify the voters wishes.

To illustrate with an example, what do the following voters really want if their wishes are expressed with the profile 500 voters prefer $A \succ B \succ C$ and 500 prefer $B \succ C \succ A$? To find an answer, ignore *votes*. After all, as emphasized throughout this book, an election outcome can more accurately reflect the peculiarities of a particular voting rule than the wishes of the voters.

Here it is reasonable to argue that C should be ranked below A because, even though both candidates are bottom-ranked by half of the voters, A fares better by being top-ranked by half of the voters, and C is only middle-ranked by half of them. Notice how the value judgment of "anonymity" is being imposed: No voter's views are more important than another, so only the numbers of voters with each ranking are relevant.

So far, the societal ranking arguably has A strongly ranked over C. In comparing B and A, both candidates are top-ranked by different halves of the voters. Candidate B, however, is second-ranked by half of the voters. In contrast, A is bottom-ranked by half of the voters. Thus, it is arguable that B should be strongly ranked over A. A similar argument comparing B and C again captures B's high standing among the voters; all of this leads to the societal ranking of $B \succ A \succ C$.

By developing a sense of the aggregate views of the voters, we can grade voting rules. The idea is simple; any voting system that fails to deliver this decisive $B \succ A \succ C$ outcome fails to reflect the views of the voters – for this particular profile. The list of the derelict includes the popular plurality vote (with its $A \sim B \succ C$ outcome) and the majority vote over pairs (with an acceptable $B \succ C$ ranking, but misleading $A \sim C$ and $A \sim B$ conclusions).

This analysis is informative; nevertheless, it suffers problems. For instance, it is ad hoc rather than systematic in nature – an analysis should be applicable for *all* profiles. The simplicity of this particular profile leads to a straightforward analysis, but acceptable interpretations need not be forthcoming with more complicated profiles. For instance, arguments applied to a difficult profile may end up being circular. Something systematic must be developed.

4.3.1 Selecting Conditions

To determine what constitutes the will of the voters, we need value judgments; to make them broad and encompassing, only four are made here. I welcome disagreements about my choices and tacit assumptions because I wish to encourage a wider, systematic mathematical exploration of this issue.

I insist on *anonymity* – a driving force behind the secret ballot. In our setting, where preferences, rather than votes, are considered, it means that the views of Joe, or a small group consisting of Joe and his friends, cannot have atypical power in characterizing the aggregate wishes of the voters. Although it is easy to conceive of settings where Joe should have more influence than Bob, for this first cut anonymity is required.

Anonymity means that permuting the identities of the voters, in any desired manner, does not affect the will of the voters (i.e., *who* ranks the candidates in a specific manner does not matter). If a profile has Bob preferring $A \succ B \succ C$ and Sue preferring $B \succ C \succ A$, the aggregated will of the voters remains the same if Sue, not Bob, prefers $A \succ B \succ C$ and Bob, not Sue, prefers $B \succ C \succ A$.

The second condition is *neutrality*; the voters' wishes are not based on the names of the alternatives. Instead, after permuting the names of the alternatives in any manner, the ranking reflecting the voters' wishes is similarly permuted. It was argued with the thousand-voter example at the beginning of Section 4.3 that $B \succ A \succ C$ captured the voters' wishes. Neutrality requires that after changing this example so that A now is called B, B is called C, and C is called A, the voters' aggregate wishes reflect this name change by being $C \succ B \succ A$.

The third condition mimics the thousand-voter analysis whereby if candidate A does as well as candidate B with the same number of voters, but A ranks higher than B with the rest of them, then A is ranked above B. Call this *positive reinforcement*. A special case is *unanimity*; if everyone prefers $A \succ B \succ C$, it is safe to say that the will of these voters is $A \succ B \succ C$.

The fourth condition captures the spirit of Arrow's independence of irrelevant alternatives. We say that the will of the voters satisfies *consistency* if this will is consistent over whatever subset of candidates is considered. So, if the will of the voters is $A \succ B \succ C \succ D$, then it must be $A \succ B \succ D$ when C is not involved. The objective is to prevent the will of the voters from changing with changes in the subset of candidates. Incidentally, consistency differs from Arrow's IIA condition because IIA is a condition on voting rules; with voting rules this condition leads to an impossibility assertion. (Also IIA negates the assumption of individual transitivity of preferences (Chapter 2).) Instead, I insist that the rankings representing the will of the voters remain the same over all subsets of candidates.

These four conditions are imposed on preferences, but by reexpressing the first three as conditions on voting rules and by leaning on the beautiful work of Peyton Young [119], it takes only a few more conditions to characterize positional voting rules. Alternatively, replacing Young's conditions with a more relaxed set leads to a wider class of voting rules, with positional rules as special cases, as developed in my book *Geometry of Voting* [63].

Indeed, if we were analyzing voting rules rather than the will of the voters, then by emphasizing the first three conditions, which are not controversial, it is easy to show that they are satisfied by a wide array of voting rules extending beyond positional voting. Such a list includes Approval Voting, cumulative voting, majority votes over pairs, agendas, positional methods, and runoffs with any of these positional methods. If fact, I am unaware of any voting rule that would have any hope of ever being treated as "acceptable" if it did not satisfy these three conditions.

This first stage ignores voting rules and emphasizes properties of what the voters want as expressed by the profile (e.g., the goal is to determine the "voters' intent" by examining a profile with these conditions). This is done without regard to how to codify this intent with a voting rule. After a sense of what the voters want is determined, the next step is to determine whether there exists an election rule that will faithfully deliver the expected outcome (i.e., the will of the voters).

4.3.2 Identifying the Voters' Wishes

The setting of three alternatives $\{A, B, C\}$ is emphasized, with admittedly loose arguments, in order to use the profile decomposition. A similar analysis holds for more candidates, but, interestingly, the answers can change.

Anonymity and neutrality require the kernel profile to be treated as reflecting $A \sim B \sim C$; the aggregate of the voters prefer no alternative over another. After all, a kernel profile has the same number of voters preferring each of the six ways there are to rank the three alternatives. If instead of a tie, A has a special distinction (ranked either above or below another alternative), a name change of the alternatives (neutrality) and/or a name change of the voters, would create the identical profile but where a different alternative now has this distinction.

Next, consider a basic profile such as the A-Basic choice where, without negative terms (by including the kernel term)

Number	Ranking	Number	Ranking
2	$A \succ B \succ C$	2	$A \succ C \succ B$
1	$B \succ A \succ C$	1	$C \succ A \succ B$

Changing the roles of B and C leads to the same profile, so neutrality requires the will of the voters to have the $B \sim C$ ranking. Consistency requires A to be top-ranked. As with the thousand-voter example, the voters' wishes are captured by $A \succ B \sim C$. A similar argument applied to any profile $\mathbf{p} = a_B \mathbf{B}_A + b_B \mathbf{B}_B + c_B \mathbf{B}_C + k\mathbf{K}$ shows that a reasonable choice for the will of the voters reflects the ranking of the coefficients a_B, b_B, c_B.

A similar application of neutrality and anonymity applied to the Condorcet profile, such as

Number	Ranking	Number	Ranking
1	$A \succ B \succ C$	1	$B \succ C \succ A$
1	$C \succ A \succ B$		

where each candidate is in first, second, and third place once, suggests that the profile must be treated as constituting a tie among the choices. Again, if one alternative, say A, has a distinguished role, then the change in the names of the alternatives (neutrality) – where B replaces the old A, C replaces the old B, and A replaces the old B, and then the names of the voters are interchanged (anonymity) – yields the same profile but where B now is the alternative with the distinguished role. A similar argument makes C the distinguished alternative. Thus, this profile should be treated as assigning a complete tie for the will of these voters. (Incidentally, a name change interchanging A and B merely creates the other Condorcet triplet, with the same conclusion.)

Only the reversal profiles remain (e.g., the same number of voters prefer $A \succ B \succ C$ as prefer $C \succ B \succ A$). Here the twin tools of anonymity and neutrality only suggest that the view of the voters must include $A \sim C$; they do not offer any insight or argument about the placement of B within the will of the voters. In fact, strong arguments could be advanced where B should be preferred, tied, or ranked below A and C. To break this indecision, invoke the fourth assumption requiring a consistent ranking when analyzed in terms of pairs, or in terms of the full ranking. (Remember that the Condorcet terms have already been removed.) Using this distinction and recognizing that we obtain complete ties with reversal terms over pairs, it follows that the choice of the will of the voters for a reversal profile is a complete tie.

We are done; we have exhausted all directions of profile space. So, it is reasonable to assert that the will of the voters is captured by the structure of the basic profiles. Indeed, quite often during lectures, both mathematicians and experts in voting theory suggest that an appropriate approach is to compute the basic profile component in a given profile and use the associated ranking. This mathematical complication is not necessary because the structure of the basic profile component is completely and accurately captured by the Borda Count outcome. Thus, the Borda Count ranking is *one* voting rule that captures the will of the voters; it is the only positional rule, or voting rule based on positional outcomes.

4.3.3 Extensions and Questions

Notice how I qualified the preceding comments. The reason is that Borda Count is *not* the only rule satisfying these conditions; for example, nothing disqualifies assigning the $A \succ B$ ranking to $\mathbf{p} = a_B \mathbf{B}_A + b_B \mathbf{B}_B + c_B \mathbf{B}_C + k\mathbf{K}$ only if some $a_B > b_B + \epsilon$ threshold is satisfied, rather than just $a_B > b_B$. (Here, the voters' intent no longer satisfies transitivity, but rather quasi-transitivity.) In terms of voting rules, this requirement leads to a modified form of the Borda Count where a tie vote is not where two candidates have the same tally, but where their Borda tallies fail to pass some threshold where one candidate receives a specified number of points more than the other candidate.

To curb obvious complaints, notice that the preceding analysis tries to determine the will of the voters, which means that pragmatic constraints such as strategic behavior are not relevant. (However, the Borda Count is the unique positional rule to minimize the likelihood that a small number of strategic voters will successfully manipulate the outcome (Saari [57, 64]).

Interestingly, different answers can arise when considering four or more candidates. This is true whenever it can be argued that certain profiles from the kernel should have a ranking different than a complete tie. Whenever this is true, positional methods cannot meet these standards.

4.4 Teaser about More Candidates

Armed with the tools to analyze everything that can happen with three alternatives, it is time to wonder what happens with more alternatives. Everything needed to understand peculiar behavior of majority votes over pairs is based on the Condorcet n-tuples (Section 4.1.6). It remains to discover relationships of positional elections over different subsets of candidates and why these outcomes can differ.

4.4.1 Designing Profile Configurations

Mimicking the approach used for three candidates, we need to identify configurations of preferences with a neutral outcome (a complete tie) over some subsets of candidates but not over others. Even though I found these structures via mathematical symmetries, the following is intended to develop intuition. To do so, consider the following kind of challenge that always arises:

Find a four-candidate profile configuration with which all majority vote pairwise elections and all positional outcomes for four candidates end in complete ties, but, except for the Borda Count, all positional outcomes over triplets of candidates are not ties.

Namely, find all configurations of profiles that are neutral over pairs and the set of all four candidates, but not with triplets.

To meet this challenge, recall that combining a preference ranking with its reversal ensures a complete tie with majority votes over pairs. So, start with a ranking, say $A \succ B \succ C \succ D$, and include its reversal $D \succ C \succ B \succ A$. This pair ensures tied outcomes for pairwise votes, but it does not ensure four-candidate positional outcomes. Instead, to ensure complete ties with all possible four-candidate positional rules, each candidate must be in each position the same number of times.

The solution now is obvious; combine the two structures. With the starting $(A \succ B) \succ (C \succ D)$, reverse the two indicated pairs to create $(B \succ A) \succ (D \succ C)$. By including its reversal $C \succ D \succ A \succ B$, the resulting configuration

$$A \succ B \succ C \succ D, \quad D \succ C \succ B \succ A,$$
$$B \succ A \succ D \succ C, \quad C \succ D \succ A \succ B \tag{4.27}$$

has each ranking accompanied by its reversal, which guarantees tied majority votes over pairs, and each candidate is in each position precisely once, which ensures that all four-candidate positional outcomes are ties.[6]

To understand what happens with triplets, dropping D, the rankings become

$$A \succ B \succ C, \quad C \succ B \succ A,$$
$$B \succ A \succ C, \quad C \succ A \succ B \qquad (4.28)$$

which consists of two three-candidate reversal pairs. Thus, the majority votes over pairs and the three-candidate Borda outcome remain ties, but all other positional outcomes must differ. For example, with $(1, s, 0)$, C is the winner with $s < \frac{1}{2}$, while $A \sim B$ are the cowinners with $s > \frac{1}{2}$.

In other words, by dropping a candidate to create a triplet, Equation 4.27 becomes a three-candidate reversal profile as described in Section 4.1.4. Thus, the kind of profile in Equation 4.27 is precisely what we need to explain how and why election rankings for triplets can differ from those of pairs and the set of all four candidates. Armed with this building block and using standard linear algebra, new relationships among election outcomes over all of the triplets become apparent.[7] This approach, of combining symmetries from different subsets of candidates, resulted in a profile coordinate system described in my 2000 *Economic Theory* papers (Saari [71, 72]).

4.4.2 An Interesting Relationship

To suggest how mathematical symmetries play a central role in creating profile coordinate systems, and even leading to results not described here, it is worth deriving an interesting relationship that holds for any number of candidates and combines different sorts of reversals.

A sense of what will be developed appeared in the discussion in Section 3.2 where I posed two conflicting sets of "axioms" for the vote-for-two rule. These conditions came from an earlier discussion [75], where I discussed the misuse of "axioms" in terms of the plurality vote. The

---

[6] By listing a ranking as $x_1 \succ x_2 \succ x_3 \succ x_4$, the configuration in Equation 4.27 is the orbit of the Klein four-group.

[7] As a hint of new kinds of "positional election" effects, by dropping different candidates from Equation 4.27, the outcomes for $s < \frac{1}{2}$ have the $A \succ C \sim D$, $B \succ C \sim D$, $C \succ A \sim B$, $D \succ A \sim B$ rankings with another kind of distinct cyclic flavor.

idea is that examples, or axiomatic representations, for one system can be translated into something for the other. The reason is that the plurality and antiplurality (vote-for-two) vote share reversed properties. As examples,

The plurality vote always ranks first any candidate who is top-ranked by most voters; the antiplurality vote always bottom-ranks any candidate who is bottom-ranked by most voters. The plurality vote can have a candidate top-ranked even when she is bottom-ranked by one less than two-thirds of all voters; the antiplurality vote can have a candidate bottom-ranked even when she is top-ranked by one less than two-thirds of all voters.

Profiles supporting plurality vote properties can be converted into supporting properties for the antiplurality properties just by reversing them; this is the immediate consequence of the tool to be developed here. This material comes from my book *Basic Geometry of Voting* [64] and my paper [81], and it is fully discussed in a paper with S. Barney [85].

For motivation, consider the following true story. In a departmental election over three candidates, the chair asked each voter to rank the candidates by placing the names next to the numbers 1, 2, 3 listed on the ballot. Presumably, a first-place candidate would be listed after 1, and so forth. After all ballots were tallied, the chair disclosed that he expected everyone to place a first-ranked candidate next to the 3 and a third-place candidate next to the 1.[8] Thus, *everyone's* ranking was tallied in the reversed order. So if the ranking using the incorrect rank ordering was $A \succ B \succ C$, what should be the election ranking when tallied with the correct ordering? Would it be the anticipated reversed $C \succ B \succ A$? As fodder for departmental intrigue, imagine the reaction if the chair announced that, after reversing all rankings, the outcome remained unchanged.

This unchanged status, or anything else, can occur; for example, with the profile

Number	Ranking	Number	Ranking
3	$A \succ B \succ C$	3	$C \succ B \succ A$
4	$A \succ C \succ B$	4	$B \succ C \succ A$

[8] Bewildering! The chair was later promoted to the Provost's office.

the plurality election ranking is $A \succ B \succ C$. After reversing each ranking exactly the same profile emerges, so the election ranking remains unchanged. This profile resides, of course, in the Reversal subspace.

To explore what can happen with any number of candidates and any profile, let ρ be a reversal mapping. For instance, for profile $\mathbf{p}$, the mapping $\rho(\mathbf{p})$ reverses each voter's ranking. Thus, with the profile $\mathbf{p} = (2, 4, 3, 0, 0, 0)$,

- Where two voters have $A \succ B \succ C$ preferences, four have $A \succ C \succ B$, and three have $C \succ A \succ B$
- In $\rho(\mathbf{p})$, two voters have $C \succ B \succ A$ preferences, four have $B \succ C \succ A$, and three have $B \succ A \succ C$

or $\rho(\mathbf{p}) = (0, 0, 0, 2, 4, 3)$.

For the $n!$ rankings generated by n candidates, let p_k represent the fraction of all voters who have the kth ranking, $k = 1, \ldots, n!$ Let $\mathbf{s} = (1, s_2, \ldots, s_{n-1}, 0)$ where $1 \geq s_j \geq s_{j+1} \geq 0$ be the general description of an n-candidate positional voting rule. Let $\tau^{\mathbf{s}}(\mathbf{p})$ be the tally of the candidates $A_1, \ldots, A_n$ using $\mathbf{s}$. The goal is to find a general description of what happens by reversing the profile; that is, describe $\tau^{\mathbf{s}}(\rho(\mathbf{p}))$.

Descriptions about $\tau^{\mathbf{s}}(\mathbf{p})$ involve another voting rule – the "reversal" of $\mathbf{s}$ where $\mathbf{s}^*$ is the rule $(1, 1 - s_{n-1}, 1 - s_{n-2}, \ldots, 1 - s_2, 0)$. For example, if $\mathbf{s} = (1, 0, 0)$ (plurality rule), then $\mathbf{s}^* = (1, 1, 0)$ (antiplurality vote). Similarly, if $\mathbf{s} = (1, \frac{1}{4}, 0)$, then $\mathbf{s}^* = (1, \frac{3}{4}, 0)$. In a real sense, $\mathbf{s}$ and $\mathbf{s}^*$ are "reversed voting rules" with complementary roles captured by Theorem 4.6.

Theorem 4.6: All normalized profiles $\mathbf{p}$ over $n \geq 3$ candidates satisfy the "reversal relationship"

$$\tau^{\mathbf{s}}(\mathbf{p}) + \tau^{\mathbf{s}^*}(\rho(\mathbf{p})) = (1, 1, \ldots, 1) \tag{4.29}$$

To answer questions about $\tau^{\mathbf{s}}(\rho(\mathbf{p}))$, use $\tau^{\mathbf{s}^*}(\mathbf{p})$ and Equation 4.29.[9] As each candidate's Equation 4.29 sum is unity, if she receives less than half of the votes with $\mathbf{s}$, she receives more than half with the reversed

---

[9] This is because $\rho(\rho(\mathbf{p})) = \mathbf{p}$ (i.e., the "reversal of a reversal" is the starting position).

profile and $\mathbf{s}^*$; that is, the $\tau^{\mathbf{s}}(\mathbf{p})$ and $\tau^{\mathbf{s}^*}(\rho(\mathbf{p}))$ rankings are opposites. This relationship captures the previous comparisons of plurality and antiplurality properties.

If $\mathbf{s} = \mathbf{s}^*$, then reversing a profile reverses the election outcome. With three alternatives, $\mathbf{s} = \mathbf{s}^*$ means that $s = 1 - s$, or $s = \frac{1}{2}$. Thus, according to Equation 4.29, the Borda Count is the only positional method whereby if *any* profile is reversed, the outcome also is reversed. *However,* with four or more candidates, a continuum of voting rules shares this property. With four candidates, for instance, the $\mathbf{s} = \mathbf{s}^*$ condition becomes $s_2 = 1 - s_3$ and $s_2 \geq s_3$. Consequently any four-candidate voting rule $(1, t, 1 - t, 0)$, $t \geq \frac{1}{2}$, fits the bill; this includes the Borda Count $(1, \frac{2}{3}, \frac{1}{3}, 0)$, $(1, \frac{1}{2}, \frac{1}{2}, 0)$, and even the vote-for-two $(1, 1, 0, 0)$ rule.

Proof of Theorem 4.6: To prove that each candidate's sum over the two profiles is unity, compute a candidate's two tallies for, say, A_j. A_j's $\mathbf{s}$ tally includes the score assigned to A_j from the kth ranking. If A_j is in the tth place in this ranking, then $s_t p_k$ points are assigned to A_j.

In $\rho(\mathbf{p})$, the kth ranking of $\mathbf{p}$ is reversed; that is, if A_j was in tth place in the kth ranking of $\mathbf{p}$, then A_j is in $n - t + 1$ place in $\rho(\mathbf{p})$. Therefore, the $\mathbf{s}^*$ contribution to A_j from $\rho(\mathbf{p})$ is $p_k(1 - s_t)$. Thus, the sum of A_j's $\mathbf{s}$ tally from the kth ranking of $\mathbf{p}$ plus A_j's $\mathbf{s}^*$ tally of the reversal of this ranking is $p_k s_t + p_k(1 - s_t) = p_k$. As A_j's tally is over all rankings, the sum is $\sum_{k=1}^{n!} p_k = 1$, which completes the proof. $\square$

4.4.3 A New Approach

A profile coordinate system exists (Saari [71, 72]) from which all profiles exhibiting different behavior can be created, new properties about voting rules can be found, and so forth. But this system proved to be more complicated to use than I had expected. So, adopting my earlier advice from Section 4.2, I developed a different approach, which will be described elsewhere, that is easier to use when searching for relationships among election outcomes over different sets of candidates. Such relationships, of course, form a central objective of voting theory.

The approach starts by emphasizing the simplest units – voting over pairs, and finding all consequences with all possible positional rules. The next level, consisting of triplets, is then analyzed, followed by quadruples, quintuples, and so on.

To suggest what is done, starting with the n-candidate binary stage, the goal is to discover a useful profile decomposition that will identify all effects of these pairwise votes. To do so, divide a profile $\mathbf{p}$ into the part that affects binary outcomes, $\mathbf{p}_{Bin}$, and the part that does not, $\mathbf{p}_{Orthog}$, to obtain

$$\mathbf{p} = \mathbf{p}_{Bin} + \mathbf{p}_{Orthog} \qquad (4.30)$$

Borrowing from the three-candidate analysis, further decompose the $\mathbf{p}_{Bin}$ into two parts. The first is where there never will be inconsistencies when considered over different subsets of alternatives; call this the *Borda portion* and denote it by $\mathbf{p}_{Borda}$. The remaining portion of $\mathbf{p}_{Bin}$, which allows cyclic and other effects, is denoted by $\mathbf{p}_{Cyclic}$. Equation 4.30 now becomes

$$\mathbf{p} = \mathbf{p}_{Borda} + \mathbf{p}_{Cyclic} + \mathbf{p}_{Orthog} \qquad (4.31)$$

Borda and Condorcet Coordinates

To relate Equation 4.31 with voting rules for three alternatives, notice that the basic and Condorcet portions define, respectively, $\mathbf{p}_{Borda}$ and $\mathbf{p}_{Cyclic}$; the reversal plus kernel portions describe $\mathbf{p}_{Orthog}$. To utilize Equation 4.31, as I will later in this chapter, the coordinate system must be described.

Definition 4.1: For n candidates, the Borda coordinate for alternative X is where $n - (2j - 1)$ voters are assigned to every ranking where X is jth ranked, $j = 1, \ldots, n$.

As is true in Theorem 4.2, $\mathbf{p}_{Borda}$ is a sum of the X-Borda profiles. The "Borda" title reflects the consistency of majority vote tallies for pairs over $\mathbf{p}_{Borda}$ with Borda tallies over any subset of candidates. To illustrate, the A-Borda coordinate for three alternatives assigns two points to each ranking where A is in first place and -2 points to each ranking where A is bottom-ranked; that is, the A-Borda vector is twice (for mathematical convenience) the A-basic profile. For four candidates, three voters are assigned to each of the six rankings where A is top-ranked, one to each ranking where A is second-ranked, -1 voters to each ranking where A is third-ranked, and -3 voters where A is bottom-ranked. The $n - (2j - 1)$ choices ensure a consistent definition for all choices of n that avoid fractions.

Important for the Borda basis vectors is that dropping alternatives creates a multiple of the Borda vector for the subset of alternatives. For instance, dropping an alternative other than A converts the four-candidate A-Borda vector into five times the three-candidate A-Borda vector.

The Condorcet terms are as described in Section 4.1.6. There exist scalars β_j so that

$$\mathbf{p}_{Cyclic} = \sum_{j=1}^{\frac{(n-1)!}{2}} \beta_j \mathbf{C}_j^n \tag{4.32}$$

the $\mathbf{C}_j^n$ terms are the Condorcet basis vectors (Equation 4.19). The program, which will be described elsewhere, identifies all consequences of these $\mathbf{p}_{Borda}$ and $\mathbf{p}_{Cyclic}$ terms on positional outcomes. Some of this was described earlier where, for instance, the Condorcet terms can force differences in the outcome of any subset of candidates.

This creates the foundation to capture all possible consequences of pairwise majority vote (e.g., see Section 4.5), so the next step is to consider positional outcomes over triplets. From the discussion based on Equation 3.8, we know that triplet outcomes can influence certain positional outcomes for sets of four, or five, or more candidates. The objective is to identify all possible connections. Again, interesting connections, similar to the cyclic behavior associated with Condorcet terms, emerge. The idea is to find the portion of $\mathbf{p}_{Orthog}$ that affects triplet outcomes, $\mathbf{p}_{Triplet}$, and the part that does not. Then, as with $\mathbf{p}_{Bin}$, the portion $\mathbf{p}_{Triplet}$ is further subdivided into the part with which there never will be inconsistencies over the different triplets, and the part that allows cyclic and other effects.

The process continues (e.g., the positional election behavior for all quadruples is examined). The new coordinates are divided into those that have consistency and those that identify consequences for elections with a larger number of candidates. Hopefully, this new approach will be easier to understand and lead to stronger conclusions.

4.5 Finding and Proving New Theorems

The casual reader interested in an overview of what has been done in this area most surely should skip the rest of this chapter and move on to Chapter 5. In the rest of this chapter, some heavy equations will start to fly around. On the other hand, pragmatic readers wondering how to exploit this information to derive new results are advised to study the following material. This is because those flying equations constitute new research tools to help us identify and obtain new results. In describing what can be done, I will emphasize the Condorcet profiles; a similar approach holds for the reversal profiles and for combinations of the two.

Before starting, recall that when harvesters enter the field to pick fruit from trees, the first ones in the orchard have the easiest time; they can pick the low-hanging fruit. Those who follow experience more difficulties; they need ladders to reach what fruit remains hidden somewhere high up in the trees.

This truism applies to research; the first researchers to use new tools or concepts in an area can harvest the low-hanging fruit by finding valued results that tend to be much easier to prove. Those who follow typically experience more difficulties in finding interesting, valued research questions. Moreover, equally as burdensome as carrying heavy ladders into the orchards, proofs typically become technically more complicated. What follows are new tools that can be used to harvest some low-hanging fruit.[10]

Start with the assertion, probably due to Nanson [42] over a century ago, that the Borda Count always ranks the Condorcet winner over the Condorcet loser. This is easy to prove; just use the fact that a candidate's Borda tally is the sum of points she receives over all pairwise comparisons. A candidate who ties in each election receives precisely the average vote of one half; in the summation, she has precisely the average, $\frac{1}{n}$th, of the total Borda tally.

A Condorcet winner does better; by beating everyone she has an above average tally in each election, so the summation defining her Borda score

---

[10] To provide tools for others, I raise issues and illustrate these tools only in illustrative settings. When questions are obvious, the tools are provided with minimal commentary.

also is above average (i.e., she receives more than $\frac{1}{n}$th of the total tally). The poor Condorcet loser does not do as well; adding less than half of the vote from each pairwise election creates a sum below the average, or less than $\frac{1}{n}$th of the total Borda vote. Clearly, the Condorcet winner must be Borda ranked above the Condorcet loser.

To identify new research issues, notice how this result states nothing about how pairs are ranked; for example, there is not even information on whether the Borda winner always beats the Borda loser in a pairwise majority vote. The answer, as described later, is "no." Thus, the new issue is to characterize when the Borda winner will beat the Borda loser in a majority vote.

To appreciate what is needed to prove such results, treat the troubling Condorcet terms as unruly guests. The Borda outcome is not affected by Condorcet terms, and the summation used to determine the Borda tallies eliminates the effects of Condorcet terms. So, treat the preceding summation argument as firmly shoving those unwelcomed guests out the door. In other words, what makes it easier to discover results about the Borda rankings relative to specified pairwise outcomes is that the summation eliminates the effect of the Condorcet terms.

But to find results in the other direction, to understand what can happen with pairwise votes, these boisterous individuals (the Condorcet terms) must be invited back to the party. The idea is to determine how many of the disorderly can participate (i.e., the amount of Condorcet terms included in a profile) without the party degenerating into some form of an animal house (i.e., enough order persists so that what we want to prove holds); for instance, the Borda winner beats the Borda loser.

Thus, results about pairwise rankings require including, rather than excluding, Condorcet terms. Headway requires using profile coordinates. As described with Equation 4.31, with respect to the Borda Count and pairwise elections,

any n-candidate profile $\mathbf{p}$ can be uniquely divided into

$$\mathbf{p} = \mathbf{p}_{Borda} + \sum \beta_j \mathbf{C}_j^n + \mathbf{p}_{Orthog} \tag{4.33}$$

The Borda outcome is determined strictly by the $\mathbf{p}_{Borda}$ terms; the corresponding pairwise rankings and tallies are transitive. But the pairwise rankings are further influenced by the Condorcet terms $\mathbf{C}_j^n$. No other terms affect differences in tallies, so, for practical purposes, they can be ignored; in other words, these coordinates minimize the curse of dimensionality. *An important point is that all properties, all relationships among Borda and pairwise majority vote rankings, are based on Equation 4.33.*

4.5.1 Special Case; Three Candidates

To avoid camouflaging concepts with notation, the notions are introduced with three candidates. The same approach, supplemented with combinatorics to handle the extra $\mathbf{C}_j^n$ terms, holds for any number of candidates (Saari [71, 72]).

For any profile, let $\mathcal{B}(X, Y)$ and $\mathcal{P}(X, Y)$ be, respectively, the difference between X's and Y's Borda and majority vote tallies. A useful relationship for any three of the n alternatives is that

$$\mathcal{B}(X, Y) + \mathcal{B}(Y, Z) = \mathcal{B}(X, Z) \tag{4.34}$$

The $\beta \mathbf{C}_1^3$ term in the Equation 4.33 profile does not affect $\mathcal{B}(X, Y)$ values, so (using $(1, \frac{1}{2}, 0)$ for Borda) the pairwise tallies become

$$\mathcal{P}(A, B) = \tfrac{4}{3}\mathcal{B}(A, B) + 2\beta, \quad \mathcal{P}(B, C) = \tfrac{4}{3}\mathcal{B}(B, C) + 2\beta,$$
$$\mathcal{P}(A, C) = \tfrac{4}{3}\mathcal{B}(A, C) - 2\beta \tag{4.35}$$

To derive this expression, notice that if a profile has a units of A-Borda and b of B-Borda, then Borda tallies for A and B are, respectively, $4a - 2b$ and $4b - 2a$ for a difference of $6(a - b)$. The pairwise votes for the two candidates are, respectively, $4a - 4b$ and $4b - 4a$ for a difference of $8(a - b)$; this explains the $\frac{4}{3}$. To explain the coefficient 2, notice that with $\beta \mathbf{C}_1^3$, A and B receive, respectively, β and $-\beta$ votes, so the difference is 2β.

What simplifies finding results is that *all possible three-candidate differences in Borda and pairwise tallies and rankings are completely captured by Equation 4.35!* Similar expressions hold for any number of candidates.

4.5.2 Condorcet Winners and Losers

To demonstrate the power of Equation 4.35, first assume that A is the Condorcet winner; in other words, assume that $\mathcal{P}(A, B)$ and $\mathcal{P}(A, C)$

are both positive. According to Equation 4.35, this means that

$$\mathcal{B}(A, B) > -\frac{3}{2}\beta, \quad \mathcal{B}(A, C) > \frac{3}{2}\beta \qquad (4.36)$$

There are two possibilities. If $\beta \geq 0$, then $\mathcal{B}(A, C) > 0$, which means that A is Borda-ranked over C. Otherwise, $\beta < 0$, which means that $\mathcal{B}(A, B) > 0$, or that A is Borda-ranked over B. This means that A beats someone in the Borda Count, so the Condorcet winner can never be Borda-bottom-ranked. This is a new three-candidate proof of the well-known result.

If, in addition, there is a Condorcet loser, say C, then $\mathcal{P}(B, C) > 0$. According to Equation 4.35, $\mathcal{B}(B, C) > -\frac{3}{2}\beta$. If $\beta \geq 0$, then (Equation 4.36) $\mathcal{B}(A, C) > 0$, which means that the Condorcet winner is Borda-ranked over the Condorcet loser. If $\beta < 0$, then both $\mathcal{B}(A, B)$ and $\mathcal{B}(B, C)$ must be positive. In turn, from Equation 4.34, we have that

$$\mathcal{B}(A, C) = \mathcal{B}(A, B) + \mathcal{B}(B, C) > 0 \qquad (4.37)$$

or, again, the Borda Count strictly ranks the Condorcet winner over the Condorcet loser. So, always, Borda ranks a Condorcet winner over the loser.

Before moving on, it is worth pointing out that Equation 4.37 and extensions play such an important role in the analysis that they should be in the toolboxes of all researchers in the area.

4.5.3 Borda Winners and Losers

Solving the Equation 4.35 equalities for $\mathcal{B}(X, Y)$ yields similar expressions, which means that similar arguments can be used to determine when the Borda winner can beat the Borda loser in a majority vote. To illustrate with the Borda ranking $A \succ B \succ C$, we want to determine when $\mathcal{P}(A, C) > 0$.

Again, β can be zero, positive, or negative. Everything agrees with $\beta = 0$. Positive β values increase the $\mathcal{P}(A, B)$ and $\mathcal{P}(B, C)$ tallies. Transitivity prevails until $\beta > \frac{2}{3}\mathcal{B}(A, C)$, when the transitive ranking suddenly becomes a cycle where the Borda loser beats the Borda winner.

Negative β values enhance the Borda winner's majority vote victory over the Borda loser, so all action involves the other two rankings. These rankings will reverse with sufficiently negative β values: The first ranking to change sign has the smallest $\mathcal{B}(X, Y)$ value. As this pair involves adjacently ranked candidates, the pairwise rankings remain transitive: The second change, however, creates the cycle. These simple observations prove the following.

Theorem 4.7: For three candidates, whenever the pairwise rankings define a transitive ranking, the Borda winner always beats the Borda loser in a majority vote; this statement holds even with one of the two possible cycles.

If the Borda tally differences between the top- and and second-ranked candidates are greater than that between the second- and third-ranked candidates, then, whenever a Condorcet winner exists, it agrees with the Borda winner.

Condorcet and Borda winners can differ, and Theorem 4.7 identifies precisely when and why this can occur. Other corollaries are immediate; for instance, imposing reasonable probability distributions over the coefficients for the basic and Condorcet terms proves that settings where there are different Borda and Condorcet winners are less likely than having agreement with the two winners (Saari [76]).

4.5.4 Low-Hanging Fruit with n Candidates

To find results involving more candidates, extend Equation 4.35. By inviting the disrupting Condorcet terms back into the fold, each $\mathbf{C}_j^n$ term adds the same amount to the majority vote of each pair in the primary cycle, a smaller fixed amount to each pair in the secondary cycles, and so forth. To see what happens, consider four candidates.

With four candidates, there are three Condorcet terms. Using the ranking wheel with $A \succ B \succ C \succ D$, let $\mathbf{C}_1^4$ be

Number	Ranking	Number	Ranking
1	$A \succ B \succ C \succ D$	-1	$D \succ C \succ B \succ A$
1	$B \succ C \succ D \succ A$	-1	$A \succ D \succ C \succ B$
1	$C \succ D \succ A \succ B$	-1	$B \succ A \succ D \succ C$
1	$D \succ A \succ B \succ C$	-1	$C \succ B \succ A \succ D$

To find a choice for $\mathbf{C}_2^4$, use the ranking wheel with some ranking not already represented, say, $A \succ C \succ B \succ D$, to obtain

Number	Ranking	Number	Ranking
1	$A \succ C \succ B \succ D$	-1	$D \succ B \succ C \succ A$
1	$C \succ B \succ D \succ A$	-1	$A \succ D \succ B \succ C$
1	$B \succ D \succ A \succ C$	-1	$C \succ A \succ D \succ B$
1	$D \succ A \succ C \succ B$	-1	$B \succ C \succ A \succ D$

Only eight rankings remain, so select one, such as $A \succ B \succ D \succ C$, to define a generating ranking for $\mathbf{C}_3^4$, which will be

Number	Ranking	Number	Ranking
1	$A \succ B \succ D \succ C$	-1	$C \succ D \succ B \succ A$
1	$B \succ D \succ C \succ A$	-1	$A \succ C \succ D \succ B$
1	$D \succ C \succ A \succ B$	-1	$B \succ A \succ C \succ D$
1	$C \succ A \succ B \succ D$	-1	$D \succ B \succ A \succ C$

So β_j describes the level of $\mathbf{C}_j^4$ in a profile. The computations are elementary; for example, the pairwise vote between A and B with $\mathbf{C}_1^4$ has A with 2 votes and B with -2 votes, so $\mathcal{P}(A, B) = 4\beta_1$. Similarly, $\mathcal{P}(A, C) = 0$.

4.5.5 Borda versus Pairwise Rankings

We need expressions that describe how tallies differ because of the β_j values. To do so, which is to develop the counterpart of Equation 4.35, remember that the Borda tallies are determined with $(1, \frac{2}{3}, \frac{1}{3}, 0)$. Let $\mathcal{B}_4(X, Y)$ be the difference in the Borda tallies of X and Y in the four-candidate election. By using the relationship between the Borda and Condorcet terms, we have the following relationships, or new tools.

$$
\begin{aligned}
\mathcal{P}(A, B) &= \tfrac{3}{2}\mathcal{B}_4(A, B) + 4[\beta_1 + \beta_3], \\
\mathcal{P}(A, C) &= \tfrac{3}{2}\mathcal{B}_4(A, C) + 4[\beta_2 - \beta_3] \\
\mathcal{P}(A, D) &= \tfrac{3}{2}\mathcal{B}_4(A, D) + 4[-\beta_1 - \beta_2], \\
\mathcal{P}(B, C) &= \tfrac{3}{2}\mathcal{B}_4(B, C) + 4[\beta_1 - \beta_2] \\
\mathcal{P}(B, D) &= \tfrac{3}{2}\mathcal{B}_4(B, D) + 4[\beta_2 + \beta_3], \\
\mathcal{P}(C, D) &= \tfrac{3}{2}\mathcal{B}_4(C, D) + 4[\beta_1 - \beta_3]
\end{aligned}
\tag{4.38}
$$

To explain this relationship, it follows from the definition of the Borda coordinates (Definition 4.1) for four candidates that with a, b, and c units of A-, B-, and C-Borda vectors, respectively, the Borda tallies for A and B are, respectively, $20a - \frac{20}{3}(b + c)$ and $20b - \frac{20}{3}(a + c)$. Thus, $\mathcal{B}_4(A, B) = \frac{80}{3}(a - b)$. Using the same coordinates for pairwise votes, A and B receive, respectively, $20a - 20b$ and $20b - 20a$ votes, so $\mathcal{P}(A, B) = 40(a - b)$. The $\frac{3}{2}$ coefficient now becomes obvious. The β_j terms are explained earlier.

To find another useful tool, notice that pairwise outcomes are difficult to analyze because they do not satisfy an expression similar to Equation 4.34. The pairwise tallies do, however, satisfy a related expression. Namely, by using Equations 4.38 and 4.34 we have that

$$
\begin{aligned}
\mathcal{P}(A, C) &= \frac{3}{2}\mathcal{B}_4(A, C) + 4(\beta_2 - \beta_3) \\
&= \frac{3}{2}[\mathcal{B}_4(A, B) + \mathcal{B}_4(B, C)] + 4(\beta_2 - \beta_3)
\end{aligned}
$$

Solving for $\mathcal{B}_4(A, B)$ and $\mathcal{B}_4(B, C)$ (Equation 4.38) leads to the new relationship $\mathcal{P}(A, C) = \mathcal{P}(A, B) + \mathcal{P}(B, C) + 8[-\beta_1 + \beta_2 - \beta_3]$. All four-candidate relationships among pairwise tallies can be found from the following.

Theorem 4.8: For four alternatives $\{A, B, C, D\}$, the pairwise tallies satisfy

$$
\begin{aligned}
\mathcal{P}(A, C) &= \mathcal{P}(A, B) + \mathcal{P}(B, C) + 8[-\beta_1 + \beta_2 - \beta_3] \\
\mathcal{P}(A, D) &= \mathcal{P}(A, B) + \mathcal{P}(B, D) + 8[-\beta_1 - \beta_2 - \beta_3] \\
\mathcal{P}(A, D) &= \mathcal{P}(A, C) + \mathcal{P}(C, D) + 8[-\beta_1 - \beta_2 + \beta_3] \\
\mathcal{P}(B, D) &= \mathcal{P}(B, C) + \mathcal{P}(C, D) + 8[-\beta_1 + \beta_2 + \beta_3]
\end{aligned}
\tag{4.39}
$$

All basic relationships among pairs come from Equation 4.39. As an illustration, solving the first expression for $\mathcal{P}(B, C)$ and using $\mathcal{P}(A, B) = -\mathcal{P}(B, A)$, we have that $\mathcal{P}(B, C) = \mathcal{P}(B, A) + \mathcal{P}(A, C) + 8[\beta_1 - \beta_2 + \beta_3]$. To go a step further, solving the second Equation 4.39 expression for $\mathcal{P}(B, A)$ leads to the expression $\mathcal{P}(B, C) = \mathcal{P}(B, D) + \mathcal{P}(D, A) + \mathcal{P}(A, C) - 16\beta_2$.

As there are many questions in the area of social choice that involve pairwise elections, it is easy to find settings where Equation 4.39 is useful.

For a trivial example, in a similar way as indicated earlier, it follows that $\mathcal{P}(A, D) = \mathcal{P}(A, B) + \mathcal{P}(B, C) + \mathcal{P}(C, D) - 16\beta_1$, or that $\mathbf{C}_1^4$ is the Condorcet term affecting the pairwise tallies of these four terms. So, with the pairwise rankings $A \succ B$, $B \succ C$, $C \succ D$, we now know that a cycle with $D \succ A$ occurs if and only if $\beta_1 > 0$ has a sufficiently large value; that is, if and only if $\beta_1 > \frac{1}{16}[\mathcal{P}(A, B) + \mathcal{P}(B, C) + \mathcal{P}(C, D)]$.

A Wealth of Expressions

The value of these tools is that they can be used to identify and resolve new issues concerning the long-standing objective of finding expressions relating Borda and pairwise outcomes. Additionally, the Kemeny rule seeks the "nearest" set of pairwise rankings that are transitive, so any results about Borda and transitive pairwise rankings is a new result about Borda versus Kemeny rankings! Whatever they are, they follow from this equation. To illustrate, start with Equation 4.38 and suppose that A is a Condorcet winner; that is, $\mathcal{P}(A, X) > 0$ for $X = B, C, D$. To find how this assumption affects the Borda tallies, notice from Equation 4.38 that

$$\frac{3}{8}\mathcal{B}_4(A, D) > \beta_1 + \beta_2, \quad \frac{3}{8}\mathcal{B}_4(A, C) > -\beta_2 + \beta_3, \quad \frac{3}{8}\mathcal{B}_4(A, B) > -\beta_1 - \beta_3$$

So, could A be Borda-bottom-ranked? If so, then all $\mathcal{B}_4(A, X)$ terms would be negative, which creates the inequalities

$$-\beta_1 > \beta_2, \quad \beta_2 > \beta_3, \quad \beta_3 > -\beta_1$$

or the contradiction that $-\beta_1 > -\beta_1$. This is *a simple, new proof showing for four candidates that the Condorcet winner cannot be Borda-bottom-ranked.* The same approach leads to a new four-candidate argument proving that Borda strictly ranks the Condorcet winner over the Condorcet loser.

To explore how the ranking of Borda candidates compares with ranking based on pairwise votes, solve the Equation 4.38 expressions for $\mathcal{B}_4(X, Y)$ and use a similar argument. For instance, the $A \succ B \succ C \succ D$ Borda ranking requires that $\mathcal{B}_4(A, X) > 0$ and $\mathcal{B}_4(Y, D) > 0$. The Borda loser could beat the Borda winner in a pairwise comparison, so the issue is to determine when this outcome cannot happen. By using the earlier comparison of Condorcet terms with unruly guests, we must determine how many of these guests (the $\mathbf{C}_j^4$ terms) can be admitted without causing so much damage to the pairwise rankings that the Borda loser beats the winner.

Assume that $\mathcal{P}(A, D) < 0$ (i.e., the Borda winner loses to the Borda loser). Also assume there is a Condorcet winner and a Condorcet loser. With $\mathcal{P}(A, D) < 0$, the Condorcet winner can only be B, C, or D. The winner cannot be D as D is Borda-bottom-ranked. A similar argument shows that neither A nor D can be the Condorcet loser. Thus, initially assume that B is the Condorcet winner and C is the Condorcet loser. These assumptions force the $B \succ D \succ A \succ C$ transitive ranking for the pairs.

By now the approach should be standard; the pairwise and Borda rankings fix the $\mathcal{P}(X, Y)$ and $\mathcal{B}_4(X, Y)$ signs. If these signs differ in Equation 4.38, an inequality with the β_j terms emerges. For instance, as $\mathcal{P}(A, D) < 0$ and $\mathcal{B}_4(A, D) > 0$, it follows that $\beta_1 + \beta_3 < 0$. The inequalities found in this manner, coming respectively from $\{A, D\}$, $\{A, B\}$, $\{C, D\}$, are

$$\beta_1 + \beta_2 > 0, \quad \beta_1 + \beta_3 < 0, \quad \beta_1 - \beta_3 < 0$$

These inequalities tell us, for instance, that $\beta_1 < 0$ (because $\beta_1 < \beta_3$ and $\beta_1 < -\beta_3$). As this information fails to provide what we want to learn, we must find ways to use information where $\mathcal{P}(X, Y)$ and $\mathcal{B}_4(X, Y)$ have the same sign. This comes from the crucial structure in Equation 4.34, which means, in particular, that $\mathcal{B}_4(A, D) \geq \mathcal{B}_4(X, Y)$ for any $\{X, Y\}$ pair.

The $\mathcal{P}(A, D) < 0$ assumption requires $8(\beta_1 + \beta_2) > 3\mathcal{B}_4(A, D)$. In turn, Equation 4.34 requires that $8(\beta_1 + \beta_2) > 3\mathcal{B}_4(X, Y)$ for *any* (X, Y) *pair*. To illustrate how to use these inequalities, notice that

$$0 < \mathcal{P}(A, C) = \frac{3}{2}\mathcal{B}(A, C) + 4[\beta_2 - \beta_3] < 4[\beta_1 + \beta_2] + 4[\beta_2 - \beta_3]$$

or that $\beta_1 + \beta_2 > -\beta_2 + \beta_3$. In this manner and by using pairs where $\mathcal{P}(X, Y)$ and $\mathcal{B}_4(X, Y)$ have the same positive sign, we obtain, respectively, from $\{A, C\}$, $\{B, C\}$, $\{B, D\}$ that

$$\beta_1 + \beta_2 > -\beta_2 + \beta_3, \quad \beta_1 + \beta_2 > -\beta_1 + \beta_2, \quad \beta_1 + \beta_2 > -\beta_2 - \beta_3$$

The middle inequality requires $\beta_1 > 0$, which contradicts the earlier $\beta_1 < 0$: This contradiction proves that, with transitive pairwise rankings, the Borda winner always beats the Borda loser in a majority vote. If C, rather than B, is the Condorcet winner, the argument is even easier.

Key to the argument is that the largest difference in Borda tallies is between the Borda winner and the Borda loser. Using this feature, and recognizing that each Condorcet term alters the Borda differences by the same amount, the following result can be proved.

Theorem 4.9 (Saari [71]): For any number of candidates, if the pairwise rankings define a transitive ranking, then the Borda winner beats the Borda loser in a majority vote election.

This result can be sharpened; for example, transitivity of majority vote rankings most surely can be replaced by just assuming the existence of a Condorcet winner and loser.

The preceding four-candidate argument uses only three of the six inequalities and never any β_j values (i.e., determine what happens if $\beta_2 = \beta_3 = 0$). Also ignored are the $\mathcal{B}_4(B, D) = \mathcal{B}_4(B, C) + \mathcal{B}_4(C, D)$, $\mathcal{B}_4(A, C) = \mathcal{B}_4(A, B) + \mathcal{B}_4(B, C)$ expressions, which most surely can be used to determine how other Borda-ranked candidates fare in pairwise votes. In other words, other low-hanging results remain within easy reach.

4.5.6 Borda versus Borda Rankings

These tools provide new ways to more fully explore a variety of research issues, but even more is possible. To motivate what follows, recall that all inconsistencies with the Borda Count are caused by Condorcet terms. It is reasonable to more fully explore this comment to determine how much and what kind of Condorcet terms are needed and to discover accompanying consequences. Again, consider four candidates.

For notation, let $\mathcal{B}_{\{X,Y,Z\}}(X, Y)$ represent the difference between the X and Y Borda tallies, for the triplet $\{X, Y, Z\}$. To list the Borda outcome over the triplets, start with $\{A, B, C\}$.

$$\mathcal{B}_{\{A,B,C\}}(A, B) = \tfrac{9}{8}\mathcal{B}_4(A, B) + 2\beta_1 + 4\beta_2 + 2\beta_3$$
$$\mathcal{B}_{\{A,B,C\}}(A, C) = \tfrac{9}{8}\mathcal{B}_4(A, C) + 4\beta_1 + 2\beta_2 - 2\beta_3 \qquad (4.40)$$
$$\mathcal{B}_{\{A,B,C\}}(B, C) = \tfrac{9}{8}\mathcal{B}_4(B, C) + 2\beta_1 - 2\beta_2 - 4\beta_3$$

Equation 4.34 requires $\mathcal{B}_{\{A,B,C\}}(A, B) + \mathcal{B}_{\{A,B,C\}}(B, C) = \mathcal{B}_{\{A,B,C\}}$ (A, C), and, as addition shows, this is the case. Thus, these three expressions reduce to two independent expressions.

To derive this expression, already it was shown that with a, b, and c units of A-, B-, and C-Borda terms, then $\mathcal{B}_{(A,B)} = \frac{80}{3}(a - b)$. When D is dropped, a straightforward computation shows that $\mathcal{B}_{\{A,B,C\}}(A, B) = 30(a - b)$. Comparing the two coefficients determines the $\frac{9}{8}$ multiple. The β_j expressions reflect the Figure 17 description of the extra candidates. With $\mathbf{C}_1^4$, for instance, dropping D to create the subset $\{A, B, C\}$ of candidates forces the Condorcet four-tuple to have a Condorcet triplet plus one $A \succ B \succ C$ ranking with β_1 voters, and one $C \succ B \succ A$ ranking with $-\beta_1$ voters. As A and B are adjacent in both rankings, the Borda Count tally difference for each ranking is one. Thus, the contribution made by this $\mathbf{C}_1^4$ term to $\mathcal{B}_{\{A,B,C\}}(A, B)$ is $\beta_1 - (-\beta_1) = 2\beta_1$. Similarly, because A and C are separated by a candidate in both rankings, the contribution of $\mathbf{C}_1^4$ term to the $\mathcal{B}_{\{A,B,C\}}(A, C)$ differences is $2\beta_1 - (-2\beta_1) = 4\beta_1$. The other terms are similarly computed.

To suggest what issues to examine, suppose Condorcet terms are added to reverse the $A \succ B \succ C \succ D$ ranking to $C \succ B \succ A$ when D is dropped. What is the accompanying behavior of pairs? For a first cut at this question and because $\mathbf{C}_1^4$ has the strongest effect on creating this behavior, assume that $\beta_2 = \beta_3 = 0$.

To study the pairs, we need to relate $\mathcal{B}_{A,B,C}(X, Y)$ with $\mathcal{P}(X, Y)$. Doing so merely involves some elementary algebra from Equations 4.38 and 4.40, which leads to

$$\mathcal{B}_{\{A,B,C\}}(A, B) = \tfrac{3}{4}\mathcal{P}(A, B) - \beta_1 + 4\beta_2 - \beta_3$$
$$\mathcal{B}_{\{A,B,C\}}(A, C) = \tfrac{3}{4}\mathcal{P}(A, C) + 4\beta_1 - \beta_2 + \beta_3 \qquad (4.41)$$
$$\mathcal{B}_{\{A,B,C\}}(B, C) = \tfrac{3}{4}\mathcal{P}(B, C) - \beta_1 + \beta_2 - 4\beta_3$$

The argument now is immediate. Because $\beta_2 = \beta_3 = 0$ and because the Borda rankings for the triplet are reversed, we have from Equation 4.40 that β_1 is negative. Thus, the first Equation 4.38 expression sums two negative terms, $\frac{3}{2}\mathcal{B}_{\{A,B,C\}}(A, B) + \beta_1 = \mathcal{P}(A, B)$, so $\mathcal{P}(A, B) < 0$ or B beats A in a majority vote; similarly, $\mathcal{P}(B, C) < 0$, so C beats B in a majority vote. For the remaining pair, notice from the middle expression in Equation 4.40 that $\mathcal{B}_{\{A,B,C\}}(A, C) - 4\beta_1 > 0$. This expression also is in $\frac{3}{4}\mathcal{P}(A, C)$, so $\mathcal{P}(A, C) > 0$. Namely, *with the described reversal of the Borda rankings, the three alternatives must define the majority vote cycle of $B \succ A$, $A \succ C$, $C \succ B$.* This result should be expected because the effects of the Condorcet terms increase by dropping candidates.

The following extends these tools to the other triples:

$$
\begin{aligned}
\mathcal{B}_{\{B,C,D\}}(B, C) &= \tfrac{9}{8}\mathcal{B}_4(B, C) + 2\beta_1 - 2\beta_2 + 4\beta_3 \\
&= \tfrac{3}{4}\mathcal{P}(B, C) - \beta_1 + \beta_2 + 4\beta_3 \\
\mathcal{B}_{\{B,C,D\}}(B, D) &= \tfrac{9}{8}\mathcal{B}_4(B, D) + 4\beta_1 + 2\beta_2 + 2\beta_3 \\
&= \tfrac{3}{4}\mathcal{P}(B, D) + 4\beta_1 - \beta_2 - \beta_3 \\
\mathcal{B}_{\{B,C,D\}}(C, D) &= \tfrac{9}{8}\mathcal{B}_4(C, D) + 2\beta_1 + 4\beta_2 - 2\beta_3 \\
&= \tfrac{3}{4}\mathcal{P}(C, D) - \beta_1 + 4\beta_2 + \beta_3
\end{aligned}
\tag{4.42}
$$

$$
\begin{aligned}
\mathcal{B}_{\{A,C,D\}}(A, C) &= \tfrac{9}{8}\mathcal{B}_4(A, C) - 4\beta_1 + 2\beta_2 - 2\beta_3 \\
&= \tfrac{3}{4}\mathcal{P}(A, C) - 4\beta_1 - \beta_2 + \beta_3 \\
\mathcal{B}_{\{A,C,D\}}(A, D) &= \tfrac{9}{8}\mathcal{B}_4(A, D) - 2\beta_1 - 2\beta_2 - 4\beta_3 \\
&= \tfrac{3}{4}\mathcal{P}(A, D) + \beta_1 + \beta_2 - 4\beta_3 \\
\mathcal{B}_{\{A,C,D\}}(C, D) &= \tfrac{9}{8}\mathcal{B}_4(C, D) + 2\beta_1 - 4\beta_2 - 2\beta_3 \\
&= \tfrac{3}{4}\mathcal{P}(C, D) - \beta_1 - 4\beta_2 + \beta_3
\end{aligned}
\tag{4.43}
$$

$$
\begin{aligned}
\mathcal{B}_{\{A,B,D\}}(A, B) &= \tfrac{9}{8}\mathcal{B}_4(A, B) + 2\beta_1 - 4\beta_2 + 2\beta_3 \\
&= \tfrac{3}{4}\mathcal{P}(A, B) - \beta_1 - 4\beta_2 - \beta_3 \\
\mathcal{B}_{\{A,B,D\}}(A, D) &= \tfrac{9}{8}\mathcal{B}_4(A, D) - 2\beta_1 - 2\beta_2 + 4\beta_3 \\
&= \tfrac{3}{4}\mathcal{P}(A, D) + \beta_1 + \beta_2 + 4\beta_3 \\
\mathcal{B}_{\{A,B,D\}}(B, D) &= \tfrac{9}{8}\mathcal{B}_4(B, D) - 4\beta_1 + 2\beta_2 + 2\beta_3 \\
&= \tfrac{3}{4}\mathcal{P}(B, D) - 4\beta_1 - \beta_2 - \beta_3
\end{aligned}
\tag{4.44}
$$

Have Fun!

These equations provide new tools that can be used in the indicated manner. Of importance, there remain many other questions that can be raised and explored, so much fun remains. What makes this exploration easier is that, armed with the tools covered in this chapter, we no longer must re-create this development; we just need to move to the next step of finding more imaginative election relationships.

FIVE

Deliver Us from the Plurality Vote

To connect theory with reality, this concluding chapter addresses certain realistic, pragmatic dangers associated with actual elections. I also critique, but only briefly, some contemporary, so-called reform efforts.

After exhibiting my tendency toward reckless behavior by sticking a toe into the dangerous waters populated by advocates of various voting rules,[1] I will hastily retreat to the safety zone ensured by theory and academics. Once back in this ivy-covered haven, I will tie together certain points made in this book by using a different approach.

5.1 Our Standard Voting Rule

The material developed in the past few chapters probably spawned worries about the accuracy of standard elections. I hope so; a strong, take-home message is that standard voting rules create real and grave problems.

These fears realistically arise whenever elections are based on, or involve, the plurality vote. As described in the past two chapters, this typically used voting rule suffers severe weaknesses causing its outcomes to compromise the wishes of the voters. To escalate the rhetoric, it is

---

[1] Regularly, but not as frequently as spam messages enticing me to become a multi-millionaire by helping the wife of some disposed dictator, I receive emails from reform advocates. One salutation started, "The lawyer MORONS in . . . ," while other messages approach religious fervor in admonishing me to change my evil ways by endorsing this or that voting rule. Wives of disposed dictators seem so much more reasonable.

realistic to fret about the legitimacy of any reasonably close election where the outcomes involve the plurality vote.

5.1.1 The 2000 U.S. Presidential Election

In Section 1.1, doubt was expressed whether the 2000 U.S. presidential election outcome involving George W. Bush, Albert Gore, and Ralph Nader accurately reflected the views of the voters. I blamed the plurality vote, but it is easy to challenge this comment on the technical grounds that the presidential outcome was determined not by the popular vote, but by the Electoral College ballot.[2] The much maligned Electoral College did play a role, but this relic from centuries past was a scapegoat rather than the deciding factor. After all, the statewide elections for presidential electors were determined by the plurality vote.

To use figures, the final certified vote for the state of Florida gave George W. Bush a 537-vote victory, or the miniscule 0.009 percent of the total Floridian vote. To be precise, the official federal vote for Florida had

- George Bush receiving 2,912,790, or 48.847 percent of the vote
- Al Gore receiving 2,912,253 votes, or 48.838 percent of the vote
- Ralph Nader receiving 97,421 votes, or 1.634 percent of the total vote

Although small in numbers, the Nader vote plays a crucial role when analyzing who the Floridian voters *really* wanted. This is due to the general acceptance that most Nader voters, many of whom supported the Green Party, ranked Gore as their second choice. The arithmetic is easy; if most of the 97,421 Nader voters preferred Gore over Bush, then one could comfortably assert that the Floridian voters preferred Gore to Bush. Contrary to what the vote registered, Gore was the Floridian's top choice. This leads to the issue raised in Section 4.3: Which election rule would have more accurately captured the voters' intent? For this *particular election*, with any voting rule taking account of second choices,

---

[2] Another argument claims that the outcome was determined by a closer vote – the split 5–4 U.S. Supreme Court decision to halt further recounts in the Florida election.

or if even a small fraction of the Nader voters had voted for Gore, Gore would have defeated Bush.

Attention focused on Florida with its twenty-five electoral votes, but had *any* state voted for Gore rather Bush, the election would have reversed.[3] This suggests examining election outcomes from other states, such as New Hampshire with its four electoral votes, where the vote differential between the two main contenders of 11,719 was about 52 percent of Nader's 22,188 votes. Yet to suggest that Gore was favored over Bush by these voters requires arguing persuasively that at least 79 percent of the Nader voters preferred Gore. This statement is probably true, but it is not clear.

Incidentally, I singled out this 2000 election because it received immense international attention and the outcome proved to have dramatic global consequences. But this is only one of many choices where doubt should accompany the plurality outcome. Most election seasons provide examples; just investigate any election where the combined vote for two candidates promoting a similar philosophy exceeds that of the winner. For a rich supply of possibilities, check the New Hampshire presidential primaries; for instance, news reports from 1996 suggested that the Republican voters strongly favored Senator Robert Dole over the conservative commentator Pat Buchanan. This will of the voters was not reflected by the plurality election outcome; with a Republican primary crowded with presidential wannabes, where many of them campaigned with messages similar to Dole's, Buchanan won.

Explanations for this violating the voters' intent are immediate. The extreme nature of plurality outcomes, as captured by the geometry of the procedure line (Section 3.5.2) with a surprisingly large likelihood (Saari and Tataru [95]) of a plurality ranking rejecting what the voters want, raises doubts about continued use of this standard approach.

5.1.2 The 2002 French Presidential Election

The shock ran the whole world through. The bombshell coming out of Paris blasted the news that Jacques Chirac and Jean-Marie Le Pen were

---

[3] Bush received 271 electoral votes; a winner required 270 votes. Each state has three or more electoral votes.

the leaders in the April 21, 2002, first round of the French presidential election. They, rather than the universally anticipated pair of Jacques Chirac and Lionel Jospin, would advance to the runoff.[4]

Le Pen, a right-wing nationalist politician whose credentials include his efforts to impose restrictions on immigration, support for the death penalty, promoting the censorship of the arts, and even having been accused of being a racist and anti-Semitic with his alleged denials of central details about the Holocaust (e.g., the gas chambers), ensured that his advancement to the runoff would attract international attention and bring about a soul-searching French nation. What a field day for journalists and commentators; they could question the changing political climate and attitudes of the French voters. Were the French becoming more conservative? Were they racist? A parallel debate about the validity of polling techniques arose.

I referred to this turmoil in Section 1.1 with my question, "Did the French electorate truly respect Jean-Marie Le Pen enough to justify advancing him to the runoffs in the 2002 French elections?" Of course they did not. The problem had *nothing* to do with the general French voters; there were *no* radical changes in French attitudes. The pundits completely missed the point: The jolting outcome was a direct consequence of using the *plurality vote* in the first round of the 2002 French elections with *sixteen* candidates. *Sixteen!*

To capture what went wrong, suppose tomorrow morning the president of a local university announces that from this date on, class rankings for students will be determined strictly by the number of As they earn. Why shouldn't rankings be determined this way? This approach appears to reward excellence – until one realizes that a student with all Bs will be ranked below the student with an A in gym and Fs in every other course. Concentrating on As is roughly equivalent to the plurality vote where a voter can register only his or her A candidate. This means that a highly respected candidate with some As but many Bs among the voters

---

[4] In round one, Chirac received 5,666,440 votes, or 19.88 percent; Le Pen received 4,805,307 votes, or 16.86 percent; and Jospin received 4,610,749 votes or 16.18 percent of the vote. In the May 5 runoff, Chirac received more than 82 percent of the vote, while Le Pen improved only slightly over his first round vote effort with less than 18 percent of the vote. It appears that Le Pen had only a hard core of 18 percent of the French voters supporting him.

could lose to a candidate with a couple more As but many Fs; this is precisely what happened with Jospin's 16.18 percent of As and Le Pen's 16.86 percent. In other words, even a candidate disliked by a vast majority of the voters could emerge victorious if touted by a reasonably sized minority.

This story explains the 2002 French presidential election. Read the press reports of that time; most French citizens were upset by the possibility of President Le Pen, they were embarrassed that he even made it to the runoff. Election figures support this comment; Le Pen's 16.86 percent of the vote in the sixteen-candidate first round increased only to 17.8 percent in the two-person runoff. As is true with the first round of the French election and the grading system for the hypothetical university, the plurality vote allows a candidate disliked by a vast majority, but solidly supported by a strong minority, to emerge victorious in a crowded field. Le Pen enjoyed A grades from about 17 to 18 percent of the voters, but much lower assessments from the rest of them.

Lessons learned from the 2002 election can be expected to introduce caution into the next few French presidential competitions; fear from past elections that may guide voters into voting for choices who more accurately reflect the general views of the French voters. If a voter's A candidate cannot win, the reality that his F candidate might emerge victorious may cause him to vote for a B candidate who *can* win. This appeared to have occurred in the April 22, 2007, first round of the French presidential elections with press reports that supporters of the six far-left candidates supported the Socialist candidate Segolene Royal in fear that another first-round elimination would prove disastrous for the future of the left.[5] This strategy also resembles what might have happened in the 2004 U.S. presidential elections: After voters were reminded about the 2000 "Nader factor," it appears that some of them did not give Nader's candidacy the same support.

If we reflect on George Santayana's comment that those who forget history are doomed to repeat it, we can expect a French constitutional

---

[5] In the first round, Nicolas Sarkozy, a conservative, received about 31 percent of the vote; Segolene Royal from the Socialist Party had 26 percent; Francois Bayrou, a centrist, had 18.5 percent; and Jean-Marie Le Pen declined sharply from his 2002 showing by receiving only 10.5 percent.

crisis in 30 or so years from now, unless the French voting system is changed. With the tendency for more and more candidates to run for office, which means that previously A-ranked candidates now must "split the vote" to become B-ranked for many voters, it is easy to foresee scenarios whereby the two choices advanced to the runoff represent extreme ends of the political spectrum. Candidates receiving just enough As, while handicapped with many Fs, could beat more moderate, representative candidates who receive slightly fewer As but many Bs. Consultants for an extreme wing of the French populace should urge them to consolidate around one candidate, and let the many moderate candidates split the vote. Should this approach be adopted by two extreme parties, however, expect a situation where neither runoff candidate reflects the views of most voters.

5.1.3 Reform, or Fighting Termites with Paint and Putty?

Reform approaches are everywhere. A currently popular proposal is the instant runoff vote (IRV). IRV is nothing special; it is just a regular runoff where everything is determined with the same ballot. Namely, after voters rank the candidates, the candidates are ranked with the plurality vote where a candidate with a majority vote wins. If no candidate receives a majority, then, *using the same ballots,* a runoff is held between the top two candidates.

There are excellent reasons to use the same ballots.

- The first is immediacy and efficiency; with modern computers, the election outcome can be quickly registered rather than incurring the wait and expense of a runoff held weeks later.
- Using the same ballots reduces strategic voting. For instance, my sincere preferences are Ann $\succ$ Barb $\succ$ Carol. However, if Barb advances to a runoff with Ann, it is possible that Barb will win. Therefore, to try to create an Ann–Carol runoff, I may vote strategically for Carol; then in the runoff I would support my sincere top choice of Ann. With IRV, however, this ploy is impossible because my registered ranking in the first round determines my runoff vote (i.e., by voting strategically for Carol in the first round, my runoff vote would also

be for my *bottom-ranked* Carol rather than my top choice of Ann). Thus, for some settings (not all), IRV discourages strategic voting.

Had IRV been used in the 2000 Florida presidential election, where neither Bush nor Gore received a majority vote, Gore would have won the IRV runoff. But remember, reform methods are intended to prevent problems in the future rather than hypothetically correcting flaws of the past. Will IRV do this? Even though IRV sounds good, it has serious deficiencies.

The most serious IRV weakness is its reliance on the questionable plurality vote. One is left with the feeling that rather than addressing the root troubles associated with the plurality vote, IRV supporters want to bandage the electoral difficulties by introducing another step. However, whenever the plurality vote is a major component of an election method, its negative consequences can prevail. For me, this "find a Band-Aid" approach resembles discovering termite damage in a house and trying to correct the problem by filling the holes with putty and painting over the eyesore. Until the basic source of the problem is removed, expect difficulties!

The type of problem IRV corrects is that manifested by the Florida election; it is where the outcome between two major candidates is altered by support for a minor candidate. Instead of providing a salvation, IRV can create serious problems in any closely contested election involving more candidates. Problems arise with three or more serious contenders, such as with the quadrennial U.S. presidential primaries or even the U.S. presidential elections that involve, not infrequently, three serious candidates. With the 2002 French presidential race, for instance, Le Pen still would have advanced to the runoff where he may have fared better with the runoff ballots being tallied than with those originally cast. Indeed, IRV cannot prevent the scenario whereby two fringe French candidates could advance to the runoff. Instead, IRV might lull voters into supporting an unlikely "Nader" in anticipation that the deciding runoff would involve the voter's second choice: If this is the case, expect fringe candidates to win. My fear is that it takes only one term served by a poorly qualified, or fringe candidate, to cause serious damage.

IRV critics may pile on my comments by arguing (as some have) that IRV also fails to satisfy *monotonicity.* I'll explain what this means with a story: Suppose that if an election among Ann, Barb, and Carol had been held yesterday, Ann and Barb would have advanced to the runoff where Ann would win. Now suppose that, after a tremendous election speech last night, more voters join Ann's bandwagon. Does Ann's added support ensure she will win more convincingly? Maybe not; with IRV, she could *lose*!

How could this happen? The answer is simple; voters who previously would have voted for Barb now vote for Ann, which means that the runoff could be between Ann and Carol. In this runoff, Carol wins. Incidentally, IRV is not the only rule that suffers this lack of monotonicity: It accompanies *all election rules* with two or more steps. After proving this result (Saari [63, 64]), I reconsidered the issue in [78] and discovered that while the difficulty is more severe with IRV than other methods (because IRV relies on the plurality vote), the problem is not as serious as many suspect.

5.1.4 Resolutions, but Other Problems

An effective reform resolution requires addressing the core difficulty; replace the plurality vote with rules that *do* recognize second and third choices. My recommendations to IRV advocates, the French government, and others is to use the Borda Count for the first stage. In this manner, as described in the past two chapters, the first stage outcome more accurately reflects the voters' views.[6] For those who are trying to minimize strategic behavior or who are caught up by a need for an instant runoff, drop all but the top two or three candidates from the first round and use the same ballots for another Borda election. Moreover, by using the Borda Count on the first stage, where the Borda outcomes and that of the runoff (over a pair) are more closely coordinated, worries about the described monotonicity problem are lessened.

My comment about recognizing second-, third-, and other-ranked candidates needs clarification. After all, as the procedure line shows, difficulties associated with the plurality vote are inherited by the

---

[6] Suppose the Borda Count is to be used with only five of the *n* candidates; give 5, 4, 3, 2, 1 points, respectively, to how they are listed on the ballot. If a voter votes for only two candidates, give them, respectively, 2, 1 points.

vote-for-two rule. Similar problems arise with all of the vote-for-k-candidates rules.

To appreciate why these vote-for-k-candidates rules can violate the voters' intent, expand on the earlier analogy of how a university ranks its students. Instead of ranking students according to the number of As, suppose they are ranked according to the number of As and Bs without distinguishing between them; this grading scheme roughly captures what happens with the vote-for-two voting rule. Namely, because a student with all As is tied with a student with all Bs, quality is not served. Similar stories for vote-for-three and other rules are obvious. The point is that distinctions, as provided by the Borda Count, are needed to evaluate students (i.e., the four-point grading system, where an A is assigned four points, a B receives three, and so forth, is equivalent to the Borda Count) and candidates.

So, to avoid distorted election outcomes, stay clear of voting methods using vote-for-k rules. This includes IRV, Approval Voting, Coombs runoff where the candidate most disliked in the first round is dropped (thus, the antiplurality loser is dropped), cumulative voting, and so forth.

5.2 Newton's Third Law of Politics

Veterans of meetings have experienced, and suffered, the effects of Newton's third law of politics:

Every proposal has an opposite and equally forceful counterproposal.

It is frustrating, but often true.

To appreciate this law, recall the dynamics of proposals and counter-proposals. As is particularly true with academics, debatable questions tend to involve several principles and issues. To create an illustrating example in Figure 18a, the issues are the stipend (x-axis) and the number of hours of service (y-axis) expected from a graduate student. A committee of three is charged with determining the final package; each member's *ideal point* is indicated by a bullet, $\bullet_j$, with an identifying subscript. Member 1, for instance, prefers low pay and low work; member 2 is more generous with a higher salary accompanied with a reasonable

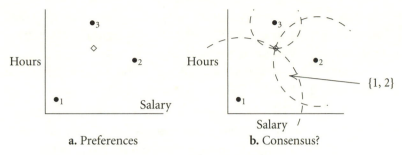

a. Preferences   b. Consensus?

Figure 18. Cycles using triplets.

number of hours of work; and tightfisted member 3 insists upon more work at a lower pay. What would this committee, with divided opinions, decide?[7]

Presumably this committee will compromise by selecting a central point in the triangle defined by the voters' ideal points, such as the one given by the diamond. But check those Figure 18b circles that pass through the proposed diamond; each circle's center is a voter's ideal point. As it is reasonable to expect a committee member to prefer counterproposals closer to his or her ideal point, the three leafs of intersecting circles identify alternatives that would defeat the original proposal.

The largest leaf, indicated by an arrow from the symbol $\{1, 2\}$, identifies all possibilities that the majority winning coalition of voters 1 and 2 prefer to the original one. Similarly, the trefoil leaf at the top right are choices preferred by the majority of $\{2, 3\}$, while the skinny trefoil region identifies the limited options preferred by the majority of $\{1, 3\}$. As each trefoil leaf consists of points preferred over the original choice by a deciding majority, some majority may be tempted to validate Newton's third law of politics by advancing a counterproposal.

This behavior is not an artifact of the Figure 18a choices. Instead, as long as the three ideal points do not lie on a straight line,[8] the circles defined by *any* proposal *must* have a nonempty intersection for at least

---

[7] This analysis, called spatial voting, is standard. Among the early advocates of this approach are Melvin Hinich, Bernie Grofman, Charles Plott, Richard McKelvey, and many others (e.g., see the book *Advances in the Spatial Theory of Voting* [16] edited by Enelow and Hinich).

[8] Even if the ideal points are on a line, if the proposal is not, the circles intersect.

two circles. Thus, whatever the original proposal, a counterproposal supported by a majority exists. Of course, any counterproposal is subject to a counter-counterproposal, that is subject to . . . *chaos reigns.*

Going beyond the theoretical, once we know what to look for, it is not difficult to find this behavior in group deliberations. An amusing one occurred at the 2003 Mathematical Association of America (MAA) annual Mathfest where during my plenary talk I motivated this phenomenon by referring to those multiple amendments that can plague business meetings. Immediately after my talk *was* the MAA business meeting called to consider proposed changes to their bylaws. The obvious happened; amendment after amendment to the carefully thought-out proposals were made – accompanied with laughter once participants recognized they were fulfilling my predictions.

A more serious example involved a gathering charged with designing the Iraqi constitution during the tense summer of 2005. The constitutional convention quickly spun out of control as change after change was proposed by different coalitions of the Shia, Sunni, and Kurd. That evening I received several emails comparing the news events reported on August 16, 2005, with these theoretical predictions.[9]

5.2.1 Comparison with Pairwise Voting

Typically, majority votes are used to decide between a proposal and a counterproposal. As such, we must wonder whether this chaotic spatial voting description is related to the Condorcet n-tuple described in Section 4.1.6.

They are essentially the same; the main difference is that the Condorcet n-tuples involve specified alternatives, and the Figure 18b dynamic indicates how to identify the counterproposals to create cyclic effects. Also, by relying on a cardinal, rather than an ordinal, measure, the figure indicates the intensity of voters' preferences over competing proposals.

---

[9] The first came from Raymond Rogers who urged me to check the PBS *NewsHour* because "The guest speaker described the Iraqi constitutional process/negotiations, and he was reiterating the points of your article (Saari [79]) to a T."

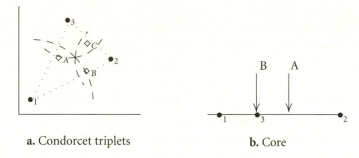

a. Condorcet triplets   **b.** Core

Figure 19. Condorcet and cores.

To sharpen the comparison, notice from the Condorcet triplet

Voter	Preferences
1	$A \succ B \succ C$
2	$B \succ C \succ A$
3	$C \succ A \succ B$

(5.1)

that

- coalition $\{1, 2\}$ can elect B over C
- coalition $\{2, 3\}$ can elect C over A
- coalition $\{1, 3\}$ can elect A over B

The similarity of what these winning coalitions can do with those in Figure 18b is not an accident. Instead, we should expect that three alternatives can be placed within the triangle formed by the ideal points to create a Condorcet triplet. As indicated in Figure 19a, this is trivial to do. (Each voter's preference over the three alternatives is as indicated in the Condorcet triplet in Equation 5.1.) Just draw the circles passing through *any* interior point of the triangle defined by the voters' ideal points. After that, it is easy to position three points $\diamond_A$, $\diamond_B$, $\diamond_C$ to have the desired Condorcet triplet structure; notice, the points need not be in the leafs of the trefoil.

A growing literature is trying to debunk cyclic behavior with claims that cycles do not exist in practice. My best guess about these mystifying assertions is that these authors don't know where to look. Part of the problem is that most elections are carried out with a plurality vote, rather than pairwise votes. To address this issue, Sieberg and McDonald [110] did the obvious, which, surprisingly, had not been done before; they determined the likelihood of cycles in terms of plurality tallies. They found it is likely for cyclic behavior to accompany close elections. Another "where to look" illustration is the Wheaton College example (Section 2.2.2), which does not resemble the standard description of a cycle; nevertheless, it is one. Also, a distinction must be made between claiming that cycles cannot exist and that one would have occurred had the voters taken another vote.

Indeed, whenever the ideal points for three voters, or parties, do not lie on a straight line, there are many Condorcet triplets providing the potential for cycles. But the possibility of a cycle does not mean one will occur; the voters may not recognize their ability to do so. On the other hand, the described amendment process and Iraqi constitutional process most surely exhibit cyclic effects.

5.2.2 Stability and the Core

To determine where stability can be found, we need to characterize spatial voting settings where the Condorcet triplet behavior cannot occur. The appropriate stability notion is provided by the *core*.

Definition 5.1: For a specified voting setting and voting rule, a core point is one that cannot be defeated by any other option. The core is the set of core points.

Figure 19b illustrates the spirit of a core point with a single issue and three ideal points placed on the line. To design a proposal that, seemingly, will withstand pressures of successful counterproposals, a reasonable choice appears to be near the middle of the extremes, such as proposal A in the figure. This proposal is easily beaten by proposal B: B is supported by the majority of $\{1, 3\}$; only voter 2 supports A. Indeed, it takes only slight experimentation to discover that no other proposal can beat B. In doing so, notice that the process of starting anywhere on the line and then continually introducing successful counterproposals, and counter-counterproposals, and so on requires the dynamic to approach the core. In terms of dynamics, the core is an *attractor*.

With majority voting, then, the key concept is not the midpoint or mean; it is the median point, which in Figure 19b is defined by voter 3's ideal point. The reason is clear; by locating a proposal at a median, the voter associated with this point combined with all voters on either side always have at least half of the votes. A nonmedian location does not have this politically attractive power. Indeed, the median voter theorem is often cited to explain, for instance, the tendency of the major political parties to move to the center. The argument is obvious, as a candidate who wants to be in the core must be associated with the voters' median view.[10]

To connect this structure with the Figure 19b arguments, draw circles with centers located at the voters' ideal points. If the common point through which all circles pass – the proposal – is not at the median voter point, then at least two of the circles have an open intersection. Whenever an open set can be constructed, a majority can successfully propose an alternative. Only at the median voter's ideal point do the circles meet without intersecting. (Voter 3's circle is a point.) In such settings, the Figure 19a construction, creating a Condorcet triplet, is not possible.

This extends to any number of voters with a single issue; again, a core point is a median point of the ideal points. As is true in statistics, the structure of the median with an odd and even number of voters differs. For four voters (as in Figure 20a), all points between the two middle voters' ideal points are core points. By definition, core points cannot beat each other, so any two points in this core lead to a tie. This comment illustrates the important feature that even though a core point cannot be *defeated*, it need not be a winner.

To connect this discussion with that of Chapter 4, the existence of a core makes it is impossible to create a Condorcet triplet. Conversely, if the core is empty, then a Condorcet triplet, or worse, exists. These

---

[10] *Successful* candidates want to be so associated; extreme candidates with no intention of winning have other agendas such as appealing to their group. With a chance for success, this can change. Flushed with the 2002 success and with the advice of his daughter and campaign manager Marine Le Pen, the 2007 version of Jean-Marie Le Pen's party tried hard to appear more palatable. As the election 2007 results proved, he was not successful.

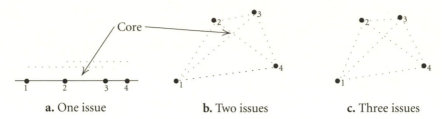

| **a.** One issue | **b.** Two issues | **c.** Three issues |

Figure 20. Core versus Dimensions.

statements hold in general, but to see why a Condorcet triplet does not exist with three voters and a single issue, put three proposals A, B, and C anywhere on the line and compute each voter's preferences according to the distances from the voter's ideal points. As some proposal (the one in the middle) never is bottom-ranked, some rankings are not admitted. The missing rankings include the Condorcet triplets (i.e., the geometry of a single issue restricts the admissible preference rankings).

Core versus Number of Issues

The core, then, is intimately related to the earlier discussions about the Condorcet triplets and circles. An interesting feature is how the existence and structure of a core depends on the number of issues.

To see this feature with four voters, all majority coalitions consist of three or four voters. For any coalition of three voters, draw lines connecting their ideal points; this enclosed convex region is the *coalition's Pareto set*. In Figure 20a, the Pareto set for coalition {1, 2, 3} is the line connecting the ideal points for 1 and 3 as indicated by the first dotted line above the issue line. In Figure 20b, the {1, 2, 3} Pareto set is one of the dotted triangles.

The *coalition Pareto set* term arises because moving any point in this region to help one voter will hurt another coalition voter. Consequently, this coalition will not coalesce around supporting different points in its Pareto set. The situation changes for any point outside of the Pareto set because there is a point in the Pareto set that is preferred by everyone in this majority vote coalition.[11] Thus, a point outside of a coalition's

[11] For a given point outside of a coalition's Pareto set, find the nearest point *in* the Pareto set. This majority coalition prefers that point.

Pareto set cannot be a core point. In particular,

a point is a core point if and only if it is in each winning coalition's Pareto set.

By using this property, it is easy to understand how and why the number of issues affects whether a core does, or does not, exist. This is because the number of issues affects the geometry of the Pareto sets. In Figure 20a, for instance, the Pareto sets for *all* winning coalitions are line segments; the geometry forces each to include voters' 2 and 3 ideal points. Because these Pareto sets must overlap, as indicated in the figure, the core is the interval between the ideal points of voters 2 and 3.

With two issues, the ideal points now reside in a two-dimensional setting as indicted in Figure 20b. In this figure, the x-coordinate for each ideal point is the same as in Figure 20a, but the second issue (the y-direction) creates a separation. The added flexibility allowed by the extra dimension makes it more difficult for all Pareto sets to intersect. Indeed, the Pareto sets for minimal winning coalitions are triangles. But one edge of any triangle must be a diagonal of the quadrilateral, and the two diagonals cross in the interior of the quadrilateral. As this intersection point is in the Pareto set for each winning coalition, it is the core point. Notice how the core dimension dropped from the previous line segment to a zero-dimensional point.

Figure 20c indicates what happens with three issues, or three dimensions. In general, the four ideal points define a tetrahedron. Each majority coalition of a triplet defines a triangular face of the tetrahedron. As all four faces cannot meet in a single point, the core is empty. So, increasing the number of issues, or dimensions, makes it increasingly more difficult for the Pareto sets of winning coalitions to have a common point, which forces an empty core. Notice how the core keeps losing dimension; in the four-voter example, it evolved from a line segment to a point to being empty.

The q-Rules

Extensions of the majority vote include the *quota*, or q-rules. This is where the winner in a pairwise comparison must receive q or more of the n votes where $q > \frac{n}{2}$. Examples are easy to find; for instance, to break a filibuster in the U.S. Senate, one needs $q = 60$ votes from the $n = 100$

senators. As one must expect, a larger quota, or q value, allows the core to persist even with more issues. The geometric reason is that by requiring more points to be in a winning coalition, the associated Pareto set is a larger dimensional object, which makes it easier for all of the winning coalitions' Pareto sets to intersect in a common point.

To illustrate this idea, for a proposal to beat another one with $q = 4$, $n = 5$, it needs four or five votes. With one issue, the core exists; it consists of all points between the second and fourth located ideal points on the line. For two issues, each winning coalition's Pareto set is a quadrilateral; it is easy to see that, in general, these two-dimensional objects have a nonzero intersection to ensure that a core exists. The general situation with three issues is that the Pareto sets for the winning coalitions are tetrahedrons; again they tend to intersect to define a nonempty core. By venturing into four dimensions, however, the Pareto sets are three-dimensional faces of the four-dimensional object defined by all five ideal points. In general, all faces of this object do not intersect, so the core need not exist. Geometry, in other words, imposes a close relationship among the number of issues, when a q-rule core exists in general, and the structure of the core.

5.2.3 McKelvey's Chaos Theorem

Without a core, Condorcet cycles create the difficulties associated with proposals and counterproposals. It is worth questioning how wild the choices can be. This question was raised and answered by Richard McKelvey.[12]

Theorem 5.1 (McKelvey [34]): Suppose there are no restrictions on what proposals can be made in a spatial voting, majority vote setting. Suppose the voters' ideal points are such that a core does not exist. By specifying

---

[12] As comments about him in this chapter make clear, Richard McKelvey (1944–2002) was a superb mathematical political scientist. He received his Ph.D. from the Center of Mathematical Political Science, developed by William Riker, at the University of Rochester. In part due to McKelvey and Plott, the California Institute of Technology became an international center of mathematical political science excellence.

any two points, an initial x_i and final x_f, there exists an agenda, $x_1, x_2, \ldots, x_N$ so that $x_1 = x_i$, $x_N = x_f$, and x_{j+1} will beat x_j, $j = 1, \ldots, N - 1$, with a majority vote.

Stated in English, if a core does not exist, it is possible to start anywhere and, with carefully designed choices of proposals and counterproposals, end up via the majority vote at any other specified location. Imagine the opportunities this result promises for a clever person to get whatever he or she wants; if stories are to be believed, this has been done.[13] This kind of impressive, depressing conclusion is what experts really enjoy in this area!

Among many other results, my former graduate student, Maria Tataru, extended McKelvey's result from the majority vote to any q-rule.

Theorem 5.2 (Tataru [116, 117]): Suppose there are no restrictions on what proposals can be made in a spatial voting, q-rule setting. Suppose the voters' ideal points are such that a core does not exist. By specifying any two points, an initial x_i and final x_f, there exists an agenda, $x_1, x_2, \ldots, x_N$ so that $x_1 = x_i$, $x_N = x_f$, and x_{j+1} will beat x_j, $j = 1, \ldots, N - 1$, with a q-rule vote.

The common message emerging from McKelvey's and Tataru's theorems is that when a core does not exist, we end up with a potentially chaotic decision situation where anything can happen. Consider what this means; beyond any conniving, even well-intended, sincere individuals could secure a conclusion that nobody really likes by making continual improvements – such behavior resembles the continual improvements that characterized the election of Fred. (See Section 4.1.7.) No wonder these results are known as the chaos theorems. Diane Richards [52], a mathematical political scientist, nicely connected voting chaos results and dynamical chaos.

The McKelvey and Tataru results raise two natural issues: When does the core exist? and What can be done to introduce some stability into the situation? These are the last two issues described in this chapter.

---

[13] In fact, it is not difficult to accomplish.

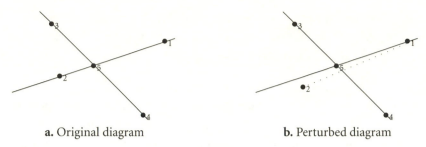

a. Original diagram   **b.** Perturbed diagram

Figure 21. Plott diagram.

5.3 Generic Stability of the Core

This description shows that, in general, a close relationship exists among the choice of a q-rule, the number of issues, and the existence of a core. But notice my cautionary "in general." This is because Charles Plott[14] showed for any number of voters and issues that ideal points can be positioned so that a core exists!

As is true with many nice ideas, after the fact, Plott's approach is simple. Start with points along a line; here the core exists for all q-rules. With an odd number of voters, the median voter's ideal point is the majority vote core. Pair off all other ideal points with one ideal point to the left of the median voter and the other to the right. Next, rotate the line connecting each pair about the median voter. The Figure 21a Plott diagram results whereby the median voter is, again, at the core. Now, with an even number of voters, the majority vote core is an interval; select any point in the interior of this interval and carry out the same construction; the pivot point will be a core point. If a point is a core point for the majority vote, it is, of course, a core point for all q-rules, $q > \frac{n}{2}$.

Plott's configurations identify an important property; the core can be highly fragile in that small, arbitrary changes in the location of any ideal point can cause the core to disappear, which puts the chaos theorems into play. This is illustrated in Figure 21b where voter 2's ideal point slipped downward a bit from its Figure 21a location. With the majority

[14] Plott, a mathematical economist at the California Institute of Technology, has made many valued contributions to social choice and voting. However, he and Vernon Smith may be better known as the founders of the important area of experimental economics.

vote, the core now disappears. This is because the Pareto sets for {1, 2, 4} and {1, 3, 5} meet only at voter 1's ideal point; this point will be the core if it exists. But this ideal point is not in the Pareto set for {2, 3, 5}.[15]

Such fragility is problematic for models in the social sciences. After all, it is debatable whether anyone has a precise and highly accurate sense of their own preferences. As such, desired results in the social sciences are those that are robust in the sense that lessons learned from a particular choice of preferences remain valid even after the preferences are slightly modified. As we have learned from Plott's diagram, the existence of the core can require unrealistic precision in locating each ideal point. The natural question, which appears to have been raised by McKelvey, is to determine when the core is "structurally stable" in the sense that if a core exists, the core continues to exist after slight, arbitrary changes in any voter's preferences. Namely, when is the core "robust"?

Most notable among articles addressing these questions were clever papers by McKelvey [35] and McKelvey and Schofield [36][16] where they used something called "singularity theory." Unfortunately,[17] Jeff Banks [4], a former student of McKelvey, discovered that these papers were incorrect.

At the 1994 Society of Social Choice and Welfare meeting in Rochester, NY, Banks told me about the problem. Perhaps because of my indirect involvement (see footnote 17), or maybe it was the challenge of the problem, but I started searching for a correct statement and proof. In doing so, I included q-rules and replaced circles and spheres with more general, smooth utility functions. After stating my result, which follows and which relates q, n, and k (the dimension of issue space), I will describe in more intuitive terms what it means. In this description, generic means that if the core exists, it continues to exist, in general, after preference functions and locations of ideal points are slightly modified in

---

[15] For a $q = 4$ rule, voter 5's ideal point remains a core point.
[16] Norm Schofield, a mathematical economist at Washington University, is a prolific contributor with many deep contributions to several different areas including social choice.
[17] The word "unfortunately" reflects the fact that these are insightful papers. More personally, in a conversation with Carl Simon about a year after these papers appeared, we discovered that we were the referees; neither of us discovered the subtle error. We were the referees because of our earlier work [92] using singularity theory in economics.

the Whitney topology on function space. (It is not necessary to describe the topology here; however, the interested reader can find a description in Saari and Simon [92] or Golubitsky and Guillemin [21].)

Theorem 5.3 (Saari [79]): For a q-rule, a core point located at a voter's ideal point exists generically if and only if

$$k \leq 2q - n \qquad (5.2)$$

Core points that are not ideal points exist, generically, for $k \leq 2$ when $q = 3$ and $n = 4$. If $n \geq 5$ and $4q < 3n + 1$, then these kinds of core points exist generically if and only if

$$k \leq 2q - n - 1 \qquad (5.3)$$

For supermajorities in which $4q \geq 3n + 1$, let α be the largest odd integer such that

$$\frac{q}{n} > \frac{\alpha}{1 + \alpha} \qquad (5.4)$$

Core points that are not ideal points can exist generically if and only if

$$k \leq 2q - n - 1 + \frac{\alpha - 1}{2} \qquad (5.5)$$

For any k and n, there exists a q-rule where core points exist generically. In particular, the unanimity rule $q = n$ has a core in all dimensions.

That's quite a mouthful! To make sense out of this, notice that the extra $\frac{\alpha-1}{2}$ dimensions in Equation 5.5 are associated with supermajorities. In part, this bonus reflects the added flexibility offered by replacing the rigidity of circles and spheres with general utility functions. To appreciate what else it means, the extreme supermajority setting is to decide by unanimity, so $q = n$. While a core exists for this rule with any number of issues, this freedom for the value of k is not captured by Equation 5.2 or 5.3; however, it is captured with Equation 5.5. This is because with $q = n$, *all* positive odd integers satisfy Equation 5.4, so the constraint for an unanimous vote specified by Equation 5.5 has no upper limit.

For further intuition, concentrate on the ideal point setting in Equation 5.2. To use an example with simple numbers, suppose $n = 100$ cardinals are locked in a room trying to elect a new pope, where, as victory requires $q = 67$, Equation 5.4 is not satisfied. Equation 5.2 asserts that a core will be stable when the core agrees with an ideal point if the considerations do not involve more than $2q - n = 2(67) - 100 = 34$ issues. To describe this upper bound on the number of issues in a more intuitive manner, notice that the minimum victory for winning side is 67 votes; the losing side has $100 - 67 = 33$ votes. For the losing side to become victorious, it needs to persuade $67 - 33 = 34$ of the cardinals in the winning coalition to change sides. Namely, a core that is a voter's ideal point can be expected to be stable with slight changes in preferences up to 34 issues. More generally,

the $2q - n$ value of Equation 5.2 is the number of voters that must change from the winning side to make the losing side victorious; issue space can have up to one issue for each changeable voter.

All of this holds when a core point is some voter's ideal point. When the core is not an ideal point, Equation 5.3 applies, which reduces by one the number of issues preserving the stability of a core. This bound on the size of issue space captures an interesting difference between a majority vote with an even or odd number of voters; with an odd number of voters, a single person can change outcome, so, in general, a core is generically stable only for a single dimension. For an even number of voters, it takes two voters to switch sides to change the outcome. Consequently, the core remains stable up to and including two issues, *but*, and this is an important "but," for $n > 4$, the core is stable for two issues only if some voter's ideal point is the core point. If not, then Equation 5.3 applies, which drops the stability of a core back to a single issue![18]

5.4 More about Cycles and Chaos

In this penultimate section, I will introduce machinery to create a deeper intuition about the Chapter 4 results concerning pairwise voting. As we learned in Section 4.1.6, all responsibility for the problems associated with pairwise voting results can be attributed to the Condorcet n-tuples.

---

[18] As an example using the U.S. Senate, let $n = 100$, so $q = 51$. Equation 5.3 asserts that the stability can be expected for k issues where $k \leq 2q - n - 1 = 102 - 100 - 1 = 1$.

5.4.1 Condorcet n-Cycles

As the Condorcet n-tuples are to blame, it should identify all spatial voting settings where these troubling outcomes can, or cannot, arise. My concern differs from McKelvey's; his result essentially creates n-candidate cycles with repeated use of Condorcet triplets over different subsets of candidates, so the tallies need not be extreme. As we will discover, the dimension of issue space, not the number of alternatives, determines whether various Condorcet n-tuples can be constructed with extreme pairwise votes.

Answers are suggested in discussion in Section 5.2.2 noting that the restricted dimensionality of a single issue limits what profiles can be constructed (i.e., Condorcet triplets never occur in a one-issue space). As an extension, maybe a Condorcet five-cycle could never be constructed in a two- or three-dimensional space. To address this issue, I will use the Theorem 5.3 results about q-rule cores.

To see why q-rules are involved, notice that a Condorcet n-tuple creates an n-candidate pairwise cycle with $n - 1 : 1$ victories. Pairs in a primary Condorcet five-cycle, then, enjoy $4 : 1$ victories. Thus, with this profile and its pairwise victory margins, the cycle persists even when using the supermajority vote of $q = 4$ with $n = 5$.

This example captures the basic idea. By combining the tallies for a Condorcet n-cycle with the stability assertions of Theorem 5.3, we can find bounds on the dimensions of issue space in which a Condorcet n-cycle can, or cannot, be constructed.

Theorem 5.4:   With at least n voters, it is impossible to construct a Condorcet n-cycle with the voters' preferences (given by Euclidean distances) in a $(k \leq n - 3)$-dimensional issue space. If the ideal points are positioned so that a voter's ideal point is a core point, then it is impossible to place n propositions in a $(k \leq n - 2)$-dimensional issue space to create a Condorcet n-cycle.

The idea of the proof is immediate; using arguments similar to those associated with Figure 19a, one can show that when, say, a Condorcet six-cycle is possible, core points are not structurally stable. As a Condorcet six-cycle has 5 : 1 tallies in the primary cycle, the profile would create a q-rule cycle with $q = 5$, $n = 6$. To avoid the instability of this q-rule, Equation 5.3 asserts that the issue space dimension must satisfy

$$k \leq 2q - n - 1 = 2(5) - 6 - 1 = 3$$

The general argument is much the same.

If the ideal points are positioned so that an ideal point is a core point, then Equation 5.2 is the relevant expression, which admits an extra dimension. In general, then, adding dimensions imposes a curse on the stability and orderliness of voting.

5.4.2 Controlling Chaos

Much more can be done. As an example, notice that even when cycles are possible, it may be possible to find ways to deter them. For instance, with carefully planned intervention, it is possible to control the "chaos theorem" damage. A way to do so is by controlling the agenda.

This approach of trying to control the agenda in terms of making appropriate counter-counterproposals to counterproposals is easier to envision with spatial voting. Wuffle et al. [118][19] developed what they call a "finagle point" that nicely captures this sense of control. In general, however, their construction appears to be limited to three voters and the majority vote with two issues.

With my graduate student Garrett Asay, I developed a more general approach that holds for any number of issues, any number of voters, and any q-rule. The idea is to stake out a position that minimizes what is needed to successfully respond to any counterproposal. This point, which I call the *finesse point* (Saari [83], Saari and Asay [84]), generalizes the concept of a core in that rather than avoiding being beaten (the definition of a core point), the point minimizes what it takes to avoid being beaten.

---

[19] Bernie Grofman, from the University of California at Irvine, has made many contributions to political science. Indeed, he has published so much that he needed to invent the lead author, Wuffle, to assume some of the burden. Scott Feld is a mathematical sociologist at Purdue University. Guillermo Owen, now at the Naval Postgraduate School, is well known for his many contributions to game theory.

In a very real sense, this finesse point is intended as a response to the McKelvey and Tataru chaos theorems; it is intended to provide control. However, as is true of almost all topics in this area, these efforts are preliminary; much more must be done.

5.5 Final Comments

I hope I kept my promise to describe some good news about social choice. I also hope to have conveyed my attitude about the direction that future research should take in this area.

In my opinion, those negative social choice results that are consistently being discovered – results that are essentially guaranteed by the dimensionality curse – should be treated only as first steps toward identifying reasonable starting points for more extensive research investigations; *never* accept them as final conclusions. After all, for a field to prosper and expand, it must offer something of value, a sense of guidance, for others.

To expand on this comment, recall that social choice enjoys an enviable position. After all, most disciplines and societal issues involve allocations or decisions based on aggregating potentially conflicting inputs – precisely the kind of questions we examine. By adopting a broader view of social choice, we can see that this area offers unexplored opportunities to help shape what happens in other disciplines. To be useful and attract the interest of others, however, contributions usually must be positive. To explain, positive breakthroughs in medicine interest many of us; negative reports describing impossibilities and failed approaches interest only specialized experts.

This desire to find the positive is the unifying theme of Chapter 2. I treat negative results as identifying what can go wrong; the challenge is to find what can go right. This is why in Chapter 2 my descriptions of selective major negative social choice conclusions, which previously have been viewed as unassailable barriers for progress, and some lesser known voting obstacles are not treated as beautiful (they are!) *final* statements, but as starting points in a search for positive conclusions. In each case, rather than immediately seeking positive results, the crucial step was to first understand *why* the negative assertion occurred. A reason is that "immediate solutions" tend to address details; they solve one problem but can disguise or even create others. More lasting solutions require an understanding of how the various concepts interact. This comment sounds nice, but the pragmatic issue is *what* concepts and *how* can they be found?

In searching for the root causes of a negative statement, my personal technique is, initially, to ignore details to explore how assumptions interact with one another. To do so, I tell stories describing the problem to *anyone* not in the field and willing to listen – or unable to politely escape. As my initial attempts almost always are clumsy and ill-formed, my patient and forgiving wife tends to be my first victim. Examples of such stories are scattered throughout this book (e.g., selecting a CD featuring Sibelius as a way to understand the source of Arrow's result). My approach is based on the reality that technical details seldom permit a story to be told, but concepts transcend disciplines so they usually do. Forcing myself to create an adequate story helps me to eventually discover appropriate concepts.

By understanding what conceptual issues cause a conclusion, I can frequently find positive alternatives. In other cases, I have been able to identify compelling reasons to avoid such rules. A consistent, unexpected theme in Chapter 2 is how innocent-sounding assumptions can inadvertently force a rule to ignore valued, explicitly intended information. It is surprising how many concerns can be resolved by applying this simple principle: Much more needs to be done, and I invite you to do so.

William Riker joins Arrow and Sen as a giant in this research area. Somewhere in his classic *Liberalism against Populism* [53] is a statement that the choice of a positional rule is subjective. His comment is not negative, but it should attract the attention of anyone wanting to make positive contributions to the area. After all, his comment indicates that when he made it, we did not know enough about the properties of positional methods and their relationships to select one rule over another. This comment offers a research agenda: Find appropriate properties and relationships to eliminate subjectivity in selecting a rule. This theme unites Chapters 3 and 4.

Finding properties and relationships for positional rules is the objective of Chapter 3. You probably join me in being shocked by the astronomical numbers and enormous variety! This complexity required developing the chaotic dynamic and other approaches to find them. As an optimist who views most water glasses – even with a quarter content – as partially full, you can easily appreciate how even though I was proud of my dictionary results, I was overwhelmed and discouraged by their implications. The dictionaries significantly simplify doing what researchers want to accomplish, but they also reveal that the problems are magnitudes upon magnitudes worse than previously anticipated. The situation is so bad that even gee-whiz comments fail to accurately convey the dire situation. After all, try to adequately describe the problems beyond comparing them (Section 3.4) to a billion times the number of droplets of water in all of the oceans of the world! With so many things going wrong, how can positive conclusions be discovered?

To find them, my approach, again, was to first investigate *why* negative conclusions occur. I started by telling stories about three alternatives [70] to discover how to tame that dimensionality curse lurking in distant corners of the domain. What emerged was my cup-of-coffee approach, which is to discover the domain structures that are associated with specified voting rules. If you reread Chapter 4, you will recognize that my "profile coordinate system" describes level sets for classes of positional rules. A clue is that reversal terms never affect pairwise rankings, so they are in the level sets for pairwise rankings. Similarly, Condorcet terms never affect positional outcomes, so they help fill level sets for positional outcome. Finding level sets is a valued way to extract hidden domain structures (see Saari [67]); others might wish to use this approach to examine other classes of decision rules. Try it; it works!

Beyond seeking good news for the area of social choice while offering a selective exposition of some of my results, I wanted to express the notions in a way to encourage others to join in the fun inherent in this area. For instance, consistent with my belief that in an exposition concepts are more important than technical details, throughout the book I emphasized key ideas while leaving specifics to the references. Let me remind the reader that this is a subject area where contributions might make a big difference: Important contributions reflecting a variety of backgrounds and talents have been and will be made by researchers. Even though this area increasingly uses the muscle power of mathematics, a clever person with a willingness to question can be expected to discover new and important results. Join us!

This area also is in desperate need of expertise to publicize the need to reform our voting rules. If this is not done, then hard-earned results may collect dust in libraries rather than influencing how decisions are made. In blunt words, by not publicizing what can go wrong, by not informing the general public how to avoid these problems, expect to experience societal consequences that are significant and serious.

To conclude in the way that I started this book in the Preface, *I warmly invite students and researchers to join this area, to help us better understand what is going on and what needs to be done!*

SIX

Appendix
Extending the Upset Child Example

An anonymous reviewer of this book accurately suspected that more was involved with the topological decision issues introduced in Section 2.1.3. To indicate other concepts (with the same assumptions), in this appendix I outline key ideas that Jason Kronewetter and I developed for [24]. As one must expect, this discussion emphasizes the connecting themes of the book – the structure of the domain and the dimensionality curse.

In introducing alternative ways to think about group decisions on domains with holes, I hope to interest others in exploring these new, fairly simple nontopological arguments. My comments start, as in Section 2.1.3, with choice problems on a circle. The motivating story was to select a beach location on an island: However, applications arise in any number of disciplines. After all, a point on a circle defines a direction, so this discussion applies to any topic where a selected direction is based on information from two or more other directions.

Consider this illustration: A current psychology project with Louis Narens involves a colored disk placed in the center of a surrounding colored background. It is well known that the perceived color of the disk in this "center-surround" framework depends on the colors of the disk and the surrounding background. A color's hue can be described as a particular point on a color circle, so understanding the behavior of the perceived color reduces to finding properties of the "perception mapping"

$$F : S^1 \times S^1 \to S^1$$

For instance, when the color of the center and surround are the same, that is the perceived color, so the unanimity condition is satisfied. Thus, whenever both continuity and Pareto are natural assumptions, one color must be more "effective" than the other in selecting the perceived color.

Related topics most surely occur in engineering. Also, this "direction" perspective makes it easy to relate these issues to Arrow's theorem. Indeed, Chichilnisky studied the properties of a group utility function based on the agents' utility functions. A level set of the utility function at a particular point can be characterized by its tangent plane or, more efficiently, by its gradient. Actually, the only information needed about the gradient is its direction, which is orthogonal to the tangent plane. By being a direction, it defines a point on a circle (or sphere in higher dimensions). Thus, a key step in her analysis was to understand how individual gradient directions define the societal gradient direction, or to find the properties of

$$F : S^1 \times \cdots \times S^1 \to S^1$$

This is the structure of the beach problem. What captures the spirit of Arrow's result is that any such function F must have a specified agent that is more effective than others.

6.1 Source of the Problem

An alternative way to describe what causes the Section 2.1.3 problems is that a circle, as well as many other geometric constructions, admit situations where the Pareto set is not uniquely defined. Recall, to avoid unreasonable outcomes, that the societal choice is required to be in the Pareto set.

The Pareto set was defined in Section 2.1.3 as the shortest arc on the circle that connects the two agents' points. This set usually is uniquely defined; problems arise when uniqueness fails. For the two-agent circle problem, this setting occurs if and only if the two pointsare diametrically

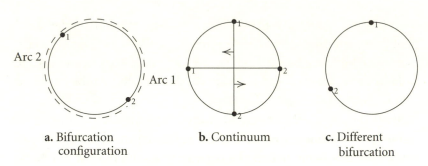

a. Bifurcation   **b.** Continuum   **c.** Different
   configuration   bifurcation

Figure 22. Circles and Pareto sets.

opposite; here the two choices for the Pareto set agree only on the agents'
preferred points.

As illustrated in Figure 22a, this Pareto set could be arc 1, which goes
in a clockwise direction from the first agent's choice to the second, or
arc 2, which goes in a counterclockwise direction. Treat a configuration
of diametrically opposite points, where the competing candidate Pareto
sets have disjoint interiors, as defining a *bifurcation*. In this transition
situation, slight changes in the agents' choices cause the Pareto set to
jump into either a slight modification of either arc 1 or arc 2. Important
for our purposes is that the modified choices are disjoint.

Step 1 is to determine the bifurcation configurations and their assigned societal outcomes. Notice that the outcome can be in either of
the two different candidate Pareto sets, which agree only at the agents'
points. With a little thought, it becomes clear that the choice must be in
the intersection of these two sets. As this intersection consists of only the
agents' preferred locations, *the societal outcome at a bifurcation configuration must coincide with the choice of one of the agents.* (If restrictions other
than Pareto sets are imposed on the outcomes, the outcome assigned to
bifurcation configurations can be different.)

To provide intuition for this assertion, compare this problem with
being at a train station knowing only that your train is either the one
to the immediate left or the one to the immediate right; the correct
one will leave in a minute. If you are inside the wrong train, it will
be impossible to change in time – without risking a dangerous jump.
Thus, the appropriate stance is to stand at a juncture point between
them so that it will be possible to board the train (or Pareto set) that

moves first. The same argument holds for selecting the societal outcome at a bifurcation configuration; just replace the two candidate trains
with the two candidate Pareto sets. Suppose the societal outcome is inside of one of the two arcs, say, the interior of arc 1. Slightly changing
the agents' points in appropriate directions causes the new and *unique*
Pareto set to be a replica of arc 2, which forces the societal outcome to
jump from the interior of arc 1 to the replica of arc 2. As it is easy to
show that this jump violates the continuity assumption, at a bifurcation configuration the societal outcome must coincide with some agent's
point.

Step 2 is to determine the structure of the set of bifurcation configurations. In our setting, it forms a continuum. Namely, it is possible to
move continuously from any bifurcation configuration to any other one
while remaining within the set of bifurcation configurations. I'll explain
why with an example. One Figure 22b bifurcation configuration is on
the vertical line; here agents 1 and 2 have their points, respectively, at the
circle's north and south poles. A second choice is where they are on the
horizontal line; one on the east and the other on the west. To move from
one setting to the other, just rotate the diameter line – the endpoints
always are bifurcation configurations – in the manner indicated by the
arrows.

This argument means that the set of bifurcation configurations has
a single path-connected component. Combining this feature with the
continuity of the choice function leads to the conclusion that *at all bifurcation points, the societal outcome must always agree with the same agent's
point.* (The bifurcation points are diametrically opposite, so changing
the choice to that of the other agent would violate the continuity of *F*.)
Thus,

on the set of bifurcation configurations, one of the agents serves as the dictator!

This agent turns out to be the effective agent.

As developed in Chapter 2, the dictator on bifurcation configurations
need not be dictatorial over the full space because what happens off the
set of bifurcation points can be selected in many ways while preserving
the continuity of *F*. To illustrate this feature, we designed our upset child
example to be as extreme as possible – *each* agent is a "dictator" on a

different domain where the domains are then pieced together to satisfy the continuity of F. Namely, the child is the dictator on the bifurcation configurations, and the mother is the dictator on a significantly larger region that is slightly separated from the set of bifurcation configurations.

6.2 Generalizations

Before describing how to extract other information, notice that the crucial feature is *not* the circle; it is the structure of the bifurcation configurations as determined by the associated Pareto sets, or by whatever structure governs the location of outcomes. Whenever ambiguity is introduced through bifurcation points – by introducing competing sets for the admissible outcomes – anticipate a dictatorial flavor for the decision mapping over each component of the bifurcation points.

On the circle, these bifurcation configurations need not be diametrically opposite; any choice will work as long as points exist where suddenly the choice of the regions governing the location of the societal outcome jumps between disjoint options. For instance, replace the "shortest arc" definition of the Pareto set with a "shortest arc" description where the distance from agent 1's point to agent 2's in a clockwise direction is defined by the actual distance, but in the counterclockwise direction, the value is twice the actual distance. This choice changes the location of the bifurcation configurations from the $180°-180°$ diametrically opposite configuration to the $120°-240°$ configuration illustrated in Figure 22c. The definition of the Pareto set changed, but the conclusion remains.

By playing with definitions of the regions of admissible outcomes (using domains with different geometric shapes and maybe more agents), it is not overly difficult to create examples where the bifurcation configurations has two (or more) disjoint components, so each agent can be dictatorial over one component. A trivial example is to have two different islands where each agent is dictatorial over the bifurcation components on a different island. (As indicated in the following discussion, when a bifurcation configuration involves multiple choices for Pareto sets, other features may arise.)

The conclusion that F is dictatorial over a component of the bifurcation points extends to other "holey domains" such as spheres of any

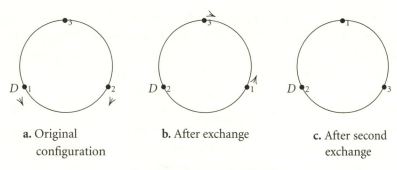

a. Original   **b.** After exchange   **c.** After second
configuration   exchange

Figure 23. Exchange problem.

dimension (where, again, the arguments center about the definition of the Pareto set), products of spheres, or the like. A sense of when bifurcation points exist comes from the Section 2.4.3 solution for this problem. If the described domain cannot be covered with a single chart, expect bifurcation configurations.

These conclusions hold for other issues, such as location problems made more complicated because the outcome can be on an arc going around one side, or the other, of a lake, or mountain, or any other obstacle. Rather than just two candidate Pareto sets at a bifurcation configuration, there can be many of them (e.g., many paths go north around a lake, and many others go south around it). The analytic trick is to collapse all the north choices into one category and the south ones into another.

The "collapse" term suggests the story that I used to describe what it means for a function to be homotopic to a dictator. Indeed, Kronewetter and I used this homotopy "collapsing" approach in [24] to collapse all of these arcs into two "classes" of Pareto sets at bifurcation configurations.

All of this extends to any finite number of agents; key to the analysis is the definition of the Pareto set. On the circle, the natural choice is the shortest arc that contains all of the agents' points. Again, the first step is to find all bifurcation configurations and the associated societal outcomes. Here, the new bifurcation configurations, as illustrated in Figure 23a, are where the agents' points define an equilateral or isosceles triangle.[1]

---

[1] One kind of n-agent bifurcation configuration on a circle is whenever the points are symmetric with respect to some diagonal. Namely, twisting about the diagonal puts

The societal outcomes at these configurations are determined by the intersections of the candidate Pareto sets. The candidate Pareto sets for the equilateral (three-set) and diagonal (two-set) configurations intersect only at the agents' points, so the earlier "train" argument proves that the societal outcome for these configurations must agree with one agent's point. With an isosceles triangle configuration, however, the intersection of the two candidate Pareto sets consists of the center vertex (the one without an equal angle) and the arc connecting the two other vertices; here the outcome can be the center vertex, or *any point in the arc*. As this arc permits freedom in the definition of F, dictatorial assertions on bifurcation configurations refer only to the equilateral triangle, diagonal, and center vertex of isosceles triangle configurations.

Step 2 determines the structure of the bifurcation configurations. To establish that the three-agent bifurcation choices have a single path-connected component, notice that isosceles triangles vary from the extremes of an equilateral triangle to where the positions are diametrically opposite. Combined with rotations, it now is easy to show that one can move through these configurations between any two choices. However, even though these configurations have a single component, an extra argument is needed to prove there is a unique dictator on the set of bifurcation configurations. To explain, the continuity of F ensured a single dictator over the two-agent bifurcation configurations because the configurations separated the agents' points. This structure, however, does not always hold with three or more agents.

The problem is to exclude the possibility of shifting the title of "dictator on bifurcation configurations" between agents along the arc of the isosceles configurations or at a diametrically opposite configuration where the dictator shares a point with another agent. What prevents this exchange is (1) that at an equilateral configuration, the outcome coincides with one agent's point, a choice that remains fixed with all rotations of this configuration, and (2) that all equilateral configurations can be continuously changed into each other through bifurcation configurations, which is the assertion that there is a single path-connected component of bifurcation configurations.

the points that were on the left-hand side on top of where the points were on the right-hand side.

To illustrate this argument, in Figure 23a, D indicates that agent 1 is the dictator at that bifurcation setting. For any rotation of this configuration, continuity requires the societal outcome to remain at agent 1's point. To demonstrate why an exchange is not possible, assume that it is. If agent 2 is a dictator on the sole point of a diagonal configuration or at the central vertex of an isosceles triangle configuration, by opening up either configuration while maintaining an isosceles triangle, it follows that the agent is a dictator on an equilateral configuration. This configuration must be a rotated version of Figure 23b where agent 1's point is the first one in the counterclockwise direction; otherwise, the configuration, such as Figure 23c, is a rotated form of 23a, where agent 1 must be the dictator.

To create a Figure 23b setting without violating the continuity of F, first collapse the Figure 23a configuration to where agents 1 and 2 are diametrically opposite agent 3. Do so via isosceles bifurcation configurations, which require the outcomes to remain in the arc between the points for agents 1 and 2.[2] Along the arc or at the diametrically opposite configuration (not shown), assume that an exchange is permitted; that is, let the societal outcome coincide with agent 2's choice; this can be done without violating the continuity of F. Keep separating these two points with isosceles triangle bifurcation configurations until reaching the equilateral configuration of Figure 23b. The D indicates that, due to the exchange, the outcome at this bifurcation configuration coincides with agent 2's point.

To create a contradiction, hold the point for agent 2 fixed and collapse the points for agents 1 and 3 in the directions indicated by the Figure 23b arrows, via isosceles bifurcation configurations. The outcome at these configurations always coincides with the point for agent 2. Once the diametrically opposite setting is achieved, keep moving the points for agents 1 and 2 in the same directions to create the Figure 23c configuration. As the D indicates, the point for agent 2 must continue to determine the societal outcome.

---

[2] The "train" argument applied to an isosceles configuration shows that the outcome is on the arc. After all, a slight change of the center vertex destroys the isosceles triangle and creates a unique Pareto set; if the outcome is not in the arc, continuity of F can be violated.

The desired contradiction arises because Figures 23a and 23c differ only by a rotation, so the societal outcomes must agree with the same agent's point. As they disagree, an exchange at diametrically opposite points is not permitted. Thus, the same agent is dictatorial over the component of bifurcation configurations (i.e., at the equilateral triangle or diagonal or when continuously connected to the center vertex of an isosceles triangle configuration). A similar analysis holds for all choices of n where equilateral triangles are replaced with equilateral n-gons and diagonal configurations, where points are on top of others, are supplemented with equilateral k-gons, $2 \le k < n$.

Notice how this argument relies on the higher dimensionality of the domain. These dimensions introduce different avenues to approach any bifurcation configuration, such as that in Figure 23c. As the continuity of F must be preserved at the Figure 23c point no matter how it is approached, the preceding argument establishing different routes to Figure 23c shows that a single dictator presides over the specified bifurcation configurations.

This construction indicates how to create an extreme three-agent setting where each agent is dictatorial over different regions. One choice extends the upset child example by using the mother, father, and child. Select the child to be the dictator over the equilateral triangle, diagonal, and center vertex of any isosceles configurations, let the father be dictatorial over most of the arc of any isosceles configurations where the mother is at the center vertex, and let the mother be dictatorial over most of the rest of the region. Again, the child is the effective agent and topological dicatator, but, in fact, he is dictatorial over the smallest region. The father is more effective than the mother, but she has the greatest overall influence in the outcome. Extreme examples involving n agents are similarly created.

6.3 Level Sets

To manage the dimensionality curse, the Chapter 2 discussion emphasized the domain structure of points with the same outcome – the choice function's level sets. In this manner, immediate explanations for classical paradoxes arose by identifying the troubling profiles with outliers in

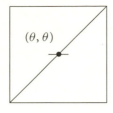

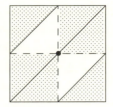

a. Segment of θ-level set   **b.** Forbidden regions

Figure 24. Geometric arguments.

particular level sets. As in Chapter 4, to understand the domain structure for this class of voting issues, emphasis was placed on level sets of positional mappings (e.g., all Condorcet configurations are in the level set of positional rules, all Reversal profiles are in the level sets of majority votes over pairs) to define a coordinate system for profile space.

In both chapters, the domain structure used to tame the dimensionality curse was determined by level sets. To see where this natural approach is used elsewhere, a dimensionality curse in statistics involves the huge mound of data, which is handled with "sufficient statistics." The values of these terms identify different "level sets" of data. Mimicking this success, it is natural to seek deeper insight into the behavior of the "beach problem mapping" by analyzing its admissible level sets. Namely, the next step is to analyze the structure of points in the domain with the same specified outcome. I indicate how to do so in the following brief description; for details and additional results, see [24] and [67].

The first issue is to identify the domain $S^1 \times S^1$. To do so, attach to each point on the first agent's circle a circle representing the second agent's choices. Moving the first agent's point around the circle forces the second agent's circle to trace out a torus, which resembles the surface of a donut.

Visualizing what happens on a torus can be difficult, so, to simplify the analysis, use the standard trick of opening up the torus to create a square. To do so, snip each circle at some point, and open it into a line segment. In doing so, remember that the ends of the segment correspond to the same point on the circle. In this way, the product of a circle with a circle can be represented as a square of dimensions 2π by 2π; in Figure 24a, the choices of agents 1 and 2 are, respectively, in the horizontal and vertical directions.

Because the square represents a torus, its top and bottom edges represent where all choices on the circle are available for agent 1, but only the same fixed value is assigned to agent 2; it is the "square's equivalent" of attaching the circle of agent 1's choices to the "snipping point" that opened agent 2's circle into a line segment. Thus, for any x, the points $(x, 0)$ and $(x, 2\pi)$ are the same. Similarly, the two vertical edges of the square represent choices for agent 2 at the same "snipping point value" for agent 1; for example, $(0, y)$ and $(2\pi, y)$ represent the same point. This equality means we could bend the square to glue the top and bottom edges, creating a cylinder. Then, gluing the vertical edges returns us to the original torus. To keep our focus on the torus, even when using its square representation, instead of using (x, y) for points in the square, I will use (θ_1, θ_2).

With this description, if agent 1 is a dictator, then the level sets of F are vertical lines; this is because agent 1's choice on the x-axis determines the outcome – the level set – that does not vary for whatever choice agent 2 makes in the vertical direction. Similarly, agent 2 is the dictator if the level sets are horizontal. Function F is homotopic to a dictator if all of its level sets can be continuously deformed into either vertical or horizontal lines. (In [67] I used this level set argument to describe Arrow's theorem.)

The unanimity assumption ensures that all outcomes are possible. So, select any point θ on the circle and find its level set $F^{-1}(\theta)$. It does not matter where the circles were snipped to create the square, so assume this cutting was done to position point (θ, θ) at the center of the square. The unanimity condition mandates that $(\theta, \theta) \in F^{-1}(\theta)$. Indeed, the unanimity line is the diagonal in Figure 24a. Because level sets cannot cross each other, each level set can pass through this diagonal line in only one point.[3]

The trick is to find where the level set *cannot* be. This forbidden region, for instance, includes all points (θ_1, θ_2) where the Pareto set they define does not include θ. For another kind of argument, the two line segments parallel to the diagonal line are given by $(\theta_1, \theta_1 + \pi)$,

---

[3] As these are the only two properties needed from the unanimity condition, it can be replaced with any conditions that ensure all image points can occur, and each level set passes once, and only once, through some continuous line that divides the square into two parts.

$0 \leq \theta_1 \leq 2\pi$. By being bifurcation configurations, the F value at these configurations must be either θ_1 or $\theta_1 + \pi$. Consequently, the $F^{-1}(\theta)$ level set cannot meet this line except possibly when $\theta_1 = \theta$ (at the top and bottom edge) or $\theta_1 = \theta \pm \pi$ and $\theta_2 = \theta$ (at the side edges). By invoking various arguments of this type, it follows that the shaded regions of Figure 24b are excluded regions. Thus, $F^{-1}(\theta)$ is restricted to the nonshaded portion of the square.

As a level set must be a closed set (point θ is a closed set, and the inverse image of a closed set with a continuous function is a closed set), $F^{-1}(\theta)$ could be a point or include a short line segment as in Figure 24a. But continuity requires that if either were the case, another level set would surround this line segment; this neighboring level set would pass through the unanimity line in more than one place, which is not permitted. Thus, $F^{-1}(\theta)$ includes a curve that passes through the unanimity line on one side and reconnects on the other. This construction requires the level set to pass through an edge of the square and emerge on the opposite edge (remember, points on one edge are identified with points on the other edge) to reconnect.

The forbidden regions depicted in Figure 24b limit how the level set can pass through an edge on the square; it must pass through either $(\theta \pm \pi, \theta)$, which is the same point but, because of the cutting, represented on the two vertical edges, or through $(\theta, \theta \pm \pi)$, which is the same point on the top and bottom edges. Both points are bifurcation configurations,[4] so the level set passing through one of them defines which agent is the dictator on the bifurcation set. For instance, if the level set passes through the horizontal edges at $(\theta, \theta \pm \pi)$, then agent 1 is the dictator on all bifurcation configurations.

Once this dictator is determined, the other point, here $(\theta \pm \pi, \theta)$ on the vertical edges, now belongs to the forbidden region, which means (by the continuity of F) that the level set must remain at least a small distance away from it. This construction mandates that there is at least a small gap between the level set and the particular edges of the square.

Even though this gap may be small, it depends on the choice of F; the fact it exists is central to all of the results. The gap, for instance, limits

---

[4] This is why the square was selected so that (θ, θ) is at the center; it places the associated bifurcation configurations on the edges.

what outcomes certain agents can impose; in other words, this limitation leads to the effective agent. (See the discussion after Theorem 2.4 for related comments and [24] for details.) Also, this gap requires the above level set to be a distorted vertical line. Because it (and the other level sets) can be deformed into a vertical line, the topological dictator is the effective agent. As the gap prevents the level sets from being distorted into horizontal lines, it follows that the other agent cannot be a topological dictator. Almost anything else is possible; indeed, the level sets for the upset child example come as close to the boundaries of the shaded regions as admissible. Because these level sets are horizontal over much of the region, the noneffective and nontopological dictator (the mother) is, in fact, the "dictator" over a much larger portion of the domain.

The conclusion requires using only the boundary of the forbidden region limiting where the level set can exit. Thus, relaxing the region of admissible outcomes in any manner so that the level set must exit only at a bifurcation configuration, $(\theta \pm \pi, \theta)$ or $(\theta \pm \pi, \theta)$, leads to the same conclusion. Also, unanimity is used only to have the separating line on which each level set meets in a unique point; unanimity can be replaced with any condition yielding a similar property.

Beyond exploring the many possible applications of these results to other disciplines, a suggestion for further study is to better understand what kinds of conditions imposed on a decision problem will determine whether there exists an agent that is more influential than effective. With the upset child example, for instance, this would entail a discussion of being able to determine in advance which agent is dictatorial over the larger domain.

References

[1] Anscombe, G. E. M., 1976, On the frustration of the majority by fulfillment of the majority's will, *Analysis* **36**, 161–68.

[2] Arrow, K., 1951 (2nd ed., 1963), *Social Choice and Individual Values*, Wiley, New York.

[3] Baigent, N., To appear, Topological theories of social choice, to appear in *Handbook of Social Choice and Welfare*, vol. 2, K. Arrow, A. Sen, and K. Suzumura, eds.

[4] Banks, J., 1995, Singularity theory and core existence in the spatial models, *Journal of Mathematical Economics* **24**, 523–36.

[5] Baker, K. M., 1975, *Condorcet: From Natural Philosophy to Social Mathematics*, University of Chicago Press, Chicago.

[6] Borda, J. C., 1781, *Mémoire sur les élections au scrutin*, Histoire de l'Académie Royale des Sciences, Paris.

[7] Black, D., 1958, *The Theory of Committees and Elections*, Cambridge University Press, London.

[8] Block, C., 1999, Truth and probability – Ironies in the evolution of social choice theory, *Washington University Law Quarterly* **76**, 975–1037.

[9] Brams, S., and P. Fishburn, 1978, *Approval Voting*, Birkhauser, Boston.

[10] Campbell, D. E., and J. S. Kelly, 1997, Sen's theorem and externalities, *Economica* **64**, 375–86.

[11] Chichilnisky, G., 1982, The topological equivalence of the Pareto conditions and the existence of a dictator, *Journal of Mathematical Economics* **9**, 223–33.

[12] Condorcet, M., 1785, *Éssai sur l'application de l'analyse à la probabilité des décisions rendues à la pluralité des voix*, Paris.

[13] Copeland, A. H., 1951, A reasonable social welfare function, University of Michigan, Mimeo.

[14] Debreu, G., 1974, Excess demand functions, *Journal of Mathematical Economics* **1**, 15–23.

[15] Duxbury, A. (6th ed., 2000), *An Introduction to the World's Oceans*, McGraw-Hill, New York.

[16] Enelow, J., and M. J. Hinich, 1990, *Advances in the Spatial Theory of Voting*, Cambridge University Press, New York.

[17] Fine, B., 1975, Individual liberalism in a Paretian society, *Journal of Political Economy* **83**, 1277–81.

[18] Fishburn, P., 1974, Paradoxes of voting, *American Political Science Review* **68**, 537–46.

[19] Fishburn, P., 1981, Inverted orders for monotone scoring rules, *Discrete Applied Mathematics* **3**, 27–36.

[20] Gehrlein, W., 2006, *Condorcet's Paradox*, Springer-Verlag, New York.

[21] Golubitsky, M., and V. Guillemin, 1973, *Stable Mappings and Their Singularities*, Springer-Verlag, New York.

[22] Haunsperger, D., 1992, Dictionaries of paradoxes for statistical tests on k samples, *Journal of the American Statistical Association* **87**, 149–55.

[23] Kemeny J., 1959, Mathematics without numbers, *Daedalus* **88**, 571–91.

[24] Kronewetter, J., and D. G. Saari, 2006, From decision problems to dethroned dictators, *Journal of Mathematical Economics*. Available online 4 August 2006.

[25] Laruelle, A., and V. Merlin, 2002, Different least square values, different rankings, *Social Choice & Welfare* **19**, 533–50.

[26] Le Breton, M., and M. Truchon, 1997, A Borda measure for social choice functions, *Mathematical Social Science* **34**, 249–72.

[27] Li, L., and D. G. Saari, 2004, Sen's theorem: Geometric proof and new interpretations, IMBS discussion papers. *Social Choice & Welfare*. (Online 1 Jan 2008.)

[28] List, C., and P. Pettit, 2002, Aggregating sets of judgments: An impossibility result, *Economics and Philosophy* **18**, 89–110.

[29] Luce, R. D., 1959, *Individual Choice Behavior*, Wiley, New York. Republished 2005, Dover Publications, Mineloa, NY.

[30] Mantel, R., 1972, On the characterization of aggregate excess demain, *Journal of Economic Theory* **7**, 348.

[31] Marcart, J., 1919, La vie et les travaux de chevalier Jean-Charles de Borda, *Annales de l'Universite de Lyon* **2**.

[32] McGann, A., 2006, *The Logic of Democracy*, Michigan Studies in Political Analysis, University of Michigan Press, Ann Arbor.

[33] McGarvey, D. C., 1953, A theorem on the construction of voting paradoxes, *Economectrica* **21** (4), 608–10.

[34] McKelvey, R., 1979, General conditions for global intransitivities in formal voting models, *Econometrica* **47**, 1085–1112.

[35] McKelvey, R., 1986, Structural instability of the core, *Journal of Mathematical Economics* **15**, 179–98.

[36] McKelvey, R., and N. Schofield, 1987, Generalized symmetry conditions at a core point, *Econometrica* **55**, 923–34.

[37] McLean, I., 2003, The reasonableness of independence: A conversation from Condorcet and Borda to Arrow and Saari, University of Oxford, Nuffield College Politics Working Paper 2003–W6.

[38] McLean, I., and A. Urken, 1995, *Classics of Social Choice*, University of Michigan Press, Ann Arbor.

[39] Merlin, V., and D. G. Saari, 1997, Copeland method II: Manipulation, monotonicity, and paradoxes, *Journal of Economic Theory* **72**, 148–72.

[40] Merlin, V., and D. G. Saari, 2000. Changes that cause changes, *Social Choice & Welfare* **17**, 691–705.

[41] Merlin, V., İ. Özkal-Sanver, and R. Sanver, 2006, Properties of majoritarian compromise, efficient compromise and related compromise rules, Presentation at the Eighth International Meeting of the Society for Social Choice and Welfare, Istanbul, July.

[42] Nanson, E. J., 1882, Methods of elections, *Transactions and Proceedings of the Royal Society of Victoria* **18**, 197–240.

[43] Nurmi, H., 1987, *Comparing Voting Systems*, D. Reidel, Dordrecht.

[44] Nurmi, H., 1999, *Voting Paradoxes and How To Deal with Them*, Springer-Verlag, New York.

[45] Nurmi, H., 2002, *Voting Procedures under Uncertainty*, Springer, Heidelberg.

[46] Pattanaik, P., 1996, On modelling individual rights: Some conceptual issues, pp. 100–28, in *Social Choices Re-examined*, K. Arrow, A. Sen, and K. Suzumura, eds., St. Martin's Press, New York.

[47] Plott, C., 1967, A notion of equilibrium and its possibility under majority rule, *American Economic Review* **57**, 787–806.

[48] Ratliff, T., 2001, A comparison of Dodgson's method and Kemeny's rule, *Social Choice & Welfare* **18**, 79–89.

[49] Ratliff, T., 2002, A comparison of Dodgson's method and the Borda count, *Economic Theory* **20**, 357–72.

[50] Ratliff, T., 2003, Some startling paradoxes when electing committees, *Social Choice & Welfare* **21**, 433–54.

[51] Ratliff, T., 2006, Selecting committees, *Public Choice* **126**, 343–55.

[52] Richards, D., 1994. Intransitivities in multidimensional spatial voting, *Social Choice & Welfare* **11** (2), 109–19.

[53] Riker, W. H., 1982, *Liberalism against Populism*, W. H. Freeman, San Francisco.

[54] Saari, D. G., 1984, The ultimate of chaos resulting from weighted voting systems, *Advances in Applied Mathematics* **5**, 286–308.

[55] Saari, D. G., 1985, Iterative price mechanisms, *Econometrica* **53**, 1117–33.

[56] Saari, D. G., 1989, A dictionary for voting paradoxes, *Journal of Economic Theory* **48**, 443–75.

[57] Saari, D. G., 1990, Susceptibility to manipulation, *Public Choice* **64**, 21–41.

[58] Saari, D. G., 1990, The Borda dictionary, *Social Choice & Welfare* **7**, 279–317.

[59] Saari, D. G., 1991, Relationship admitting families of candidates, *Social Choice & Welfare* **8**, 21–50.

[60] Saari, D. G., 1992, Symmetry extensions of "neutrality": I. Advantage to the Condorcet loser. *Social Choice & Welfare* **9**, 307–36.

[61] Saari, D. G., 1993, Symmetry extensions of "neutrality": II. Partial ordering of dictionaries, *Social Choice & Welfare* **10**, 301–34.

[62] Saari, D. G., 1992, Millions of election rankings from a single profile, *Social Choice & Welfare* **9**, 277–306.

[63] Saari, D. G., 1994, *Geometry of Voting*, Springer-Verlag, New York.

[64] Saari, D. G., 1995, *Basic Geometry of Voting*, Springer-Verlag, New York.

[65] Saari, D. G., 1995, A chaotic exploration of aggregation paradoxes, *SIAM Review* **37**, 37–52.

[66] Saari, D. G., 1996, Election relations and a partial ordering for positional voting, in N. Schofield (ed.), *Collective Decision-Making: Social Choice and Political Economy*, Kluwer.

[67] Saari, D. G., 1997, Informational geometry of social choice, *Social Choice & Welfare* **14**, 211–32.

[68] Saari, D. G., 1997, The generic existence of a core for *q*-rules, *Economic Theory* **9**, 219–60.

[69] Saari, D. G., 1998, Connecting and resolving Sen's and Arrow's theorems, *Social Choice & Welfare* **15**, 239–61.

[70] Saari, D. G., 1999, Explaining all three-alternative voting outcomes, *Journal of Economic Theory* **87**, 313–55.

[71] Saari, D. G., 2000, Mathematical structure of voting paradoxes 1; Pairwise vote, *Economic Theory* **15**, 1–53.

[72] Saari, D. G., 2000, Mathematical structure of voting paradoxes 2; Positional voting, *Economic Theory* **15**, 55–101.

[73] Saari, D. G. , 2001, Geometry of voting, UCI preprint. To appear: Mathematical and Computer Modelling.

[74] Saari, D. G., 2001, *Chaotic Elections!*, American Mathematical Society, Providence, RI.

[75] Saari, D. G., 2001, *Decisions and Elections: Explaining the Unexpected*, Cambridge University Press, New York.

[76] Saari, D. G., 2001, Analyzing a "nail-biting" election, *Social Choice & Welfare* **18**, 415–30.

[77] Saari, D. G., 2002, Adopting a plurality vote perspective, *Math of Operations Research* **27**, 45–64.

[78] Saari, D. G., 2003, Disturbing aspects of voting theory, *Economic Theory* **22**, 529–56.

[79] Saari, D. G., 2004, Geometry of stable and chaotic discussion, *American Mathematics Monthly* **111**, 377–93.

[80] Saari, D. G., 2005, *Collisions, Rings, and Other Newtonian N-Body Problems*, American Mathematical Society, Providence, RI.

[81] Saari, D. G., 2005, The profile structure for Luce's choice axiom, *Journal of Mathematical Psychology* **49**, 226–53.

[82] Saari, D. G., 2006, Which is better: The Condorcet or Borda winner? *Social Choice & Welfare* **26**, 107–30.

[83] Saari, D. G., 2007, Hidden mathematical structures of voting, pp. 221–34, in *Mathematics and Democracy: Recent Advances in Voting Systems and Collective Choice*, B. Simeone and F. Pukelsheim, eds. Springer, New York.

[84] Saari, D. G., and G. Asay, 2006, Finessing a point: Augmenting the core, UCI Institute for Mathematical Behavioral Sciences, Working Paper.

[85] Saari, D. G., and S. Barney, 2003, Consequences of reversing preferences, *Math Intelligencer* **25**, 17–31.

[86] Saari, D. G., and V. Merlin, 1996, Copeland method: I. Dictionaries and relationships, *Economic Theory* **8**, 51–76.

[87] Saari, D. G., and V. Merlin, 2000, A geometric examination of Kemeny's rule, *Social Choice & Welfare* **17**, 403–38.

[88] Saari, D. G., and A. Petron, 2006, Negative externalities and Sen's liberalism theorem, *Economic Theory* **28**, 265–81.

[89] Saari, D. G., and K. Sieberg, 2001, The sum of the parts can violate the whole, *American Political Science Review* **95**, 415–30.

[90] Saari, D. G., and K. Sieberg, 2001, Some surprising properties of power indices, *Games and Economic Behavior* **36**, 241–63.

[91] Saari, D. G., and K. Sieberg, 2004. Are part wise comparisons reliable? *Research in Engineering Design* **15**, 62–71.

[92] Saari, D. G., and C. P. Simon, 1977, Singularity theory of utility mappings I: Degenerate maxima and pareto optima, *Journal of Mathematical Economics* **4**, 217–51.

[93] Saari, D. G., and J. Van Newenhizen, 1988, The problem of indeterminacy in approval, multiple, and truncated voting systems, *Public Choice* **59**, 101–20.

[94] Saari, D. G., and J. Van Newenhizen, 1988, Is approval voting an "unmitigated evil?", *Public Choice* **59**, 133–47.

[95] Saari, D. G., and M. Tataru, 1999, The likelihood of dubious election outcomes, *Economic Theory* **13**, 345–63.

[96] Salles, M., 1997, On modelling individual rights: Some conceptual issues: Discussion, pp. 129–33, in *Social Choice Re-Examined,* vol. 2, Ed. by K. J. Arrow, A. K. Sen, and K. Suzumura, St. Martin's Press, New York.

[97] Salles, M., 2000. Amartya Sen: Droits et choix social, *Revue Économique* **51**, 445–57.

[98] Schofield, N., 1983, General instability of majority rule, *Review of Economic Studies* **50**, 695–705.

[99] Seidl, C., 1975, On liberal values, *Journal of Economics* **35**, 257–92.

[100] Seidl, C., 1990, On the impossibility of a generalization of the libertarian resolution of the liberal paradox, *Journal of Economics* **51**, 71–88.

[101] Sen, A., 1970, The impossibility of a Paretian liberal. *Journal of Political Economy* **78**, 152–57.

[102] Sen, A., 1970, *Collective Choice and Social Welfare,* Holden Day, San Francisco.

[103] Sen, A. K., 1970, The impossibility of a Paretian liberal. *Journal of Political Economy* **78** (1), 152–57.

[104] Sen, A. K., 1976, Liberty, unanimity and rights, *Economica* **43** (171), 217–45.

[105] Sen, A., 1983, Liberty and social choice, *Journal of Philosophy* **80**, 5–28.

[106] Sen, A., 1987, *On Ethics and Economics,* Basil Blackwell, Oxford.

[107] Sen, A. K., 1992, Minimal liberty, *Economica* **59** (234), 139–60.

[108] Sen, A. K., 1999, The possibility of social choice, *American Economic Review* **89** (3), 349–78.

[109] Sieberg, K., 2001 (2nd ed., 2005), *Criminal Dilemmas,* Springer-Verlag, New York.

[110] Sieberg, K., and M. D. McDonald, 2007, Probability and plausibility of cycles in three-party systems: A mathematical formulation and applications, Department of Political Science, Binghamton University, Binghamton, NY, preprint.

[111] Sonnenschein, H., 1972, Market excess demand functions, *Econometrica*, **40**, 549–63.

[112] Sugden, R., 1978, Social choice and individual liberty, in *Contemporary Economic Analysis*, M. Martis and A. Norbay, eds., Croom Helm, London.

[113] Sugden, R., 1985, Liberty, preference and choice, *Economics and Philosophy* **1**, 213–19.

[114] Tabarrok, A., 2001, Fundamentals of voting theory illustrated with the 1992 election, or could Perot have won in 1992? *Public Choice* **106**, 275–97.

[115] Tabarrok, A., and L. Spector, 1999, Would the Borda count have avoided the civil war? *Journal of Theoretical Politics* **11**, 261–88.

[116] Tataru, M., 1996, *Growth Rates in Multidimensional Spatial Voting*, Ph.D. Dissertation, Northwestern University.

[117] Tataru, M., 1999, Growth rates in multidimensional spatial voting, *Mathematical Social Sciences* **37**, 253–63.

[118] Wuffle, A., S. Feld, G. Owen, and B. Grofman, 1989, Finagle's law and the Finagle point, a new solution concept for two-candidate competition in spatial voting games without a core, *American Journal of Political Science* **33**, 348–75.

[119] Young, P., 1975, Social choice scoring functions, *SIAM Journal of Applied Mathematics* **28**, 824–38.

[120] Young, P., and A. Levenglick, 1978, A consistent extension of Condorcet's election principle, *SIAM Journal of Applied Mathematics* **35**, 285–300.

[121] Young, P., 1995, Optimal voting rules, *The Journal of Economic Perspectives* **9**, 51–64.

Index